Nervous

Nervous Energy

HARNESS THE POWER
OF YOUR ANXIETY

Dr. Chloe Carmichael
Clinical Psychologist

ST. MARTIN'S
ESSENTIALS
NEW YORK

First published in the United States by St. Martin's Essentials, an imprint of St. Martin's Publishing Group

NERVOUS ENERGY. Copyright © 2021 by Chloe Carmichael. All rights reserved. Printed in the United States of America. For information, address St. Martin's Publishing Group, 120 Broadway, New York, NY 10271.

www.stmartins.com

The Library of Congress Cataloging-in-Publication Data is available upon request.

ISBN 978-1-250-24121-4 (hardcover)
ISBN 978-1-250-24120-7 (ebook)

Our books may be purchased in bulk for promotional, educational, or business use. Please contact your local bookseller or the Macmillan Corporate and Premium Sales Department at 1-800-221-7945, extension 5442, or by email at MacmillanSpecialMarkets@macmillan.com.

First Edition: 2021

10 9 8 7 6 5 4 3 2 1

This book is dedicated to everyone who has ever felt a sense of excess energy that they didn't know quite how to direct. Especially if you've ever been to a therapist who kept telling you to "sit with" your feelings, but you wanted to *do* something instead of just sitting there, this book is for you. If you have goals and take comfort in plotting out your next steps, this book is for you. If you would like to grow and build new skills, and if you like to learn new ways of thinking about old issues, then this book is definitely dedicated to you!

Contents

A few strong instincts and a few plain rules suffice us.

—RALPH WALDO EMERSON

PART I

The Foundations

1.

Introduction

Life isn't about finding yourself. Life is about creating yourself.
—GEORGE BERNARD SHAW

Amy shifted nervously on my leather sofa. Her manicured finger-nails fiddled with the hem of her knee-length skirt as she glanced around the room awkwardly and kept tucking an imaginary piece of hair behind her ear. It was her first visit to my office, and Amy was uncomfortable: she was afraid that coming to see a psychologist meant there was something wrong with her. A lifelong perfectionist who practically *prided* herself on being "a little OCD" (her words, not mine), it was quite difficult for Amy to admit that she might need help managing herself. Self-discipline was her *specialty*, for goodness' sake—How could this have happened? Ironically, the iron fist with which she had successfully ruled herself for so long had now ceased to create order and progress; it was now creating feelings of isolation and stagnation. Amy felt stuck—and the worst part was, she was keenly aware that *she* was actually the person holding herself back. Her "nervous energy," which had once been a friend that provided an excited drive to be "on point," was now becoming a "rabbit hole" of excessive self-criticism, anxiety, pessimism, or analysis paralysis.

Rest assured, Amy actually started to experience moderate relief later that very same session, when she learned that many bright, productive people have successfully freed themselves from the very same patterns that were ensnaring her.[1] They do this by learning how to harness their nervous energy rather than let it drain their creativity and overrun their motivation. Oftentimes, adolescents and young adults reach a moderate level of success through deliberately being their own worst critic and obsessively double-checking homework or presentations to ensure every flaw or error is detected and corrected before it is exposed; or they push their feelings aside so they can focus exclusively on "putting one foot in front of the other" to work toward their goals. **This strategy is seductive because it *actually does work*, at least up to a certain point.** When you're a college student or an early-career professional, your work is generally defined and parceled neatly into a syllabus or work plan. At this stage in your education or career, there is usually a "correct" answer, or at least the one you know will please your boss or endear you to your professor. All you have to do in those earlier stages is channel your nervous energy into constantly reviewing or preparing for the assignment in front of you, and you will progress.

The problems arise once you advance beyond college, graduate school, and early-career stages. The higher you climb, the more complex, voluminous, and sometimes amorphous the projects you're given. For example, the boss just wants "sales to climb" or "the global team to get on track"; oftentimes there's no clear direction beyond that *you're* supposed to make it happen. Suddenly, there's more work to do than any human being could *possibly* double-check, there's no syllabus or clear-cut objectives, and there's a *team* of people whose approval you're seeking rather than just one person, like a single direct manager or class professor. Or you suddenly realize it's time to "find a partner," "get closer to your spouse," or at least "get into a good relationship," but the ambiguity around exactly *how* this is supposed to happen, or figuring out *how* to manage perfectionist tendencies in the process, feels overwhelming. Meanwhile, you may have gotten *so good* at putting your emotions aside in certain situations that it's become hard to smoothly reconnect with them in a balanced way that sparks the high level of meaning and fulfillment you're seeking in work and relationships. This is when the old tools no longer suffice. This is when people like Amy often seek my help.

I've found that the nine tools in this book that can help you harness your nervous energy are extremely helpful to the Amys of the world who want to live more productive *and* more fulfilling lives. I'm very excited to share those tools with you here in this book. In the upcoming sections, you'll find a menu of techniques, some tips on how to approach the learning process, and some personal stories from my own life, illustrating how I've used the Nervous Energy Approach . . . and of course you'll also find step-by-step instructions along with optional homework to help you try the techniques for yourself!

The techniques in this book are intended to help you harness your nervous energy as a productive force that moves you forward, so that you don't feel overwhelmed or stuck. If managed correctly, the nervous energy that some people label as anxiety can actually be your friend. It can be a source of stimulation, productivity, and fulfillment—so let's capitalize on that nervous energy!

Question: What Exactly Is Nervous Energy?
Does It Mean What I Think It Means?

It's probably intuitive to you on a certain level, but just to be totally clear, let me spell it out. For the purposes of this book, the term "nervous energy" puts a label on something that many intelligent, cognitively active, goal-oriented, generally responsible people feel and want help managing: it's that "extra" part of yourself that frequently wants to double-check things that feel important (which is fine, till eventually *everything* starts to feel important and double-checking everything is impractical); that wants to rerun (and maybe overanalyze!) conversations in your head sometimes; or that wants to find ways to break complex goals down into manageable and executable steps (unless you get stuck because you're really worried about failure or parts that may be out of your control).

Sometimes people with nervous energy can be vulnerable to going into overdrive during which they overthink things or overwhelm themselves. However, **the beauty of nervous energy is that, with a few relatively simple tweaks, it can be harnessed as a valuable tool that can actually begin to shape itself in a positive way.** The good news is that just like we can quickly "go down a rabbit hole" into a negative thought spiral when we have a lot of mental speed and acuity, we can actually use that very same mental energy to train our minds to work in a more efficient, harmonious way that helps us reach our goals, increase personal fulfilment, and decrease stress. If this sounds desirable to you, then you've found the right book!

Why I "Get" People Like Amy

Amy's story is actually quite common, at least in my private practice on Park Avenue in Manhattan. In fact, I'm a bit like Amy myself. I started my practice in 2012 shortly after getting my clinical psychology license, unsure if I would even be able to attract enough clients to stay afloat. But private practice with high functioning[2] clients was my dream: I had worked independently as a private yoga and meditation teacher for years prior to becoming a clinical psychologist, and I had realized during the course of this earlier work that my true calling was actually helping high functioning people through private therapy and coaching sessions. I was determined to venture out on my own and fulfill this goal. I took a deep breath, made a draw on my tiny postgraduate school IRA, paid thousands of dollars on what felt like an enormous deposit on my first office, and quit my day job as soon as I was earning enough in private practice to squeak by. (This was actually only about six weeks after getting my license; I was thrilled that my message seemed to resonate almost immediately when I announced my practice in New York City.[3]) I'd spent much of my life studying for academic exams or licensing exams; accruing thousands of hours of training in hospitals and other clinical settings; writing (and publishing a few) academic papers and case studies; participating in academic case conferences and practicums to develop my clinical skills; brown-nosing professors even if I totally disagreed with them in order to get excellent grades (yep, I'm really goal-oriented); getting glowing letters of recommendation and signatures of approval on my dissertation; and completing whatever "next step" was needed in my goal of becoming a clinical psychologist with a successful private practice.

All of these efforts had resulted in gold-standard academic and clinical credentials, but what would it all amount to in the real world? I was painfully aware that many excellent clinicians struggle in private practice because although they do really well in a highly structured academic environment, they were never taught how to succeed on their own.[4] I was scared that I might not be one of the "lucky" therapists who were able to start successful practices (I put "lucky" in quotes here because at the time, I really had no idea why some therapists were successful and some were not—for all I knew it was just dumb luck). I desperately wanted to be one of the therapists who would be able to survive (and even thrive) doing what I loved: seeing fascinating, high functioning clients in stimulating, goal-oriented private sessions; but I felt really unsure of whether or not I had whatever "magic ingredients" might be required for success. I started my practice with four clients whom I had begun seeing after hours during the time when I still had my day job, and I needed more than that to survive. To manage my anxiety, I decided to apply what I know as a psychologist: we can manage our emotions by managing our behavior. With this in mind, I made two simple rules for myself:

1. I would report to my office for eight hours every day, five days per week, whether I had clients or not.
2. During those hours, I would spend my time seeing clients or building my practice.

Following the first rule was relatively simple—I just had to physically go to the office. The second rule was a little tougher. Sometimes I was full of ideas, and sometimes I was full of doubt. Sometimes I felt very creative, and sometimes I yearned for a simple, straightforward task. To make life easier, I took advantage of my psychology training about learning and cognition to create structured-yet-flexible work plans so that I didn't have to constantly ask myself what to do next. Oftentimes, trying to generate work plans or decide which task to do at any given moment is actually more difficult than the tasks themselves. So I kept a very long list of tasks: the list included everything from researching online forums where I could blog or post about my practice, to creating attractive and branded client invoice forms, to approaching seasoned psychologists on social media platforms for informational interviews. If I was feeling creative, I'd tackle tasks that involved writing or designing; if I was feeling less creative, I'd build lists of forums or contacts to have handy for days when I was feeling more social and ready to connect with the network I was slowly beginning to build.

The list of things to do was endless, but that was actually by design. I wanted *never* to feel helpless, as if there was nothing I could do. My long list actually gave me *comfort* because it helped me channel my nervous energy into healthy steps forward.[5] When we're feeling anxious or like our survival is on the line, we sometimes get an extra shot of adrenaline. If we use this energy wisely, then it is a boost; if we don't know what to do with that energy, then it just manifests as extra cortisol leading to tension or depression (cortisol is a hormone associated with stress). This is why having a clear way to focus our energy, like drawing up the lists I made for myself or the exercises offered in this book, can help convert nervous energy into productive zeal. I realize that my actual *survival* wasn't really on the line, but honestly it felt that way somewhere in the back of my brain. I was a single woman in my mid-thirties with a mountain of student debt, with my financial future riding on my new private practice. Many clients in my practice who are passionate about their goals tell me they feel similarly when important goals are at stake, especially if the goals relate to major milestones like finding a life partner or a job in which they will feel fulfilled and successful.

We usually get a boost in mood and productivity from a sense of organization when we're facing complex goals, so taking the time to strategize saves us energy in the long run. It can be difficult or draining to think clearly about strategy during our day-to-day busywork. That can lead to feelings of helplessness, which can leave us feeling paralyzed and overwhelmed. Similarly, when we see a mountain of things to do but those things are not well organized, we feel like we're "shooting in the dark," which can be anxiety provoking and overwhelming, as well as inefficient.

The interactions between organization, emotion, motivation, and productivity I've described are why people like Amy and me (and possibly you!) take such comfort in lists, worksheets, or exercises that help us know our "next step": these things help us be more organized and strategic about goals; they help us manage our nervous energy in a productive and calming manner. With a good set of lists, all we have to do is pick a task and get to work; and we'll suddenly have the sense that we're moving forward—and in fact, we *will* be moving forward. This knowledge tends to **increase feelings of motivation and engagement.** Organizing yourself with a deliberate strategy and specific action steps works very well for goal attainment and for many of the therapy skills that I want clients to practice between sessions.[6] This is why you'll find **each tool in this book has an exercise to help you stay on track for success, well-being, or whatever your goal may be.**

The Good News About Structure

The good news is that people like Amy generally respond very well to a structured, skills-based approach that plays to their strengths of intelligence, discipline, and persistence. By structuring myself with this system, plus all the other lessons I learned along the way, I'm proud to say that after less than a year in private practice, I had to hire another therapist to help keep up with demand for my sessions. By the third year, I employed six therapists plus a full support staff and was occupying three offices. In the meantime, I somehow started getting calls for national and international television networks. It started with VH1's *Love & Hip Hop*, then grew to CBS's *Inside Edition* and a host of other lifestyle and news programs on which I've been privileged to connect with millions of people globally. Sometimes I still can't believe that it all started just a few years ago with a brand-new degree and a lot of well-harnessed nervous energy.

My practice now uses video technology to see clients all over the world as well as quiet towns here in the United States—high functioning people are everywhere! In New York, my office works with successful Broadway actors, artists from world-class museums, and professionals in the city's most prestigious banking, law, and publishing firms. Of course, we also see many people who consider themselves to be "just regular everyday people." However, in my view, many of these soccer moms, prerevenue entrepreneurs, and other clients who quietly lead excellent lives, rich with a cognitive and emotional depth that stirs me, actually aren't much different from many of my more high-profile clients.

The common thread is that all of these clients feel a strong personal drive and desire for success, however we define it. We love to keep growing, and we crave tools to help us do that. I believe the reason my practice has been so successful is because it gets great results for people who have a strong desire to succeed and who have the basic raw materials to do so. Learning skills to both harness and embrace our nervous energy helps these clients (and me!) reach greater levels of productivity, fulfillment, and self-compassion as well as practice truly effective, strategic self-discipline that centers around doing what we want to do and feeling how we want to feel.

This book is here to share the tools that I have found essential to my own success, as well as to the success of my clients. Anxiety's healthy function is to stimulate preparatory behaviors, or to signal that there are emotions or situations that need our attention. By giving this extra energy the right format before it becomes frantic, frenetic, or stagnant, it can become a gift rather than an obstacle. Some of the techniques in this book are mine entirely; others are based on common cognitive-behavioral therapy interventions, mindfulness meditation, or even yogic techniques. I hope you will experiment with them, keep what works, and leave the rest. The idea is to discover which techniques help you move forward in a way that feels both **joyful and steady,** all the while bringing you closer to fulfilling your goals and deepening your relationship with yourself.

2.

What Are "High Functioning Clients" and Why Does It Matter?

My mission in life is not merely to survive, but to thrive; and to do so with some passion, some compassion, some humor, and some style.

—MAYA ANGELOU

Since opening my practice in 2012, it has been my privilege to work with over a thousand bright and successful clients visiting my New York office, as well as many other driven, motivated people around the world via video. I believe the reason my practice has grown so quickly and attracted such a strong following among successful, driven people is that my approach is specifically designed around what psychologists call "high functioning" people. A person's level of functioning is a term used by psychologists to describe a person's ability to meet his or her own basic needs, form meaningful and healthy relationships, and generally navigate life within his or her given culture's norms. Psychologists can assess functioning through a variety of methods, such as numerically scored measures or open-ended interviews; but to get a basic sense of what the term means, check out the lists that follow.

As you read, please know that "higher functioning," while being used as a psychological term by psychologists, absolutely does not equate to being a "better" person. On the contrary, many of my most fulfilling clinical experiences were in my early training days working with cognitively disabled adults who were quite unable to meet their own basic needs of food, clothing, and shelter—but they were wonderful, warmhearted people whose company I very much enjoyed and who taught me many important lessons, both personally and professionally. I'm extremely glad that our society makes allowances to care for those who cannot care for themselves. Conversely, many high functioning people are not necessarily as warm and enjoyable as the lower functioning clients I've described. In other words, a person's functioning is not to be confused with his or her intrinsic value or desirability as a human being. **Functioning is also not to be confused with socioeconomic status: for example, although Bernie Madoff was very wealthy, his functioning was likely significantly compromised as demonstrated by a lifelong pattern of blatant disregard for others.**

It is also important to know that a person does not have to be in perfect mental health in order to be high functioning. Many high functioning people have diagnoses like generalized anxiety disorder, panic disorder, or dysthymia. Many high functioning people also work hard to manage their substance use or abuse. ("Work hard play hard" is a common motto for those in the high functioning crowd, who often find that a stiff drink feels like the only way to "turn off" their constantly moving mental wheels, unless they have learned specific techniques to wind down.[1]) The distinctive feature is that they are able to manage any clinical-level disorders without having a pervasive pattern of posing a risk of serious imminent harm to self or others, including being unable or unwilling to meet their own basic needs on a habitual basis. In fact, there is almost no diagnosis[2] that would prevent someone from being high functioning. For example, a person with schizophrenia could be very high functioning if they were compliant with medication and did not have delusions or hallucinations that caused them to pose a danger to themselves or others, or to be unable to meet their own basic needs. There should be no stigma in acknowledging any disorder or any level of functioning.

"Functioning" is simply a term that psychologists use to describe people's ability to care for themselves and participate in their community in a full and healthy manner according to accepted norms in the field of psychology. A psychologist's assessment of functioning takes into account cultural, environmental, and socioeconomic factors. (For example, a parent struggling to feed his or her children due to a local shortage of food would absolutely not be considered lower functioning simply for having undernourished children in that circumstance; whereas a parent whose children were undernourished due to the parent's forgetfulness or lack of willingness to feed them would be evaluated differently.)

This book is not intended to replace a psychologist's assessment when a formal appraisal of functioning is needed. This section is just here to give you a basic understanding of the concept of functioning in psychology, especially as used in countries with norms that are at least somewhat similar to those in the United States where my practice is based. However, I do see clients all over the world via video, and the concept of "functioning" is used by psychologists globally.

POTENTIAL MARKERS OF BASIC FUNCTIONING

- Finding and keeping simple employment
- Being able to feed, clothe, and house yourself
- Establishing at least a few normal relationships
- Taking at least basic care of your body and grooming
- Not having a current pattern of multiple arrests or mental health hospitalizations
- Making sure your children's basic needs are met, if you're a parent
- Not engaging in physical abuse
- Not struggling with serious thoughts of harm to self or others

In addition to these points, high functioning people tend to display a few "extra" markers of achievement, such as:

POTENTIAL MARKERS OF HIGH FUNCTIONING[3]

- Having a great relationship with a spouse or significant other ("great" meaning a relationship in which trust, respect, good communication, healthy conflict resolution, and mutual support of each other are the norm, and there is an absence of physical or emotional abuse)
- Good academic credentials and/or taking classes in subjects that interest you even beyond graduation (nonacademic, community-based classes in things like salsa dancing or pottery making do count! They show an interest in learning, and a willingness/ability to function within a group).
- Having *some* sort of retirement plan or way to care for yourself later in life, even if the plan is nowhere near perfect (or at least having this concern on your radar as something you need to figure out)
- Having a career that brings fulfillment and/or excelling in your field
- Creating a beautiful home (Even if everything is from thrift stores or funds are too tight for anything even remotely luxurious, putting thought and effort into keeping your space tidy and welcoming definitely counts)
- Having good credit, or at least being on a path to getting there
- Maintaining a healthy body through being mindful of your diet and/or exercising and/or taking supplements; and/or taking really good care of your appearance through excellent personal grooming and/or dressing with clothing that is always clean and coordinated in a

socially appropriate manner that demonstrates thoughtful attention to detail

- Being an attuned and thoughtful parent (if you choose to become one) who invests time and energy to provide enriching activities and helpful structure for your kids through regular "reading hours" at home, curating TV or other media, learning about the child's academic and social situations on a regular basis, and providing emotional or practical support if the child struggles; planning at least occasional trips to museums or providing other opportunities for exposure to the arts or sciences; facilitating involvement in sports, volunteering, or other deliberate ways of stimulating and caring for the child beyond his or her basic development
- Having hobbies such as regular participation in a sports league, book club, or church group; being active in a volunteer network; hosting frequent dinner parties or making great meals for your family on a regular basis; travel; and/or any other recurring activity that demonstrates an ability for sustained focus and planning around healthy pro-social goals

It is important to emphasize that **a person absolutely does *not* need to do *all* of these things to be high functioning.** The idea, in my experience as a psychologist, is that high functioning people tend to have a few markers of personal or professional achievement such as the items just mentioned.

Even if you haven't achieved some of these things but you are working toward realistic plans to do so, or if you've found viable alternatives, you could still be considered high functioning. For example, you may not have a great relationship yet, but you're actively dating in a healthy partner-oriented manner; or you are comfortably single by choice. Or you aren't in great shape yet, but you're on a slow-and-steady pattern of healthy weight loss; or you're still in school but you're attending class regularly and on track for graduation; or you've been able to develop a career without an academic degree. The markers in this list are just examples to help you understand the general idea of a high functioning person as someone who knows how to create and adhere to multistep, healthy life plans that are a "step beyond" the basics.

High Functioning People Aren't Without Problems!

Because high functioning people tend to have their basic "bases covered" in life, it's easy to think they don't have problems. In fact, their accurate recognition that their life is running relatively smoothly sometimes leads them to feel they don't really have permission to experience feelings of distress or discontent; this pattern of minimizing their feelings can actually be hard on their self-esteem. While it's true that they're unlikely to have total breakdowns that prevent them from living what they feel is a normal life, **high functioning people actually have their own unique vulnerabilities.** For example, they can struggle with perfectionism, overthinking ("analysis paralysis," as clients in my office often say), social or performance anxiety, and getting "stuck in their head," to name a few common issues. Here are a couple of examples of high functioning people and some of the struggles they might face:

- **An early-career financial analyst who would like to earn an MBA from a top-ranking program to advance his career. Although he has the experience and raw materials to build a strong application, he is overwhelmed with anxiety as his perfectionist side anticipates the logistical** and emotional effort required for him to attain this next milestone in his climb to success. Like many perfectionists, he feels the need to seamlessly execute a stellar application instead of allowing himself to have a healthy, messy struggle with a complex process. He thinks frequently about how wonderful an MBA would be and feels a significant amount of internal pressure to move forward, but he has trouble getting started on the application process because "analysis paralysis" has him stuck at trying to choose which program is the "perfect fit," or endlessly pondering what to say in his personal statement.

This client would seek my help to create and adhere to a detailed (but not *too* detailed!) plan that would help him stay focused and emotionally balanced as he executes each component of a complex and intimidating process: determine a list of schools and complete each one's intricate application forms, earn competitive scores on the relevant standardized tests, write a compelling personal statement, obtain strong letters from influential recommenders, and fly around the country for grueling interviews. This client has the intelligence and drive to succeed; he just needs help creating and maintaining an approach in which he tackles the goal in logistically and emotionally manageable pieces instead of as one overwhelming behemoth.

- A woman whose career has thrived from her hard-driving energy, but is now growing nervous as she reaches her mid-thirties. She is concerned that her lifelong pattern of putting her career first may be competing with her parallel goal of dedicating time and energy to finding a potential husband who is just as accomplished as she is, and then cultivating the flexibility required for a romantic partnership. Yet she is justifiably concerned about becoming *so* flexible that she loses her sense of self or personal boundaries. This client would seek my help to create a dating plan including plenty of first dates and increased openness to "thinking out of the box" regarding men while still holding firm to certain deal breakers. She will need support to adhere to the plan despite the emotions that inevitably arise as this confident, powerful woman enters a realm in which she is no longer able to control and shape each element of the process. Instead, she must face vulnerabilities or insecurities as she tries to "just go with it" for the first time in her life.

At the same time, she needs help making sure the pendulum doesn't swing *too far* to the point where she ends up "working too hard" at the dating process by becoming overaccommodating or emotionally vulnerable before the man has really proven himself as stable, interested, and trustworthy through both objective and subjective standards. She knows that all of this amounts to a pretty tall order, and she sometimes wonders if it is *too* tall. Always willing to start with "the person in the mirror" and manage her expectations, she sometimes questions if she's being reasonable: she is frequently conscious of each year passing by. On the other hand, she's always been someone who goes "above and beyond," so why not expect the same from her partner, too? Like many successful women, she found learning about "imposter syndrome" (when a person feels like an imposter or poseur in certain domains such as a prestigious occupation, despite actually having earned the position legitimately) to be illuminating in giving her confidence that she has every right to "reach for the stars" in her professional life, so why not do the same in her romantic life?

As you can see, this woman's cognitive and emotional wheels are nearly always turning. **This extra energy is an asset, but she** needs to make sure it is focused in a productive manner rather than becoming a fuel for incessant second-guessing of herself that ultimately leads to a skittish approach to dating, one in which she vacillates between extremes of rigid rules ("I absolutely never call men") and total impulsivity ("I know he's been evasive and ignored me for a week, but I feel like calling him right now after these three glasses of wine, and so, dammit, I will!").

In short, high functioning people have complex goals with significant logistical *and* emotional components; there is often overlap and interplay between these components. High functioning people have a lot of mental energy coupled with a high drive to succeed; this can amount to "nervous energy" that has actually helped them reach impressive goals in their personal or professional lives. Personal and professional goals become increasingly complex each time we achieve a new level of success, thereby becoming more difficult to manage solo. High functioning people are often self-aware and solution-oriented enough to seek and benefit from targeted, action-oriented tools from a credible source so they can continue on their high functioning paths.

Many People Are Surprised to Learn They Are High Functioning

Many high functioning people don't even realize they're high functioning. To them, the following things are just part of everyday life: being steadily employed, participating in Sunday brunch or happy hour with their "core group" of friends, enjoying regular family gatherings, taking at least basic care of their body, not having a pattern of psychiatric hospitalizations or criminal arrests, and/or having a slice of their life in which they enjoy some extra challenges, like attending (or even contemplating!) grad school, reading regularly or finding some other way of learning new things, putting money into their retirement account at least occasionally, saving up to buy a home and/or improving the home they have (even if funds are scarce, finding ways to make their space tidy and inviting), maintaining a regular gym membership or finding other ways to keep themselves fit, volunteering, being a responsible parent, or organizing social gatherings. **Because high functioning people tend to be surrounded by other high functioning people, they don't always realize quite how special they are.** This can skew their sense of what's normal,[4] so they can sometimes get really down on themselves or feel like a failure for struggling with things like finding an amazing life partner, mastering anxiety or negative thoughts, or finding meaning in their professional lives as much as they feel they should.

While it's important to help high functioning people solve these problems, it's also important to help them keep these problems in perspective. **High functioning people can sometimes be really hard on themselves, to the point where their motivation and engagement will suffer; it's often helpful for the high functioning person to realize that many of the stumbling blocks he or she is facing are actually present because the person *is* so high functioning in the first place.**[5] For example, many first- and second-year law associates at white-shoe firms will call my office in a panic because suddenly they're surrounded by a bunch of Ivy League senior associates who seem to have it all figured out; the younger ones no longer feel like the smartest person in the room, and it's actually a little unnerving. Or a successful entrepreneur finds herself in a self-flagellating panic when it's time to run payroll because she just used a lot of funds to cover inventory on a large customer order (um . . . okay, that one was me once!). These people forget that **the reason they're even *having* these sophisticated problems in the first place is because their pattern of high performance has placed them in higher-stakes, complex situations.** It can be helpful to realize that, to a certain degree, these are actually *good* problems or high-level growth opportunities to be embraced rather than viewed as signs of failure or inadequacy.

The Nervous Energy approach is for people who are high functioning, whether they realize it or not. Sometimes, the realization that they *are* high functioning is actually therapeutic in itself because it helps them put their issues into perspective, appreciate their strengths, and understand their vulnerabilities. Many high functioning people think they're just doing what they're "supposed to do" or what's "normal," until they come to therapy and get some perspective.

High-Functioning Therapy and Coaching

Because my clients have always been high functioning (since my second year of training in my doctoral program in psychology studies, and from day one as a yoga teacher), I developed an approach that has a tremendous respect for their abilities. A common theme I noticed among these high functioning clients was that they often had a lot of "nervous energy": they would arrive armed with information and ideas about their situations and what might help them. They had studied my bio and scrutinized my credentials, and they would constantly ask about the "next step" so they could "move forward" (I put those phrases in quotes because they seem to be buzzwords with the high functioning crowd). They were more than willing, as well as quite able, to participate in a rigorous therapeutic process of self-examination, learn new skills, and do homework between sessions. They were eager to do whatever was needed to help them get from point A to point B (point A being their current state of distress, and point B being a place where they felt the issue was resolved).

You might be thinking, "Well, duh, of *course* a person experiencing distress would want to take the approach you've described," but as a psychologist who has actually worked with lower functioning people during my training, I can tell you this is not always the case. Many lower functioning people lack the insight to realize that much of their distress may originate from their own behaviors or attitudes (such as a meth addict who repeatedly gets into meth-fueled rages in which he aggresses physically upon others and then somehow feels persecuted and blames everyone else when he faces arrest, mandatory rehabilitation, and jail time) or from an extreme lack of boundaries around problematic situations in their lives. An example of the latter would be a profoundly codependent woman who briefly tries to refuse the violent meth addict's demand for bail money, but after a few minutes of being berated, she begins to feel irrationally guilty for "upsetting" him; she then seriously compromises her own financial future by doing a large, early withdrawal from her modest, hard-won retirement fund so she can "lend" him bail money for the umpteenth time, only to have him predictably skip bail without repaying the loan, thereby increasing an ever-growing pile of unpaid "loans" made by the self-sabotaging enabler to the addict. She feels genuinely shocked and increasingly indignant *each time* he skips bail and repeats the same addictive, violent pattern with cavalier disregard for her dwindling retirement fund.

One could say the meth addict needs support because he is clearly very sick; and that would be absolutely correct: he is so sick that his functioning would be considered very low, as it is marked with profoundly self-sabotaging behaviors that pose a threat to self and others; and he likely needs a great deal of intensive, mandatory, ongoing clinical support from a team of medical doctors, psychologists, and social workers. While the codependent enabler's functioning would probably be considered somewhat higher, since she is not posing an immediate danger to self or others, her functioning would still likely be considered significantly compromised because she's unable to enforce basic boundaries around her initial decision not to continue a repetitive pattern of "lending" her much-needed retirement funds to a person who is too ill or disturbed to be reasonably trusted with such an important debt (and who is, in fact, likely to use the bailout as an opportunity to continue his pattern of placing himself and others in physical danger).

What both the addict and the codependent enabler have in common is that **they both lack basic insight** into how their own behaviors are directly linked to their difficulties; and this **lack of basic insight prevents them from seeking tools to bolster their own skill sets,** thereby impeding their functioning. The addict **feels** persecuted and victimized rather than taking ownership of his need to control his drug use and stop aggressing on others both physically and financially. Meanwhile, the codependent enabler **feels** mired in resentment of the addict's repeated broken promises to pay back loans, yet she doesn't take ownership of a need to learn better boundaries so she can stop facilitating an unhealthy dynamic that produces deep resentment and financial distress. The addict's and the enabler's lack of insight into their own roles in perpetuating the cycle would make it very difficult to use a therapeutic approach centered around providing tools to actively manage their choices differently. Before people are ready to use tools, they must *want* tools. To want tools, they must be willing and able to have insight around the problems in their lives.[6]

Of course, higher functioning people also sometimes struggle to see their own roles in problems as well. This is certainly true of me: as a lifelong consumer of therapy and a professional psychologist, I can attest that I *definitely* have blind or stubborn spots, just like everyone else! However, the ability to have insight into your behavior and be able to see (and therefore address) your role in creating or prolonging problems is a marker of higher functioning. The ability to take ownership of one's own role in problems is a big factor in choosing what type of therapy will be effective. My approach tends to work best with people who have insight into their own roles in many of the problems they face, or at least insight into their own roles in *managing* the problems they face. **The techniques in this book are geared toward people who recognize there is something about their own thought patterns or skills that they'd like to change or improve,** and who welcome the chance to see how they can potentially change for the better.

Because many therapists are trained in environments where the emphasis is often on helping clients stay clear of crises, improve their basic daily living skills, or learn to practice simple self-care and maintain essential interpersonal boundaries, many therapists never really learn how to work with high functioning people.[7] I believe this prevents them from fully appreciating the need to offer appropriately stimulating, challenging treatment that fully engages high functioning people as the "live wires" they are. One of the first things I noticed with high functioning clients was that they were refreshed by my willingness to give them sophisticated tools and use their nervous energy as an asset to learn new ways of harnessing that very same energy, rather than keeping up a never-ending loop of "How do you feel about that?" or constantly asking them to "sit with their feelings" or giving them cookie-cutter worksheets.

When I'm training therapists in my approach, I often find they are quite surprised to realize that many high functioning people are totally able to grasp and apply sophisticated psychological concepts quickly—in fact, I believe that if therapists fail to offer high functioning clients this type of information and teach them how it applies to their own situations, they will often get bored and disengage. Oftentimes, I'll sit with a therapist under my supervision who will explain what she feels a client's barriers to reaching his or her goals are, and then she'll ask me how to communicate this to the client. I'll often reply, "Exactly like you just told it to me; this client will be able to understand and apply what you're saying *easily.*"

Another important distinction in therapy for high functioning people is that they don't necessarily need to come every week.[8] Many therapists automatically direct clients to do this, because that's how it was generally done in their training. However, they may be forgetting that their training was mostly with *lower functioning people*. Lower functioning people generally benefit from weekly therapy because the mere act of sitting with a higher functioning person (the therapist) is often beneficial to them: the therapist is teaching and modeling things like simple social skills, reliability in terms of scheduled appointments, appropriate boundaries, basic insight, and many other points of healthy interaction that are therapeutic in themselves for a person whose functioning doesn't necessarily encompass those skills. This type of therapy is called "supportive therapy," wherein the goal isn't necessarily to help the person make changes, but instead to help ensure his or her functioning doesn't decline (or at least make sure any signs of decline are treated promptly) and to provide a relationship that facilitates growth through stability, healthy social modeling, and the opportunity to learn basic life skills.

In contrast, higher functioning people will typically already have at least a couple of good, reliable high functioning friends or family members they can call for a heart-to-heart or stimulating conversation on any given week. They're seeking therapy or coaching to provide something *more* than "just" a supportive, healthy, one-to-one relationship with a reflective, reliable, empathetic person who takes a genuine interest in their life, teaches basic life skills and can monitor for declines in functioning. While I do see certain clients every week because it is specifically helpful to their particular goals or because it helps them to ensure that their mental fast track includes time to pause and reflect, it isn't an automatic assumption that weekly sessions for the indefinite future are the default, and my clients appreciate this as different from the typical approach of many therapists who don't consciously specialize in high functioning people.

It is important to know that functioning can increase with time and with learning, whether through therapy, self-help, or other resources. However, **sometimes it can be harder for a high function-ing person to find helpful resources, since he or she may already be functioning at a level beyond the majority of available resources.** The process of choosing a therapist or coach for high functioning people is discussed more fully later in this book, if that is of interest to you (see Special Considerations for High Functioning People Seeking Therapy, chapter 6). But here I'd like to share a bit with you about the role that therapy and coaching played in my own path to becoming a higher functioning person, and how that path shaped the approach offered in this book.

How Therapy Helped My Functioning as a Person and a Psychologist

To really explain my therapeutic approach and its appreciation for the needs of high functioning people, it's important to acknowledge that my own functioning increased dramatically over the course of my life, and I believe that was partly due to my experiences as a consumer of therapy long before I became a psychologist. I attended my first regular therapy session when I was seventeen years old, with a therapist at a clinic ca-tering to lower functioning people, and frankly that was probably appro-priate for me at that time: I had poor personal boundaries, I had been living on my own since the age of fifteen due to some very dysfunctional family dynamics, and the simple fact of a weekly appointment with a caring adult was actually very therapeutic for me.

At first, I was actually attending the appointment to try to persuade my then boyfriend to go, since attending therapy was part of his required after-care plan following a very frightening suicide attempt (frightening for me, because I had awakened to the sight and sound of his body literally bounc-ing off of our apartment walls due to seizures following a deliberate drug overdose he had taken after I went to sleep). He had intended the overdose to be fatal, and it likely would have been fatal if I hadn't awakened and called an ambulance. He was a very troubled yet charming person strug-gling with profound substance-abuse issues; he has since passed away.

Although he didn't get the help he needed, attending sessions in support of him was a catalyst for my own functioning to improve—particularly in terms of setting healthy boundaries with others. Thanks in large part to time spent in therapy, my functioning increased over time (and, of course, my neurological development progressed: the executive lobe of the brain doesn't fully develop until the mid- or late twenties), and I gradually began seeking different types of therapy. I found it much more difficult to find a good therapist for my level of functioning as my needs became more sophisticated.[9]

Over the years, I came to understand firsthand what it is like to go to a therapist who just doesn't seem to "get" the needs of high functioning people. While it was relatively simple for me to find a therapist who could help me when I was lower functioning—since having regularly scheduled visits with almost any stable, healthy, and socially mature person was beneficial to me—I found that as my functioning increased, it was harder to find a therapist who could really challenge me and stimulate further growth. It's kind of like how finding the right personal trainer can sometimes be harder for someone who already has a good exercise routine than it is for a total novice whose workout will likely be enhanced by receiving basic fitness instruction from most any trainer.[10] These experiences shaped my desire as a psychologist to offer high functioning people sessions that would celebrate and utilize their unique strengths.

The bottom line here is that a therapist or coach working with high functioning people must understand that **a high functioning person's nervous energy is looking for something to *do*, something to *try*, something that will feel *proactive* in a search for anything from practical solutions to inner peace.** The Nervous Energy approach offers tools that guide you to reflect on yourself and then create a structure to take action on your insight. High functioning people tend to respond very well to this type of approach because they are good at learning and applying new approaches in a strategic manner.

3.

Menu of Techniques

*When it is obvious that the goals cannot be reached,
don't adjust the goals, adjust the action steps.*
— CONFUCIUS

In my experience, one of the hallmarks of high functioning people is intellectual curiosity. Are you getting curious about what the tools of the Nervous Energy Approach actually *are*? Well, you've come to the right place. Here you will find a list of the nine techniques and a brief description of each one. In the next section we'll talk about which technique or techniques you might want to choose as a starting point based on your particular situation and personality style. Part 2 of this book will fully explain each technique so you can try it yourself. But here is a "quick and dirty" list to help you understand the Nervous Energy Approach with a straightforward overview of the techniques in the chapters.

THE THREE-PART BREATH

NERVOUS
ENERGY
TECHNIQUE
#1

The Three-Part Breath leads users to reconnect with themselves and better understand their nervous energy on a physical and cognitive-emotional level.

Many high functioning people have been able to achieve a great deal by "white-knuckling" their way through challenging situations and "playing through the pain." This allows them to overcome certain challenges and obstacles that sideline others. However, at a certain point, disconnecting from self-awareness becomes counterproductive. Methodically reconnecting with the breath increases self-awareness, along with self-control, on both a physical and intellectual level.

This chapter guides readers through the Three-Part Breath and prompts them to examine their thoughts and feelings. Shallow, rapid breathing triggers the "fight, flight, or freeze" reaction that in turn can cause multiple symptoms of nervous energy gone wild, including compromised mental functioning. It all begins with breathing. By deliberately slowing the inhale and starting to breathe deeply and mindfully, in an exercise that offers just enough of a structure to create a "mental challenge" that distracts the user from excess cognitive chatter, the "fight, flight, or freeze" cycle is interrupted. Once the cycle is interrupted, the reader is guided to unpack the thoughts and emotions underlying his or her nervous energy, and then make productive use of that insight by taking appropriate action for targeted self-care.

This chapter presents a step-by-step discussion on the Three-Part Breath, along with an explanation of how high functioning people can use it to convert excess nervous energy into insight, attunement, and productivity.

NERVOUS
ENERGY
TECHNIQUE
#2

ZONE OF CONTROL

Zone of Control is a very popular technique in my practice. It helps clients focus their energy on effective, productive actions in dealing with whatever may be worrying them. The key is to break down an issue into two categories: things we *can* control, and things we *cannot* control.

Every situation is comprised of factors that we have control over and factors that we cannot change. By writing specific, doable actions that target what is in our control, we can direct energy toward factors we are capable of changing.

By breaking down aspects of a situation into a "worry" Zone of Control and further threshing that into a list of specific, actionable items, the result is that each time the worry is triggered there is a corresponding list of actions on which we can focus our energy.

The chapter discusses a few examples of how the Zone of Control is applied to real-life situations that often lead to worry.

NERVOUS
ENERGY
TECHNIQUE
#3

MENTAL SHORTLIST

There are cases when people get stuck in emotional states that they genuinely *want* to shake but can't; or they yearn for mental distance from a particular project or situation. Since emotional states are generally controllable by our thoughts (a foundation of cognitive-behavioral therapy principles as well as Buddhist tenets), learning to control our thoughts is essential. However, because high functioning people often have very intense thoughts swirling around from their high levels of mental energy, they can quickly get "down in the dumps" about a business meeting that didn't go as planned, or an ex who is taking up too much mental space.

The goal here is finding a way to move forward by redirecting our thoughts toward more productive, fulfilling material. This sounds good in theory, but the difficulty is determining what to think about instead. Many people have a hard time finding something helpful to focus on when they're in a low mood, but high functioning people face the additional challenge of requiring a *more* stimulating "distractor task" than your average bear. That's why the Mental Shortlist technique is so helpful for them, especially when they are guided to think of stimulating examples that will captivate their attention during difficult moments.

Generating a Mental Shortlist of everything you would rather be thinking about than ruminating on an undesirable or unproductive topic makes it easy to distract yourself from any counterproductive thinking that makes you feel stuck.

NERVOUS
ENERGY
TECHNIQUE
#4

TO-DO LIST WITH EMOTIONS

Breaking down a complex goal or task list into smaller steps imbued with emotional awareness facilitates accomplishment, momentum, and fulfillment.

While breaking down complex tasks into smaller steps is intuitive, many high functioning people often neglect to think about the accompanying emotions. In fact, sometimes they have been able to achieve a certain degree of success precisely by *not* getting too focused on emotions, and focusing instead on simply "putting one foot in front of the other." This works up to a certain point. But oftentimes, as the goals get bigger (which happens frequently with high functioning people!) the emotions get bigger. Eventually, learning to address and incorporate these emotions is necessary. Doing so can even provide a springboard for greater passion, connection, and drive. Thinking about which emotions arise in response to each step makes it easier to manage those emotions and stay focused on the task. By integrating emotions into the to-do list, people can plan accordingly with ways to address and soothe those feelings.

The chapter also combines specific examples and ideas on how emotions (and preplanned self-care plans for managing them) can be structured into to-do lists.

MIND MAPPING

The chapter on Mind Mapping explores how high functioning people can use word maps to gain clarity, increase emotional connection, and discover meaningful connections between complex goals and personal values to create engagement. Writing down words and phrases, and then connecting them to a central theme, is the core of the technique. Recognizing latent subconnections also serves to complete a Mind Map, and can generate insight as well as increased motivation.

High functioning people may have especially complex thought patterns, which can actually make it harder for them to have a "bird's-eye view" of their thoughts. A Mind Map geared to the high functioning person illustrates the web of cognitive and emotional connections relating back to a larger task, goal, or idea. Clarity gained from this exercise brings self-awareness and stress relief, as well as increased energy and sense of purpose.

WORRY TIME

Many high functioning people constantly review their concerns as a way to keep focused on how to resolve them. While their drive to keep these issues "front of mind" is productive to a certain degree, it eventually becomes counterproductive if they reach a point where they "can't turn it off." This style also becomes problematic as the high functioning person takes on more and more complex projects over a lifetime. The strategy may keep a college student on top of final exams, yet be inadequate once that college student evolves into a gallery director managing multiple new artist openings, a museum collaboration relationship, hiring a new assistant, and keeping abreast of her teenage children's academic performance. This chapter introduces a simple exercise to alleviate the need to endlessly circle around important issues, while still ensuring that they are given their appropriate attention.

Having to worry about everything all the time is exhausting and unproductive. At the same time, it is difficult (and irresponsible) to just ignore these worries. The Worry Time technique guides readers to list the issues and then set aside a regular block of time to go through the list to "worry" about it. Knowing that time is literally scheduled to worry about these items unburdens the mind and allows it to focus on other things, because the fear of these items "drifting away" is resolved.

RESPONSE PREVENTION

This technique frees you to stop a compulsive behavior, such as checking for texts or emails. By taking away the option to do the behavior, you will interrupt the cycle and free yourself up to focus on other things.

High functioning people often have a mental tenacity that is usually an asset—but it can sometimes become a liability if it runs wild in certain situations. For example, a stock trader's ability to stay hyper-focused on minute changes in market values for hours on end has an obvious value during the workday—but what if that same trader struggles to quit scanning constantly for text messages from her latest romantic interest? Her mind's wonderful ability to "latch on and not let go" suddenly becomes a source of stress.

Response Prevention techniques help redirect nervous energy into areas where it will be productive rather than pernicious.

THOUGHT REPLACEMENT

High functioning people, by nature, are typically intellectual and thought-driven. This means that when one of their "automatic thoughts" or "rules about the world" is maladaptive, they're vulnerable to falling down a major rabbit hole. For example, if they struggle with perfectionism and have been let go from a job, they may have a mental script that says, "I was let go because I wasn't good enough," and this thought can become active anytime they even attempt to begin job searching—even if they were actually let go for other reasons. Naturally, the automatic thought of just "not being good enough" can be uniquely challenging for a high functioning perfectionist.

Thought Replacement zeroes in on exactly which thoughts need replacing and guides the reader to supplant them with deliberately chosen, constructive phrases. Maladaptive automatic thoughts have a nasty, intrusive effect on anyone, and they can be especially troublesome to a very cerebral, intellectual person who tends to think often and rapidly. The good news is that we can harness that same cognitive power to better understand and shape the cognitive process with more constructive thoughts in order to override and replace any maladaptive thought patterns.

NERVOUS
ENERGY
TECHNIQUE
#9

ANCHORING STATEMENTS

Many high functioning people become suddenly and intensely "keyed up" to the point of near panic when they realize they've made a mistake, have entered a social situation they feel ill-prepared to navigate, or have noticed some other way in which they have not lived up to their normal high functioning pattern. Because high functioning people are usually able to cruise through many of life's twists and turns without much struggle, they are sometimes thrown off-kilter when hitting a bump. The irony is that many high functioning people have actually *trained* themselves to go into "five-alarm-fire mode" in these situations because they think it will help summon their resources and flag the situation as an exception rather than an everyday occurrence.

Ironically, this approach can produce a rapid and counterproductive vortex of negative thoughts and physiological overstimulation, which many high functioning people dub a "panic attack." This chapter explains how to use Anchoring Statements to teach the mind to respond with a logical, comforting statement designed to quickly harness the jolt of nervous energy that arises in situations that many high functioning people find panic-inducing. Readers create tailored Anchoring Statements to remind themselves that the "panic attack" is a temporary state of mind; these statements help the reader maintain a sense of control and navigate as smoothly as possible.

4.

How to Use This Book

Channel Your Nervous Energy for Success

May all beings have happy minds.
—BUDDHA

The Nervous Energy Approach is comprised of nine tools my clients have reliably found to be practical and helpful. The chapters in part 2 are structured to lead you to reflect on how your own experiences connect to issues that are faced by high functioning people everywhere, and then they offer techniques to apply this reflection toward meaningful progress. The structure of each chapter may vary depending on the technique, but here's a general sense of what to expect:

1. **Client stories:** Each chapter introducing a technique begins with a clinical vignette from my practice or with a description of a challenge commonly faced by high func-

tioning people. Common situations include feeling ob-
sessed by a stumbling block on the path to a complex goal
or feeling so consumed by a lofty ambition that it feels
daunting to step back and strategize the most logical plan
for reaching it.

2. **Deeper look:** I'll normalize the challenge and cast it as a
    manageable issue that actually signifies something posi-
    tive about you (such as your high need for cognition,[1] or
    drive for success). Next, I'll share a technique to help you
    learn how to surmount this type of challenge.

3. **DIY:** You'll be guided to apply the technique to your own
    life through step-by-step do-it-yourself (DIY) instructions,
    troubleshooting ideas, or worksheets.

Our busy world, high expectations of ourselves, and living in
the information age can combine to set up a "spinning wheel" feeling in the mind of a person who has a lot of cognitive horsepower
and personal drive. This can almost feel overstimulating if we
don't have tools to shape, harness, and direct our mental energy.
That's when it's time to use the techniques in the Nervous Energy
Approach!

Getting Started

Depending on your particular situation or personality, certain tools
might feel more applicable than others at different times in your
life. While each of the tools is likely to be helpful to you in its own
way, **you'll probably get the most from them (and enjoy the process more!) if you start by choosing the tools that are most relevant to *your situation right now,*** especially if you're feeling under
pressure at the moment. If you're not experiencing a lot of pressure

right now and you just want to learn about some helpful tools for high functioning people, then simply go ahead and read the tools in order or browse using the approach described below.

If you'd like to select which tools to read first, then see which of the emotional experiences being faced by the three characters in the following section seem to resonate with you the most *right now* and then flip to the tools recommended for that person. We all have tendencies that likely relate to each of the three character profiles below, but just choose the one that seems to reflect you best *at this moment.* I encourage you to read all of the tools eventually, but **learning is often most effective when it feels immediately applicable;** so feel free to start with whatever tools seem to be calling your name.

The exact circumstances faced by the characters in the examples don't need to mirror yours; what's more important is *how* **the character is facing the situation.** For example, a person could think obsessively about a romantic breakup or a possible job promotion; the commonality is that *the person is thinking obsessively,* so he needs tools to help him learn how to take a step back. Similarly, a different person could be facing the same problem of a breakup but deal with it by completely ignoring or denying her emotions until she finally bursts into overwhelming panic. The initial problem of a romantic breakup is the same for these two clients, but their ways of dealing with it are completely different: one has a habit of obsessing about issues, while the other has a habit of avoiding issues. So if you read about a character struggling to get a breakup out of his mind, yet you can't relate to breakups because you're happily married, you might swap in whatever relationship or issue *you're* obsessing about, such as a defiant teenager or a coworker who gets under your skin. **The point is to look at** *how* **the character manages their thoughts and feelings around challenges rather than to compare your issues to the exact problems the character is facing.**

You may also notice that I use terms like "OCD" or "panic" and wonder if this means you need to have clinical-level symptoms of obsessive-compulsive disorder or panic disorder to use these techniques. The answer is that you absolutely do *not* need to be at a clinical level to benefit from these techniques. People could have obsessive *tendencies* or sometimes experience *feelings of panic* and benefit from learning how to manage those feelings or tendencies, all without having anything "wrong with them" or identifying as having any sort of "disorder." It is my experience that *many* very smart, driven people sometimes experience intense feelings—maybe in part because they have very **strong and rapid cognitive processes that feed their emotions.** When they get a certain thought "stuck in their head" or when they have labeled a certain thing as "overwhelming" to the point where they start avoiding it, they often experience a great deal of benefit by learning a **fresh way to think** about the stressor. That's what this book is here to offer: think of it as **a user's manual for certain parts of your mind.**

You'll notice that all of the suggested starting-point tools listed for the three example clients in the following section include the Three-Part Breath. That's because the Three-Part Breath is almost always a good idea; it can simultaneously calm and focus both mental and physical nervous energy. It also helps build your ability to pause yourself and deliberately consider your approach to a problem, and then shift into whatever additional technique will be most helpful to you in the moment. **Many people say they've "tried deep breathing before," but the Three-Part Breath involves more than simply breathing deeply, so I do encourage you to be open to giving it a try.** However, if breathing exercises just aren't for you, no worries—you can still benefit from the other tools that feel right for you.

Three Examples of Typical High Functioning People and Good Starting Points for Each "Type"

1. Christina: the "OCD Queen"

Christina has always joked that she's "a little OCD." She double-checked her homework answers religiously in high school and college, attached color-coded tabs to separate the chapters in her textbooks, and made flashcards on color-coordinated index cards for easy reference, with each set in a case labeled by semester and subject. Although some of her classmates thought she was uptight, her supercharged conscientiousness really helped her GPA. Her lab partners never had to worry about getting stuck with extra work, and teachers were always impressed by her dedication. If she's being totally honest, Christina actually **prides herself on those OCD tendencies, at least a little bit.** Christina's worst fear is being unprepared. When she has a responsibility, she *cannot* get it out of her mind—and she actually likes it that way, since this dynamic keeps her safe from having important responsibilities slip her mind. At least it used to, before her life eventually became complex enough that she had too many responsibilities for her to obsess over each and every one without completely losing track of the others.

Christina's OCD-like style may have been born of necessity. She grew up with an absent father and a hardworking mother who was so preoccupied with two backbreaking jobs and making ends meet that there was simply no time to help little Christina manage the long- and short-term planning required for a successful homework schedule.[2] It was clear to Christina from a very early age that if she was going to succeed in life, she'd have to stay on top of book-report due dates, keep up with the teacher's test schedule for memorizing multiplication tables, plan ahead to strategize and execute science-fair projects, and remain vigilant to achieve other early success milestones that required a structured and persistent approach rather than enjoy the luxury of a helicopter parent making sure she kept pace with her peers.[3]

Christina didn't want a life of toil like she saw her mother enduring, and she was painfully aware that her mother's efforts were primarily focused on creating a better life for Christina. From a very young age, Christina recognized that academic success was the most likely path to help her avoid a fate similar to her mother's, as well as a way to honor all the hard work her mother was doing to give her a chance at a better life. Whatever the reason, Christina has always maintained a nearly hypervigilant focus on anything related to work or academics, and she has actually felt really good about doing so.

Until recently, Christina's style has helped her to stay 100 percent organized and on top of things, just the way she likes it. However, she has now earned a position as a junior associate at a law firm, where the partners give her so much work that it's *impossible* to double-check everything. She is also given so many responsibilities that it's totally impractical for her to keep *everything* "front of mind" all the time. Just thinking about the big projects she needs to execute makes her feel very overwhelmed, since of course she wants to do them *all perfectly and slightly ahead of schedule.* She's now in a situation in which her old tools of making flash cards to review study materials endlessly, meeting frequently with professors to "make sure she's on the right track," combing through each brief to make sure it's completely polished before passing it along to partners, and practicing every presentation till she knows it *perfectly* are no longer practical. Clearly, Christina needs some new tools if she's going to keep rising. **This is something I see a lot: because completing milestones successfully will generally lead to being given more complex assignments, our old tools eventually need revamping in order to remain viable.**

On the personal front, Christina's boyfriend recently broke up with her. She can't stop thinking about him. It's like her mind is stuck in a gear and can't shift out of it. It's normal to think about someone a lot after a breakup, but Christina's mind is really working overtime. She feels like a failure, as if his leaving must signify there's something wrong with *her*—and in fact, maybe there *is* something she needs to learn about herself from this breakup. She can't tell if it's best to quit beating herself up about it and view his departure as *his* issue, or if there is something helpful she can learn about herself. Was she emotionally distant? Did her obsessive tendencies drive him away? Her internal monologue never stops!

Even if the breakup *was* more about her ex-boyfriend's commitment issues than anything about Christina, she still wants to understand how she could have spotted these issues earlier so she doesn't wind up making the same "mistake" twice when she returns to the dating world. She reviews the relationship constantly, wondering if she should reach out to him or not, or perhaps she should, or maybe that would look desperate, but on the other hand maybe there are certain things she really just needs to say. . . . All of this has been going on for a month, keeping poor Christina up nights and unable to either move past the breakup or give it another shot. It's "analysis paralysis," a state that Christina knows all too well.

GOOD STARTING POINTS FOR CHRISTINA

- **The Three-Part Breath.** The Three-Part Breath is extremely grounding for Christina. By feeling exactly where her breath is moving through her body, she roots herself in the "here and now" instead of letting her mind spin out into hypothetical scenarios in which she calls or doesn't call her ex-boyfriend, aces or doesn't ace a meeting, et cetera ad nauseam. By slowing her breath, she slows her thoughts. Of course, Christina has a tendency to want to do the Three-Part Breath perfectly, but that's okay at first; her desire to do it perfectly actually motivates her to practice. The Three-Part Breath also guides her to practice to observe herself *without* judgment, which helps her recognize and manage her perfectionist tendencies.

■ **Mental Shortlist.** Christina has a "love-hate" relationship with her exceptional ability for mental tenacity. Her ability to focus like a laser beam can be a cognitive blessing or curse, depending on the situation. For example, when Christina was in law school, her mental tenacity was a boon: she studied every case till she knew it like the back of her hand, and she studied for the bar exam with a fervor that made the actual exam seem easy. However, when it comes to managing sudden urges to call or text her ex-boyfriend, that same mental tenacity can be a real vulnerability. Even though she ultimately feels it's best for her not to reach out to him at this point, she sometimes feels *totally overcome* with the urge to call him, mentally replays vivid positive memories in her mind that only make her miss him even more, or finds herself worrying obsessively that perhaps she is making a mistake by deciding not to reach out.

As a psychologist, of course I help Christina review whether or not reaching out to her ex might in fact possibly be a good idea (sometimes reaching out is a good thing). But once Christina reaches the point of being certain about her choice not to call him and just wants help in adhering to that choice—even when her mind starts behaving like a "dog with a bone" that can't quit focusing on the idea of calling him—the Mental Shortlist can be helpful. Basically, the Mental Shortlist technique helps Christina to redirect her thoughts away from a topic when she realizes that she's *ruminating* rather than really engaging in productive thought. This isn't a panacea, but it does facilitate Christina's goal of diverting her tenacious focus in moments of stress or nostalgia.

- **To-Do List with Emotions.** The To-Do List with Emotions brings Christina peace on multiple levels. Christina has always been a list maker who enjoyed the obvious benefits of organization and planning that lists provide. Adding in the step of emotional awareness and self-care plans helps Christina to stay connected to *why* she's doing the things on her list, which brings a sense of fulfilment. It also helps Christina to stay attuned to herself, since she has a tendency to override her emotions and "power through" tough situations. The ability to put feelings aside and get things done helps productivity and even well-being to a certain degree, but Christina does at least need to stay aware of what the feelings are that she's overriding in the first place so that she can remember to get the emotional support she needs. Otherwise, she is vulnerable to experiencing burnout or an amorphous feeling of anxiety that she can't quite source.

Just like marathoners might make a strategic decision to "run through the pain," they still need to be aware of the pain so they can get follow-up care afterward or take stronger measures to minimize injury during the race. The To-Do List with Emotions also helps Christina make sure to notice and celebrate positive moments when she experiences pride, security, or even joy as she accomplishes meaningful items on her list, such as the time-intensive task of locating and arranging a health aide for her mother. Of course, Christina is not happy that her mother needs a health aide, but she does feel fulfilled to be able to "give back" and provide care for the woman who sacrificed so much to give Christina the chance for a better life. The To-Do List with Emotions keeps Christina connected to what she's feeling as she goes through her list, and guides her to practice self-care if needed.

2. William: The Scrutinizer

William is an accountant of average height with a slim build, in his early thirties, with carefully groomed hair, eyeglasses that are somehow always impeccably clean, and a facial expression that always seems slightly tense, even when he's having a good time. The reason for the constantly tense expression is that William is a bit of a worrywart. Whether he's going on vacation or shopping at the grocery store, he's *always* scanning for potential "issues," like subpar online reviews of the hotel property, signs of uncleanliness in the produce section, or noticing what appears to be an unattended child near the checkout lane and wondering where her guardian might be. We all do things like this to a degree, but for William it's more a way of life. Sometimes he comes across as pessimistic or even a little snobby, since he seems to find "issues" with almost everything and frequently rejects people, places, and things that don't pass scrutiny.

William is a little embarrassed about how "fussy" he can be sometimes, but on the other hand, he prides himself on the fact that most of his careful decisions actually *do* turn out favorably. He believes, probably somewhat accurately, that his life has generally gone pretty well, partially because of his meticulous scrutiny of any potential involvement before actually getting involved with almost anything or anyone. He's aware of the irony that sometimes his search for potential issues can actually *become* an issue, but overall he has found the benefits outweigh the risks in his approach to life—at least until recently.

Since William thinks so carefully about even relatively minor issues, he thinks *very* carefully about bigger issues: for example, he'd like to leave his current job at a large accounting firm and find a job as an in-house accountant for a smaller company instead. Job recruiters were initially very eager to work with him, since he has a great résumé, but he's been so picky about every single potential employment match that they've basically quit calling him with new ideas. William has earned a reputation for being *so* selective that he's boxed himself into a corner because the recruiters are sick of having their suggestions picked to death.

On the personal front, William would love to meet the right woman and settle down. However, as you might guess, it's really hard for him to find someone who passes scrutiny. She must be well educated, intelligent, fit, have long hair, be within two years of William's age, be close with her family, be interested in home-making but not overly so; she must have a career but not be too distracted by it; she must like wine but not drink too much; she must be sophisticated but not seem uptight; she must eat a healthy diet but not be neurotic about it. . . . The list goes on and on.

Moreover, there's the matter of William's scrutiny of *himself.* Whenever he does meet someone acceptable, he starts mentally and physically reviewing everything about himself to see if there are any "issues" that could render him undesirable to his paragon of a date. He worries that men in the background of her photos appear slightly taller than William; or since her profile notes that she is new to the city, he frets that she might feel overwhelmed by the idea of a relationship; or she uses a particular slang word in her profile that he doesn't use himself, and so he worries whether that means they are just too different. Even getting out the door for the date itself can take hours, as he worries about whether he's overdressed, underdressed, or somehow just doesn't "look right." A little mental back-and-forth is normal for many singles, and to a certain degree a little predate scrutiny helps us to put our best foot forward—but William takes it to an extreme. Ironically, all of this cognitive overdrive around engineering the perfect match often backfires on him and makes him come across as nervous, unconfident, or just so extremely reserved that it's hard for women to connect with him.

One of the most frustrating parts for William is that sometimes he *knows* when he's "doing it" (judging himself or others in a neurotic, counterproductive manner or worrying to the point of absurdity). However, the kicker is that he then judges himself *for being this way* or worries about how much he worries. It's like a mirror that just keeps reflecting another mirror, to the point of infinity, with William stuck in the middle.

GOOD STARTING POINTS FOR WILLIAM

- **The Three-Part Breath.** William uses the Three-Part Breath to slow himself down and ease up on his self-judgment, as well as his tendency to judge others. By learning to observe his breath in a neutral and nonreactive manner, he increases his ability to experience himself and others with less scrutiny. This fosters a lighter attitude. It also cues him to literally "take in" the space around him, creating a wonderful human level of connection instead of the constant inspecting and evaluating that gets him stuck in a sterile silo. Moreover, it gives him something else to focus on when his mind would otherwise default into a worry loop. As William learns to observe himself, he also learns to recognize when he's going down a mental "rabbit hole," such as ruminating about the possible sanitation challenges of his grocery store while shopping for produce. Learning to stay focused on the Three-Part Breath teaches him to recognize when he's veering off track and calmly redirect himself back to the moment, without judging himself or overreacting to having gone off track.

- **Zone of Control.** William finds the Zone of Control to be a helpful tool to determine what to focus on and what to let go of. For example, he recently met a woman he really likes; he's actually quite smitten. Since part of his way of showing he cares about her is to get a little obsessive about scrutinizing himself and his plans for their dates to make sure he doesn't commit any "blunders" (often actually just minor missteps, but of course he would imagine them to be enormous), William can end up spending a *lot* of time and energy worrying about things he can't control. He is also at risk of second-guessing himself to the point of total insecurity if he doesn't have some sort of boundary around which to focus his scrutiny and where to just "let go." The Zone of Control's step-by-step process of evaluating his considerations in terms of whether or not they are actionable items within his control (such as making sure to choose a restaurant with great reviews and a romantic atmosphere), or simply a "fact of life" that he must just learn to accept (such as the fact that he's five foot eight and she may prefer taller men) is great for him because it lets him focus his mental energy where it is appropriate and productive rather than draining and destructive.

- **Worry Time.** William loves structure. It makes him feel safe. In a peculiar way, he also actually *likes* worrying and actually finds it reassuring: worrying helps him feel less likely to get blindsided by problems, since worrying somewhat frequently proves that he's clearly someone who is on the lookout for potential problems. The way William sees things, it's better to be someone who worries a lot than someone who bumbles through life and is constantly getting caught unawares. This approach worked well for William as a young person, because learning how to think critically and anticipate problems is a skill that takes years to fully develop; and till he was about twenty-five he was still on the "learning curve" for the skill of thinking ahead. However, since his late twenties, William has almost gotten *too good* at this skill. It's become his cognitive "go-to" habit that he can't seem to "turn off." He'll be standing in line at the grocery store and suddenly find himself mentally reviewing everything from his homeowner's insurance policy to whether his taxes are done, and sometimes even his end-of-life planning. It can get a little out of control; but he doesn't feel comfortable just telling himself not to think about these things, since they are actually legitimate issues . . . but there has to be a better time and place for this than the grocery store line, right?

Worry Time helps William put boundaries and structure around his worries so that he no longer feels he's stuck in a binary choice between constant worry and total negligence. He makes a list of all the important things he needs to worry about and adds to it anytime he wants (he keeps the list in his smartphone). Every Tuesday night for a predetermined length of time, he focuses on the list. This helps him to make sure he keeps track of these worries, instead of those *worries* keeping track of *him*.

- **Mind Mapping.** William's mind works in a very detailed manner. His ability to focus on any given topic is really quite astounding; it can be a gift in many situations (colleagues are often simultaneously impressed and dismayed by his ability to spot errors in their reports at lightning speed). However, he sometimes focuses to the point of myopia: he misses the forest for the trees. For example, when he considers the list of potential employers in his job search, he can literally spend hours analyzing endless factors related to each company's geographical location: Is it headquartered in his city? If not, would he eventually be asked to relocate? Would relocating be costly? What would the social scene be like there? What is that city's weather like? How is its crime rate? Does it have good hospitals?

William can "spin his wheels" on this one facet so much that he actually disregards other important information, such as the company paying a higher salary that offsets the cost of relocation, or that the extra income boost might allow him to live in a very nice, low-crime part of town. Mind Mapping guides William to put all of the various components on paper and then literally "connect the dots" so he can synthesize all of his thought streams and get an overall perspective on them without having to hold each one in mind simultaneously. This helps him gain insight and find solutions that would be impossible if he were trying to "do it all in his head," since he tends to think through each component so deeply.

3. Greg: Grinning and Bearing It

Greg is a quintessential salesperson: At age forty, he still has a boyish charm and easygoing confidence that help him to "move the ball forward" (one of his favorite phrases) to close deals and lead his sales team effectively. He avoids delving too deeply into feelings or personal vulnerability. Instead, his perspective has always been to just stay active and keep smiling, or "keep dancing," as he likes to say, and this approach has generally served him pretty well. However, lately Greg has found himself facing some unexpected difficulties. For example, his sales team has a routine in which every Monday the team members sit at a round table and each person takes turns giving updates. Greg has done these Monday-morning updates a thousand times before, but lately he finds himself getting sweaty palms and drawing a total blank as his turn approaches. Similarly, he went to a client meeting recently where he found himself suddenly feeling so self-conscious that he had a difficult time even focusing on what the client was saying. Normally, Greg is able to "power through" most situations, and he was somehow able to get through the recent client situation—but he's concerned because these "little breakdowns" or "mini panic attacks" really don't feel normal to him. It was actually a huge step for Greg to even call my office: he generally thinks of therapy as "something for other people." But Greg knows he doesn't want to get sidelined by whatever has been "zapping" him lately.

On the personal side, Greg is recently divorced and actually pretty excited to date again. He's not looking for anything serious, but he does enjoy dating attractive and accomplished women who share his (usually!) easygoing style. Greg experienced a similar "mini panic attack" recently while chatting up an attractive woman at a friend's barbecue party, where he suddenly felt like a nervous high school boy all over again, and not in a good way. Most frustrating of all, this attack seemed to happen for no apparent reason: everything seemed totally normal one minute, and the next minute he was having trouble breathing, feeling sweaty, silently repeating to himself what a "loser" he was, and feeling unable to snap back to normal. He had to end the flirtatious conversation he was having somewhat abruptly in order to go be alone in the bathroom to calm himself down. All of this made him feel pathetic and frankly scared of when the next attack might strike.

Greg then started having a hard time going to big meetings or parties because he never knew when one of these little jolts might happen again. He suspected that he might be at a point of just "psyching himself out" with nerves, because the fear of these jolts got him so nervous that he actually felt even *more* prone to having them when he started thinking about them so much anytime a big event drew near—yet he felt powerless to stop thinking about them, because he was so worried about them. The Franklin D. Roosevelt quote "We have nothing to fear but fear itself" captures Greg's predicament well. Greg even went to a medical doctor to be 100 percent sure he was physically healthy, and the doctor confirmed it appeared to be stress-related. The doctor told Greg to "just relax." If only he knew how!

As Greg told me about his situation, he mentioned several times, in a conspiratorial tone, with a striking combination of great pride and profound shame, that no one in his life knew he was seeing a therapist. He took pride in how well he was hiding his struggle, but he also clearly viewed the struggle itself as a major vulnerability. **I often find that clients who experience physiological symptoms of anxiety have a personal rule that it's always best to keep your problems to yourself and even try to tune them out of your own awareness if possible.** They tend to reason that if you don't do this, then others may find you weak or needy. (Actually, the ability to locate and discuss your needs bodes well for strength and social relationships.) These clients sometimes get so good at their strategy of "acting fine" that they actually decrease their own awareness of their stressors. Denying awareness of stressors seems like a handy trick, until the anxiety eventually bursts out in the form of a "jolt," like Greg's did (similar to how spending as if you don't see price tags works great until you get a credit card bill).

To grow, Greg must both learn to manage the jolts and revise his personal rule that acknowledging and potentially sharing your problems makes you weak. This allows Greg to start dealing with problems *before* they start causing feelings of panic that he doesn't understand. Ironically, **disconnecting from his awareness of stressors is actually what sets Greg up to experience panic in the first place:** it's like purposely ignoring an overheating appliance in a state of deliberately ignorant bliss till it bursts into an overwhelming fiery blaze.

GOOD STARTING POINTS FOR GREG

■ **The Three-Part Breath.** The Three-Part Breath helps Greg in two major ways: First, it helps him learn to control his breathing so that he can regain his footing during those "mini panic attacks" he's been having. Second, it helps him recognize, label, and face the thoughts and emotions that he was previously working so hard to ignore.[4] Greg had become so good at his strategy of just "powering through" and not letting things get to him that he actually started to lose touch with his own sensitivities. That's why they burst upon him in the form of "mini panic attacks" that he didn't understand. He experienced those attacks as coming from nowhere, yet the truth was that they related to actual events in his life that he just didn't want to think about. He thought that ignoring irksome things would make life easier, which it did, until he began ignoring things that actually really needed his attention.

The Three-Part Breath teaches us to observe our own experiences in a nonjudgmental way. Greg's judgment of certain types of thoughts and feelings is what makes him so afraid of them; but by learning to just acknowledge that these thoughts and feelings occur and then handle them in a less reactive manner, Greg is able to face issues in a conscious manner instead of shunting them into his unconscious, where they have no choice but to fester and then foist themselves upon him in a bursting, panicky "jolt."

- **Anchoring Statements.** Greg finds Anchoring Statements to be a lifesaver—almost literally. When his "jolts" arise, he sometimes actually works himself up into thinking he might be having a heart attack or some other serious medical event. Naturally, this is terrifying and makes it almost impossible for him to "act normal" in a sales meeting or social situation. Worst of all, the more terrified he becomes of the jolt, the more intense the jolt will feel: his attitude of fear actually conditions him to experience the jolts as more terrifying than if he were calm about them (for example, imagine how even hitting your funny bone could build into a frightening experience if you had labeled the temporary pulsing numbness as a sign of a serious physical problem). By having a precrafted script—like, "I've seen my medical doctor and confirmed I'm fine; this will pass in three minutes flat"—Greg is better able to let the moment pass without getting completely derailed. By creating the Anchoring Statements during a calm, rational state, Greg can reground himself into that calm state by using them when a "jolt" might otherwise knock him off kilter.

- **Thought Replacement.** Anchoring Statements are great for grounding yourself when your body is spinning out into a spell of panic and you otherwise have no words other than maybe, "Oh my God, I'm having a heart attack!" They help you take a body-felt panic state and wrangle it into a calm, language-based state of mind. In contrast, Thought Replacement is used when we want to change cognitive habits that we experience so often that they're almost like what psychologists call "automatic thoughts." When we have automatic thoughts that we realize are actually not accurate or helpful, Thought Replacement is a very helpful tool for changing those patterns in a methodical manner. Greg is using Thought Replacement to break out of the "Can't tell anyone about my problems" belief that was causing him to bottle up all of his anxiety till it burst out in jolts. When a trusted friend or family member asks Greg how he's doing with the divorce, he overrides his automatic thought of, "Have to convince them I'm 100 percent fine" with the replacement thought, "Opening up is the right thing to do here." Even if it doesn't feel natural in the moment, Greg repeats it to himself a few times anyway, since he knows he has already evaluated the statement in therapy and accepted it as true.

Thought Replacements often *don't* feel natural during moments of stress, but that's actually normal: the whole point of adopting a Thought Replacement is that we're deliberately breaking out of our mold and doing something different because a part of us recognizes that it's to our own benefit to do so. Greg is successfully using Thought Replacement strategically during discussions involving personal vulnerability in order to create a "new normal" that helps him learn to develop awareness and acceptance of vulnerabilities through sharing and to enjoy the support that comes from opening up to the right people in a judicious manner. People use Thought Replacements for a variety of reasons, but they are generally best deployed when you have an ingrained way of thinking that you know you want to revise in a deliberate and methodical manner.

- **To-Do List with Emotions.** Like many clients who say they experience "mini panic attacks" and that they happen totally "out of the blue," Greg is someone who has recently taken on some new responsibilities. Recently divorced, he now has to manage living on his own, as well as coordinating visits and navigating a newly precarious relationship with his six-year-old daughter. Because he likes to "keep things light," he wasn't really processing emotions like fear or shame that arise when his errand list now includes items such as planning weekend visits with a little girl who is suddenly prone to angry outbursts as she grapples with the loss of a live-in dad.

  Similarly, his "simple stuff," like grocery shopping, now carries a new layer of emotion, since this used to be done by his wife; doing it himself reminds him of the divorce. By creating an errand list that includes spaces for him to enumerate the emotions that arise from each errand, along with healthy self-care steps to manage the emotions, Greg found that his "jolts" actually started to occur less frequently, likely because he is now dealing with emotions proactively instead of "powering through" them or even ignoring them altogether. Up to a certain point, powering through worked for Greg, but he was wise enough to recognize that certain situations are actually handled most productively with conscious awareness.

Whether you're "a little obsessive" like Christina, "kind of a worrywart" like William, or "going over the top" like Greg, or some combination of all three, the **Nervous Energy Approach has techniques to help build your skills to manage your nervous energy for increased well-being while simultaneously facilitating progress toward your personal and professional goals.**

Set Yourself Up for Success

- **Be patient with yourself.** The techniques in this book will be easiest to learn if you are patient with yourself. While *some* techniques may seem intuitive for you, please don't expect yourself to master *every* technique immediately. Some techniques may be extremely easy for you and you may even have your own enhancements or ways to personalize them. If you do, please let me know via social media or private contact, because I'd love to hear! But some of the techniques will likely take some time and practice before you truly feel comfortable using them.

- **Trust yourself, and get more help if you need it.** You should (generally) always trust your own judgment on what is best for you. If you have concerns about anything you read in this book or if some of it just doesn't seem right for you, then please feel free to take whatever parts of this book work for you and discard the rest. And, of course, remember that this book is not a substitute for psychotherapy. If you ever feel you might benefit from speaking to a therapist, please know that there are many qualified therapists who are willing and able to help. See chapter 6 for help with choosing a therapist if you're considering a professional. High functioning people often have unique therapeutic needs!

- **Embrace your energy.** Remember that the goal here is to harness your nervous energy, not to get rid of it. A person with zero anxiety or without a reservoir of extra cognitive energy is oftentimes a person without awareness of threats, without goals, and/or without resources to navigate threats and goals. If you find yourself feeling keyed up or a little on edge, don't automatically categorize that feeling as a bad thing. Instead, face whatever is on your mind that is causing you to feel this way, then consider which strategy (perhaps involving tools in this book!) would help you to make progress in that situation.

If you can't figure out what's causing the feeling in the first place, try the Three-Part Breath, Mind Mapping, or To-Do List with Emotions to search for clues. However, if you really just need help learning to wind down sometimes, check out the variations on the Three-Part Breath (the "S-L-O-W" on page 131 and "Cocoon Breathing" on page 132), try the Worry Time technique, and make sure you're exercising or finding other healthy outlets for extra energy—and remember you can always get more help if you need it!

A Word About Written Exercises

If you decide to try any of the worksheets or exercises in this book (which I hope you will!), I generally suggest completing them on paper, or at least digitally (meaning you literally use your "digits," or fingers, to type them into your phone or an online document). **Many high functioning people are used to doing things "in their head" and feel that they glean so much benefit just from *reading* the steps of an exercise that they don't actually *do* the exercise, because they feel like they've gotten the main points of the exercise just by *thinking* their way through it.** While it may be true that you're able to gain significant insight or awareness just by reading about an exercise and even doing certain steps of it in your head, please know that doing the exercises on paper or at least typing your responses into your phone forces you to focus longer and more deeply than if you're just scanning your eyes across a page to read. This is why students who study with a pen in hand tend to get better grades. By harnessing your hands to write or type your thoughts, and choosing exact words to express yourself in written exercises, you'll generally process the material on a deeper level than if you just spend a couple of minutes eyeballing an exercise and thinking about it in a broad, less specific way that doesn't require specific word choices. Deeper processing increases insight, awareness, memory, and overall learning; writing is your ticket to this type of processing.

Moreover, if you write by hand and notice your mood demonstrated by the style of your handwriting (for example, hurried and nervous writing, or slow and careful writing), you're creating a richer visual record of your mental work and your personal experience. This also applies to the material upon which you wrote (writing captured on a cocktail napkin at a restaurant, or writing done in a special notebook you keep on your nightstand). When you glance at that writing a month later randomly as you reorganize your household or office drawers one day, **you'll be cued back to a rich memory that awakens the same neural channels as when you did the exercise, which stimulates greater memory and context for the material you learned.** This memory will likely be more valuable to your learning and recall process than if you merely think your way through an exercise without leaving any trace or record of your work. Learning is generally deeper and richer when we slow our mental pace enough to write things down, but it takes more time to actually do that—and high functioning people may balk at the extra time because they do tend to be very busy. Ironically, the extra time spent focusing is actually yet another hidden boost: spending more time on material generally increases your ability to learn the material. **So if you can spare five minutes or more (or even two!), I urge you to try the exercises with a pen and paper, or at least a smartphone.** One of the most frequent complaints I get from high functioning people is that they feel "stuck in their head." Taking the time to write will help you get your thoughts *out of your head* and increase your objectivity about them.

The exercises described in this book are deliberately simple enough that you can do them on any plain sheet of paper, but you may also find online formats available at www.NervousEnergyBook.com. But even if you don't have a pristine sheet of paper handy, fret not: most of the exercises can be scribbled on a cocktail napkin or the back of an envelope, emailed to yourself, or captured in whatever way is best for you at any given time or place. The point is just to **do yourself a favor and set yourself up for success** by taking a moment to actually *write down* your responses when called for—just as you'd do for any important material you wanted to learn and master in your personal or professional life.

5.

Essentials of Nervous Energy

Self-Discipline, Perfectionism, and Mindfulness

Inspiration exists, but it has to find you working.
—PABLO PICASSO

Self-Discipline

Did you know that self-discipline is a finite resource? This means that each person can only discipline themselves to do a certain number of things at any given time, especially if they want to do those things *well*. For example, it takes self-discipline to dance the waltz well (you have to discipline your mental focus to keep the dance steps in mind, stay aware of the musical rhythm, notice what your dance partner is doing, and hold your body in a unique posture). It also takes self-discipline to sing the national anthem well (you have to focus on remembering the words of the song, monitor the pitch of your voice, and consider your tempo). While you might be able to sing the national anthem on key *or* dance the waltz with grace, you might struggle to do *both at the same time;* and you would almost certainly demonstrate a decline in the quality of your output on each task compared to if you performed the tasks one at a time. This applies to self-discipline for other challenging tasks, such as trying to learn new cognitive techniques like the ones in this book.

A simple way to understand how self-discipline applies to your learning is to remember that it may take a fair amount of your "cognitive horsepower" to learn new techniques and then practice them a few times—so please **be patient with yourself and consider giving yourself a little leeway on other areas that may compete for your self-discipline while learning something new.** For example, if you don't often treat yourself to meals out, consider taking this book along with your pen and notebook to a restaurant so you can enjoy a nice meal as you focus yourself to read and practice the techniques you are learning. Or, if you are lucky enough to enjoy great food and drink so often that studying over a meal doesn't feel like an indulgence, but you find yourself starved for quiet time, then try reading this book and/or practicing the techniques in a peaceful environment like a beautiful park or beach. The idea is just to indulge yourself a bit in one area while you increase your self-discipline in another area as you focus on learning something new. By easing up on one area of self-discipline even briefly, we make "wiggle room" for other areas.

Some people worry that if they allow themselves strategic latitude in some areas so that they can hone in on certain skills for growth, they'll end up "running wild" rather than actually adhering to the strategy. While it's important to make sure you stay accountable to yourself and do actually *use* your newly freed self-discipline to focus on your new goal, don't worry too much about "running wild" unless you've had problems with addiction or bombastic behavior before. **Generally speaking, granting yourself a** little leeway in a targeted manner will not become a "road to perdition" for you: learning the techniques in this book will actually help you to better organize your thoughts and make use of your emotions in a productive way that will ultimately *increase* your capacity for attention, concentration, and self-discipline.

Think of the initial investment of time and energy required to learn new techniques as similar to the way that you might seem to "lose" a little time and money initially by disciplining yourself to join and attend a gym. Although the investment is greater during your learning curve, you ultimately gain time and efficiency (and pleasure!) by having a healthy body that is stronger, more agile, and better able to meet your needs. Investing in your mental dexterity works the same way: **learning ways to manage your thoughts and emotions takes some initial effort, but the process can actually be fun as you get to know your mind better, and the rewards are great.**

Learning new skills, piloting new perspectives, and trying new exercises requires at least mild attention and concentration. Self-discipline is often a driver of attention and concentration. This means that your ability to learn new skills may benefit from giving yourself some temporary "breathing room" and easing your self-discipline for *some* things in service of your goal to learn new skills—skills that will ultimately increase your ability to achieve the things you had temporarily paused in order to bolster your skill set!

How I Used My Knowledge of Self-Discipline for Dissertation Success

When I was a poor graduate student working on my PhD, a big source of stress was, naturally, my dissertation. It was by far the most complex piece of work I had ever had to complete: over a multiyear period, I had to design an original research paradigm, get it approved by my dissertation committee as well as the university's research approval board,

(continued)

and then execute said research by personally staffing 100 percent of data collection sessions in which I administered a lengthy battery of psychological tests to hundreds of undergraduates in small groups of approximately fifteen at a time. Next, I had to analyze mountains of data (which was especially hard for me since I struggle with math). Meanwhile, I had to write a 100-plus-page dissertation about the entire investigation that would demonstrate a breadth of knowledge beyond anything I'd ever had to show before, then prepare a live presentation. Finally, I had to go through a process known as "defending your dissertation," during which your dissertation committee deliberately asks challenging questions during and after the live presentation of your research, just to *really make sure* that you are truly qualified to call yourself a PhD. During this process, I also had to complete what felt like an endless cycle of feedback, reanalysis, rewriting, and refining with my dissertation committee. Even just corralling all of those professors together for a meeting was often a feat in itself, much less getting them to agree on which of their (often-divergent) ideas should be implemented for the next round of edits.

While I truly felt privileged to have the chance to conduct my own psychological research and work under the esteemed professors on my dissertation committee, I'll admit that I also felt quite daunted by this massive, multiyear undertaking: the process of doing the type of dissertation required in order to graduate from a reputable clinical psychology doctorate program can take anywhere from two to four years *post–master's degree*. From what I had observed in students ahead of me in my program, it was clear that the timeline would be largely dependent on how quickly I would be able to create drafts for my committee to read, gently but firmly hound the members to approve certain sections or give me clear feedback, incorporate their feedback for further drafts, and then rehound them to read the new drafts and provide more feedback. I was also carrying a significant burden of time pressure in relation to finances: the longer my dissertation process took, the longer it would be before I could get my PhD. The longer it took to get my PhD, the longer it would be before I could start earning any real income (doctoral students in clinical psychology are paid notoriously small stipends). I had no safety net or parental support; and student loans were piling up as I tried to stay financially afloat while living in a single room at a women's rooming house on the outrageously expensive yet breathtakingly divine island known as Manhattan.

These circumstances created a feeling of pressure to work as much as humanly possible on my dissertation (and on my committee!), while also taking three subway trains each way to the hospital where I worked *full-time* doing my required clinical training. (Perhaps this is the modern-day equivalent of Grandma telling you she had to walk barefoot uphill in the snow for three miles to the schoolhouse, but I just want you to understand that I was really "in the trenches" during these years!). As you can imagine, managing my self-discipline was mission-critical.

My knowledge that self-discipline is a finite resource led me to a solution that was extremely fun, wildly productive, and ultimately financially sound: I made a deal with myself that as long as I was working on my dissertation, I was allowed to eat or drink anything I wanted, anywhere I wanted. I spent countless hours with my laptop at glamorous, expensive places where I would normally never have allowed myself due to my graduate-student budget and my otherwise careful diet. One of my favorite spots was the jaw-droppingly elegant restaurant in the Carlyle, one of New York City's finest hotels. I would regularly sign checks for a hundred dollars after a feast of decadent food and drinks (the Old Cuban cocktail there is still the best drink I think I've ever had in my life!) and pay the bill with my student-loan money. The only "strings attached" were that I had to have my laptop open with my dissertation on the screen and my hands on the keyboard—unless my fingers were lifting a glass to take a sip of my Old Cuban or a forkful of heavenly food, they were glued to the keyboard. I wouldn't even let myself place an order for food or drink until I had that laptop open and connected to Wi-Fi, with my dissertation document live on the screen.

While the strategy I used might initially appear to be financially reckless, and the mere *idea* of paying for meals at New York City's mind-blowingly luxurious (and mind-blowingly expensive) restaurants with student loans probably strikes fear in the hearts of accountants everywhere—it actually worked beautifully for me both personally and professionally. By allowing myself to strategically "loosen up" in certain

(continued)

areas, I found the energy to "buckle down" in others. I completed my dissertation and graduated in the minimum number of years my doctoral program required (five years postcollege; we have longer minimums because of the requirement of thousands of hours of supervised clinical work). Completing my degree increased my earning power dramatically; so my strategy was ultimately cheaper than if I had languished in that doctoral program for another year or two, living on a pittance and forcing myself to try to write my dissertation in my lonely SRO with a spartan glass of water and a bowl of ramen noodles (something I considered for about a minute before heading to the Carlyle).

In short, I guess you could say that I ate and drank my way to dissertation success!

A Word About Perfectionism

Many high functioning people struggle with perfectionism, for several reasons:

1. They're used to being able to learn things quickly and do them reasonably well, if they're giving an honest effort; they are intuitively aware that this has to do with their relatively high level of intelligence and drive. This context can lead them to regard mistakes as signs that they must not be trying hard enough, or to regard mistakes as threats to their identity as intelligent, capable people.

2. They have found that by shooting for the moon, they will at least reach the stars (sorry for the cliché, but it's such an apt one that I couldn't help but use it!), so they aim for perfection as a way to at least do well.

3. They find that taking a critical look at their performance helps improve their output, so they habitually scan for errors. To a certain degree, this is helpful because it is con-

sonant with a high level of conscientiousness;[1] but if it goes too far, then it can result in a person imagining that they should not make *any* mistakes, or in feeling so negatively about mistakes that their engagement begins to suffer. This dynamic can impede rather than aid the learning process.

If you're like many high functioning people, you've achieved a fair amount of success through being "a little hard on yourself" (okay, maybe "really, really hard on yourself" is more accurate for some of you!). **While there is a healthy value in being willing and able to be the first person to take an honest look at yourself so that you can recognize issues and build awareness of areas you want to improve, please do yourself a big favor and beware of the tipping point where healthy self-discipline becomes perfectionist-driven self-flagellation.**[2]

In a Nutshell

Self-flagellation is basically beating yourself up to the point where it's hard to find the joy and motivation necessary to remain engaged in the process of learning and improvement. **Self-discipline** and a desire to do your best are great—but if they morph into self-flagellation, then your motivation, ability, or energy to learn can suffer.

The chart that follows can help you understand the difference between healthy self-discipline and perfectionist-driven self-flagellation.

Imagine the following scenario: you're attempting to follow a new low-sugar diet because you've noticed that excess sugar provokes mood swings, energy crashes, and belly fat for you. You made it through about seventy-two hours, and now you've just "cheated" a bit by eating a cupcake at your best friend's birthday party. You're already feeling a jittery sugar buzz that you're sure will soon result in a sluggish crash.

Healthy Self-Discipline vs.
Perfectionist Self-Flagellation

HEALTHY SELF-DISCIPLINE	PERFECTIONIST DRIVEN SELF-FLAGELLATION
Okay, that cupcake was definitely a mistake. But I'm very proud of myself for being willing and able to recognize this after just one cupcake so that I can quickly get back on track. Maybe I'll even call a friend to talk this through and perhaps even have a laugh together as I move forward.	I'm such an idiot—barely a few days into this and I'm already eating a cupcake. I'm destined for failure. I better not tell anyone about this; it's so embarrassing and such a stupid problem in the first place.
The whole reason I'm trying to eliminate sugar is because I tend to get a little (okay, a lot) carried away around it, so I guess it's not surprising that part of what I need to learn is how to manage cravings even in high-emotion situations like a good friend's birthday party. I wonder if a part of me thought that partaking would be a way to show that this event mattered to me, or maybe a part of me just wanted to indulge, so I used "being nice" as an excuse? Is there some way I could gracefully turn down the cupcake next time, if I want to, without making my friend feel like I wasn't participating in her birthday? Or maybe I could offer myself a special diet-friendly treat in situations where I know I'll be facing extra temptation?	Obviously I just go hog-wild around sugar, like a total moron. I feel like such a disgusting pig. I made big, lofty promises to myself about giving it up, but at the first sign of real temptation, I gave in. I'm such a loser.
Let me sit down and review the factors that led to this relapse so I can better understand my triggers and prepare for next time. This happened when I attended a birthday party on an empty stomach, which I know is a setup for failure—but I got caught up in work stuff and mistakenly thought I could wing it this time. I certainly can't promise I'll never get caught up in work stuff again, and I actually don't want to prioritize skipping a random cupcake over something important at work—so what can I do? Maybe I should start carrying protein bars or packets of mixed nuts in my bag for "emergencies" when I don't have time to eat a proper meal. I think I'll put some in my bag right now so I can leave this episode behind me and move forward.	For goodness sake, I idiotically skipped eating the entire day—of *course* I lapsed into my old habits. I'm such an idiot. Who on earth would expect that they could skip meals and still make good food choices? I've been down this road a hundred times and I keep making the *same* mistake. How stupid can I be?!

Many people who are aware that their perfectionism regularly leads to self-flagellation are afraid to address the issue, because they think that their perfectionism may actually have helped them do pretty well in life so far. They are afraid that reducing perfectionism will require them to toss out even healthy self-discipline, thereby turning them into complacent slobs. As you look at the comparisons in the chart, I hope you'll see that **the idea is not to just replace self-flagellating thoughts with Pollyanna-ish, wishful thinking,** like, "I'm totally sure I'll get it right next time; and even if I mess up royally then it's no big deal"; or, "I'm 100 percent great just the way I am, and I don't need to change a single thing." Done right, good self-discipline addresses areas of struggle squarely and productively; yet it does so in a way that facilitates motivation and engagement.[3]

Here's a little trick to help you stay on the right side of the self-flagellation versus self-discipline equation: When you notice yourself lapsing into old behaviors or cognitive habits that you're trying to change using the tools in this book, don't mentally beat yourself up for mistakes or lapses. Instead, **congratulate yourself in that very moment for your awareness of the lapse and your willingness to remedy it, then practice a technique to help yourself improve the situation.** By framing your awareness of the mistake as a positive (which it is, compared to nonawareness of it), you will empower yourself to address the mistake in a pragmatic, healthy manner.

Another rule of thumb for self-talk is to **speak to yourself in the same way that you would talk to a good friend who wanted your honest input as she tried to work on a stumbling block.** You would use a tone that was both honest *and* tactful. Try to give yourself the same courtesy and respect as you learn to apply some new tactics to old cognitive or emotional habits: be firm, but also be fair and compassionate—and maybe even have some fun! This is usually the way that people get the best results when learning new material to change old habits.

To avoid the pitfalls of perfectionism while retaining your high level of conscientiousness and drive for success, remember that **the key word here is "practice."** It would be unreasonable (and even grandiose!) for you to think that you would immediately master *all* of these techniques after just one or two attempts. Certainly, this *can* happen in some cases when a person has an epiphany or "aha moment" with certain techniques, but even in those situations, it's wise to understand that during times of stress you might be vulnerable to sliding into old habits. Habitual reactions and behaviors are actually how the brain saves energy and moves quickly. The goal here is to learn *new* cognitive habits, which takes an initial investment of time, energy, and patience with yourself.

So if and when you do catch yourself engaging in perfectionist-fueled self-flagellation as you work to develop new habits, remember to **congratulate yourself on your awareness during moments of lapse or struggle, and then pivot to get back on track.** Otherwise, you run the risk of demotivating yourself or making the recognition of errors so unpleasant that you push them *out* of your awareness. The goal is to **strike a balance between honest awareness of how you've slipped and the supportive compassion you would show to a good friend who was hungry for real-yet-courteous feedback**. This is the recipe for *true* perfection that leads to positive, lasting change.

The Need for Achievement

Psychologists study many factors of personality, and one of the factors often of interest to high functioning people is a factor called "need for achievement" (Murray, 1938). Just like it sounds, this factor measures an individual's drive to achieve. Some people care a lot about achievement, while others really couldn't care less. High functioning people tend to care. Sometimes they actually care *so much* that they end up getting in their own way.

Ironically, the higher an individual's need for achievement is, the more likely he or she is to struggle to complete complex goals—at least when we compare people with a high need for achievement against people with a medium need for achievement. (People with a low need for achievement don't tend to accomplish much at all, not surprisingly.) Research suggests that this is because people with a high need for achievement can get so addicted to external validation or intrinsic enjoyment of achievement that they become resistant to projects that could take longer or require more grappling, since those projects delay the gratification of achievement. But grappling is how we make meaningful gains in our skill set. That's why the Nervous Energy Approach encourages you to be patient with yourself. Instead of expecting overnight results, be willing to slow down and practice the techniques, greeting foibles with curiosity rather than harshness. Learn to embrace difficulties sometimes (this is not to say become complacent about difficulties; it just means to be willing to allow yourself some latitude as you negotiate a challenge). This not only makes life less stressful, it is associated with greater success for complex goals.

Struggle is nothing to become panicked by; but at the same time I want to validate and recognize that discomfort with struggle is normal—in fact, it's healthy! Discomfort is part of what motivates us to learn how to resolve the source of the struggle. So we don't want to be in denial of struggle or invalidate the idea that struggle can be unpleasant. We don't want to be complacent about it, but we also don't want to be afraid of acknowledging it.

Some high functioning people have actually achieved a lot by deliberately amping up their sense of alarm to signs of imperfections, faults, or struggles. They do this on purpose because they believe that intentionally overresponding to small problems will nip those problems in the bud and help stave off the development of bigger problems. To a certain degree this is true, but there's a tipping point where this tactic can become demotivating and counterproductive. (Ever tried to learn something new with a Negative Nancy leaning over your shoulder whispering harsh words every five seconds?) So do your best to remain forgiving-yet-focused as you grapple with new things, including what you learn in this book. Sometimes experience and practice are the best teachers if we are truly open to them.

The Role of Mindfulness in the Nervous Energy Approach

The Nervous Energy Approach is comprised of nine tools my clients have found reliably practical and helpful. You are more than welcome to browse the book and start with whatever tool feels most applicable if a certain one "jumps out at you," but I encourage you to make sure you *eventually* check out the Three-Part Breath. In fact, unless any of the other techniques are screaming your name (and if they are, then by all means please start with them!), I recommend you consider starting with the Three-Part Breath. There is a reason that this technique is listed at the start of the package of techniques: it builds mindfulness skills that will help you to understand which of the *other* techniques in this book will be most helpful at any given moment. What are mindfulness skills, and why do they matter so much (besides just helping you to select the most helpful techniques from this book)? I'm glad you asked! I'd like to share more about this with you and help you understand why I'm so passionate about mindfulness, both personally and professionally, as a foundational tool for high functioning people like yourself.

My History with Mindfulness

I want to share with you here a little more about my background with mindfulness, since high functioning people tend to be (rightfully!) curious about a person's history and credentials, especially in the context of learning skills from said person. My credentials as a psychologist are easy to grasp because psychology is such a highly regulated profession; but a person's level of knowledge in mindfulness can be harder to gauge, especially for someone who might not have an extensive background in the subject. Mindfulness knowledge is gained partly through memorization of facts and techniques, but it flourishes through the experience of practicing those techniques and applying them in day-to-day life.[4] So let me tell you how I came to develop a deep relationship with mindfulness and yoga—which was actually long before I became a psychologist.

Most people who meet me today assume that I had an idyllic life, but I actually had some pretty big challenges. I believe these challenges were fundamental to my growth, and prepared me to embrace mindfulness when the opportunity arose. I began learning mindfulness skills when I was seventeen, as a beginning yoga student. My life was quite chaotic at the time: I had moved out of my parents' house at the age of fifteen, and the court declared me an emancipated minor at the age of sixteen. This means I was on my own and legally considered an adult the summer before my junior year of high school. I was definitely in need of mindfulness skills.

After a couple of years of chaos, I somehow found my way into a rather austere Ashtanga yoga studio that had a strong emphasis on mindfulness meditation. Soon after attending that first class, I was going on yoga retreats and learning to use yoga and meditation to find the focus I needed in order to see (and change) my own role in creating chaos in my teenage life. I continued learning about mindfulness as I built my personal yoga and meditation practice, and even more as I became a yoga teacher in my early twenties, before I even knew that I would eventually become a clinical psychologist. I continued studying mindfulness at Columbia University with the esteemed Dr. Robert Tenzin Thurman, the Oxford scholar and first American to be ordained as a Tibetan monk, and later in my doctoral studies as I assisted with research on the role of mindfulness in psychology. I'm still a student of mindfulness, and I will always consider myself a "student." In fact, one of the first lessons in Buddhism is that "beginner's mind" is the ideal mindset, the one we all want to cultivate, so I actually take refuge in knowing how much more I have to learn about this important field.[5]

By my early twenties, I had become a certified yoga teacher. I worked as an assistant in group classes with other teachers I admired as a way to develop my teaching skills, but I was primarily a private teacher for individual lessons. The thing about private yoga lessons is that they're somewhat costly (frankly, that's partially why I was teaching them—I needed to make ends meet). Perhaps because of the cost, most of the students I had were high functioning Manhattanites with busy lives and demanding careers. Like many New Yorkers, these students had an unusual level of drive and self-discipline. They were eager to strategize how they used their time; that's probably why they hired a private yoga teacher in the first place. They would often ask me to create customized yoga and meditation programs to help them increase their focus or calm their minds—or both. I soon realized, working with these remarkable students on their personal goals, that the most impactful changes I helped them make were more mental than physical. At first, I was a little shocked at how positively they responded to mindfulness meditation, but it soon became clear that **they just loved having an overview of their mind and their reactions to themselves or life in general. Having a mindful overview was soothing to them, and it enabled them to *manage* themselves better.**

The experience of *teaching* mindfulness skills as a yoga teacher in a private setting was an amazing opportunity for growth in my own mindfulness skills. We often learn a topic much more deeply by attempting to teach it to others (I rediscovered this the hard way as an early-career adjunct professor fielding questions from clever psychology undergraduates, but that's another story!). Teaching mindfulness, along with other forms of meditation and yoga, helped me see how fulfilling it is to give people the tools to create real, lasting change in their lives. These experiences are what stimulated me to earn a doctorate in clinical psychology so I could learn *more* about how the mind works and be even more effective with thoughtful, driven people who were willing to sweat a little (literally and figuratively) in order to grow.

As a graduate student in clinical psychology, I was pleasantly surprised to learn that the field of psychology was incorporating mindfulness skills as helpful tools for everything from problem-solving and relationship-building to stress management and anxiety reduction. Although I am pleased to see that mindfulness meditation, a practice I've known and loved since before I even took a professional interest in psychology, is now widely recognized for its psychological benefits, I have noticed that the term "mindfulness" has become a bit of a buzzword—to the point that it now gets thrown around by many people, including members of my profession, in ways that can be confusing or inaccurate. So I'm really grateful for the opportunity to clarify and share with you my own perspective on mindfulness and how it fits with the psychology techniques in this book. **If you already have a foundation in mindfulness, that's great—this book will capitalize on your skills and hopefully expand them—but if you don't have any previous knowledge of it, you will likely develop some skills, especially as you learn the Three-Part Breath technique.**

The field of psychology has embraced mindfulness for many reasons, but three big ones are that it reduces stress, helps people make better decisions, and helps them enjoy more fulfilling relationships. High functioning people are usually excited about all three of these benefits. My own personal background as a mindfulness aficionado and clinical psychologist makes me especially passionate about wanting to share more with you about this invaluable skill.

What Is Mindfulness?
(Pssst—It's Metacognition)

In a nutshell, mindfulness is thinking *about* your thoughts and feelings without getting "caught up" in any of those thoughts or feelings. I'll delve more into the benefits of it later, but for now just understand that **mindfulness helps you maintain awareness and perspective about your thoughts, feelings, and the impact of external factors in your everyday life.** This type of awareness helps you to understand which strategies will be most helpful for managing stress, meeting goals, and practicing self-care. A good mindfulness practice also improves your ability to **put your awareness into words.**

Mindfulness is rooted in Buddhist traditions, but as a psychologist and a yoga teacher, I have found that a key component of its relevance to therapeutic progress is that it builds a capacity for what psychologists call "metacognition." High functioning people tend to value cognition, and in my experience they tend to get really excited about metacognition (myself included; when I first learned about the word in a psychology class, I swear my eyes lit up). "Meta" has Greek origins meaning "higher, beyond." (As long as we're doing Greek etymology here, let me share another interesting word fact: "psychology" comes from the Greek word *psychē*, meaning "soul.") Metacognition is the awareness of your own thought process; mindfulness is intrinsically embedded within this definition. This is why metacognition is also included in the upcoming list of benefits and examples of mindfulness. Understanding the connection between mindfulness and metacognition may be helpful for anyone inclined to dismiss mindfulness as "new age woo-woo stuff"—if you feel intellectually interested in metacognition, then you may want to explore mindfulness.[6] And if you're already into mindfulness, then you'll enjoy learning about metacognition too, since overlap abounds between mindfulness and metacognition.

What Is Metacognition?

Metacognition is part of what mindfulness teaches us. Metacognition is basically "thinking about thinking," or taking the proverbial "thirty-thousand-foot overview" of your thoughts. In my experience as a psychologist and as a consumer of therapy, this is beneficial in the same way that it is helpful when a therapist observes a client over a period of time and sees broader patterns, then helps the client see those broader patterns. Each time you observe yourself in a focused mindfulness practice (or you allow a therapist to observe you in a session) provides a "snapshot" of your mental state. **The more snapshots you have, the better able you are to discern patterns; and you become better able to notice and manage those patterns in real time.** If we "just go with" each and every thought without ever noticing our *patterns* of thought or understanding the thoughts within their *contexts*, then we're vulnerable to losing track of the broader picture.

For example, if the idea to quit your job or leave your relationship crossed your mind and you realized this was the very first time you had ever harbored such an idea, that context would be very different than if you were having the same idea but simultaneously realizing that such thoughts occur quietly "in the back of your mind" somewhat regularly and they were finally coming to the fore. The ability to easily and automatically differentiate between these contexts, rather than getting swept away in the recognition of the idea itself, would be helpful as you considered possible ways to manage the idea. **Metacognition and mindfulness help us do this so we can navigate with awareness of the bigger picture.**

Six Benefits of Mindfulness

In my experience, high functioning people love to understand the purpose and benefit of everything they do, so let me highlight some of the benefits of mindfulness here (six benefits, to be exact). If the benefits sound good to you, make sure you don't skip over the Three-Part Breath technique in part 2, chapter 7, and consider trying some of the "above and beyond" techniques listed later in that chapter.

MINDFULNESS BENEFIT #1: IT'S RELAXING

When people first practice mindfulness, they often describe it as relaxing. And it can be—sometimes in part just because it helps you breathe deeply or nurture yourself. The mere act of slowing down and paying attention to yourself often soothes anxiety, depression, or restlessness because it is reassuring to know and feel that our distress will be attended to rather than tuned out or ignored. This is similar to the way that people sometimes find nonchallenging therapy sessions pleasurable or relaxing, just because it feels good to know that your thoughts and needs are really being noticed by a caring, attentive person. But even better news is that there's much more to mindfulness than mere relaxation. You can absolutely use mindfulness even when you actually need to be super "on point" or self-aware. However, if you don't practice it much, your first layer of contact with mindfulness will probably be the simple and wonderful awareness that, yes, it is inherently reassuring and relaxing to spend time with someone (in this case, yourself) who is noticing you in a nonjudgmental, fully present manner.

MINDFULNESS BENEFIT #2: YOU LEARN HOW TO TRANSLATE YOUR INNER EXPERIENCE INTO WORDS

Observing yourself and then putting your observations into words helps you communicate better with others. Being able to know and describe your internal experience increases your chances of having good relationships, managing conflicts smoothly, and getting your needs met—all of which help reduce stress and increase your productivity and well-being. One of the ways that mindful observation helps people to relieve stress is that it facilitates their ability to put their observations into words.

Putting feelings or states of being into words helps us sharpen our awareness, and it puts something abstract (thoughts and feelings) into an organized system (language). Psychologists have known for decades that **learning to label thoughts and feelings with words is not only soothing—it empowers people to become more objective and proactive about handling challenges, plus it facilitates communication with others.** As we all know, the ability to "speak your mind" or "find the right words" to say what you're feeling is a huge advantage in life. A key part of mindfulness is that it guides you to put your observations into fact-based, nonjudgmental, objective language.

MINDFULNESS BENEFIT #3: YOU LEARN YOUR "BASELINE," AND THIS GIVES YOU STRATEGIC KNOWLEDGE ABOUT YOURSELF. YOU AVOID "SURPRISE FREAK-OUTS" AND YOU MANAGE THEM BETTER WHEN THEY ARISE.

By practicing mindfulness techniques like the Three-Part Breath and some of the variations described in that chapter, even when you're not especially stressed, you will develop an exquisite awareness of your "baseline." This will help you develop an early awareness of when you're getting frazzled, stressed, angry, lonely, or any other vulnerable state in which it's helpful to have that important layer of contextual knowledge about yourself. **While it might seem at first blush like you would never need *help* to know when you're getting frazzled, stressed, or any other of the states just mentioned, consider whether you've ever found yourself suddenly realizing** that you haven't eaten all day and you're completely famished, or whether you've ever been surprised to hear yourself snapping at someone and then suddenly realized that you're actually under a lot of stress. These states have a way of sneaking up on high functioning people because we can sometimes get so good at overcoming minor obstacles as we focus on the task at hand until those "little things" start becoming *really* pesky.

In order to fully enjoy the benefit of mindfulness as an early warning detection system on stress, it's important to practice mindfulness skills as a tool to observe our mental state even when we're *not stressed*. **When we practice observing ourselves in our "normal" state, we develop an exquisite knowledge of our baseline.** We're then more attuned to deviation from our normal patterns and better able to understand and respond to stressors in a calm, strategic, nonjudgmental way. The better we get at observing and "studying" ourselves through even a few minutes of mindfulness exercises every day, the better we're able to notice and predict stressors and then handle that stress effectively rather than becoming reactive and "stressed about stress."

To help demonstrate the benefits of "knowing your baseline," let me share an example of how mindfulness skills came to my rescue in everyday life.

My Celery Cyclone

I was in my kitchen by myself, chopping celery for some houseguests seated in my living room. Suddenly, I realized that I was chopping in a really frantic manner, as if an army of celery connoisseurs had arrived at my home and demanded a mountain of perfect celery, *stat*.[7] My mindfulness skills allowed me to step out of that frantic state for a moment to *realize* that I was feeling frantic, and let me label my experience as frantic. Prior to the realization, I wasn't even really aware of my emotional state. As is often the case with intense feeling states, I wasn't consciously labeling or noticing the state: I was simply *living* it. *Realizing* my state of mind created an opportunity for me to step into a moment of self-aware reflection and become curious about *why* I was feeling so frantic in the first place. In other words, **mindfulness skills were key to helping me** *realize* **that I was feeling frantic and begin to understand** *why* **I was feeling that way rather than just continuing to** *be* **frantic.**

In psychology, we call the two layers of experience I've described "the observing ego" and "the experiencing ego" (Miller and Haggard, 1965). The experiencing ego is the part that's just "living the experience" (in this case, the part of me that was chopping celery like a madwoman). The observing ego is the overarching part of yourself that puts your moment-to-moment experience into context by recognizing how each moment fits in comparison to the rest of your life (the part of me that said, "Hey, wait a minute—why does chopping the world's most perfect celery as fast as humanly possible seem to be such a big deal right now?").

Having the metacognition skills to *observe* that I was frantic was helpful, but the "nonjudgmental and nonreactive" component of mindful observation was really helpful, too. **Instead of becoming self-critical or self-conscious or just trying to "stop it"** upon realizing that I was acting like a celery freak, **I was able to become** *curious* about my "over-the-top" frantic state—and quickly had the insight that my frantic state was due to the fact that I actually felt desperate to impress my guests because of some professional and social factors at play. (This was a fact that pride, busyness, fear of feeling in a one-down position, or just a lack of awareness had previously hidden from my conscious mind until my frantic celery chopping and mindfulness skills finally clued me in that something was up.)

This process allowed me to figure out how to self-soothe and

strategize productively rather than taking it all out on that poor celery. The ability to recognize and respond to all of this without spiraling into self-criticism is one of the myriad benefits that mindfulness brings. I took a deep Three-Part Breath and refocused my nervous energy onto brainstorming professional and social topics to discuss with my guests, since I had realized *this* was my real goal, rather than creating amazing celery slices at the speed of light.

MINDFULNESS BENEFIT #4: YOU CAN RESIST URGES AND
BREAK HABITS MORE SUCCESSFULLY

As we all know, staying "ahead of the curve" on urges makes them much easier to fight—like an ex-smoker who takes a time-out to review his reasons for quitting the moment he feels an urge brewing, rather than waiting till he's about to light up before he even fully realizes what he's doing. While the smoking example is really cut-and-dried, some problematic patterns are more nuanced; mindfulness is very helpful in those situations, too.

Here's an example of how Christina, a lawyer introduced earlier in this book, used mindful awareness to break her habit of obsessing about whether she is liked by others (and trying to get people to like her) to the point of chasing men she didn't even actually like.

Breaking Christina's "Do You Like Me?" Habit

Christina knew she had ingrained patterns of people-pleasing, but she was constantly frustrated with herself because she would frequently find herself having overaccommodated people to an extreme degree before she even realized she was doing it. She would then be upset with the people she chose to accommodate for having "made her give too much." She soon came to understand it was actually incumbent on *her* to *notice* when she was overaccommodating and then *choose* not to do it rather than expect others to alert her when she was giving too much. Her pattern of overaccommodation often manifested in her dating life as bending over backward to win the attention of men that she would lament "aren't worth all this energy." Realizing her own role in this self-defeating pattern was an important step, but actually changing her pattern was difficult: trying to please was so automatic to Christina that she would often fail to realize she was even doing it, until she found herself in the midst of full-on chasing a man she didn't even like.

Christina's mindfulness skills prompted her to realize that the early stages of her chasing behaviors usually began with a frenzied postdate mental analysis to determine how much her date liked her. It had become like a "mental reflex" to engage in a postdate analysis of the entire evening to see how much she was liked, regardless of how much *she* even liked the person. This realization helped her to create a new postdate routine specifically designed to consciously hijack her thought process away from automatically focusing on whether her date liked her: As soon as she and her dates parted company, she deliberately forced herself to journal at least ten sentences about how much (or how little!) *she* liked the man before allowing herself to consider what he thought of her.

Christina knew that although she was *particularly* obsessive about whether her dates liked her, she had a habit of thinking compulsively about whether she was liked by *everyone*, not just dates. Mindful observation allowed her to realize that she was particularly vulnerable to those thoughts whenever a moment of quiet or boredom arose. Focusing on whether she was liked was a "go-to" habit that she was repeating almost on autopilot whenever a lull arose in her day. This realization cued her to use the Mental Shortlist technique anytime she found herself "autotracking" onto the "Do they like me?" hamster wheel throughout the day.

Mindfulness helps us to choose effective tools to **fight habitual urges and problematic patterns;** and it helps us quickly realize when we're in a mental state that makes us vulnerable to lapses so that we can nip those urges in the bud.

MINDFULNESS BENEFIT #5: YOU GAIN INSIGHT AND CLARITY ABOUT WHAT THOSE "PROBLEMATIC PATTERNS" ACTUALLY ARE

Taking time to observe our own thoughts on a regular basis in a nonjudgmental way helps us increase awareness of our thought process and realize how we may want to *shape or refine* that process, in the same way a student realizes how she wants to shape or refine an essay by rereading it several times over different days. The review process helps her notice gaps in her thinking about the subject, recognize biases in her perspective, find better ways to express herself, or even discover different ways of thinking about a subject as she reflects on her own writing. **Spending time *observing* her thoughts increases her awareness and clarity.** A regular mindfulness practice works in a similar way. This is actually also similar to the therapeutic process: by talking to a therapist and explaining or reflecting on their internal process, clients build awareness of areas where they would benefit from trying a new approach.

Here's an example of how spending time noticing yourself in a mindful way can help you realize things about your own thought process that might otherwise escape your awareness, and how that knowledge can be helpful.

Greg's Zingers

Greg, the single father introduced earlier in this book, had noticed that every time he was in the same room as his ex-wife's new boyfriend, he felt strong urges to make the new boyfriend look bad, whether by obnoxiously touting his own accomplishments in a competitive manner or even through petty things like correcting the boyfriend's pronunciation of certain words. He called these remarks "zingers," and felt a guilty pleasure each time he made one. Greg felt a little embarrassed to admit all of this, even to himself— especially because he was doing some of these things in front of his daughter. He knew that his pettiness was only making it harder for his daughter to have good relationships with both her mom and him, yet he found himself constantly reduced to what he acknowledged were juvenile and counterproductive tactics.

People with zero mindfulness skills wouldn't even realize what they were doing, like Greg did (they would just get consumed by a belief that the new boyfriend was an annoying idiot); and people with basic mindfulness or self-awareness skills would maybe *realize* they were being harsh but get so caught up in shame or self-judgement over it that they wouldn't be able to address the pattern—they'd just write it off as "normal; of course I don't like my ex's new guy." **But Greg's well-developed mindfulness skills prompted him to review these interactions several times, in a curious rather than judgmental way that gave him a deeper insight:** he was able to put a fine point on his mental process and articulate that his pride was hurt by his ex being with another man. He was also able to realize that by focusing his displeasure on the new man, he was covering up anger he had with his ex-wife over the financial settlement of their divorce, especially as he noticed that her new boyfriend appeared to be benefiting from some of Greg's alimony checks. Finally, he was able to acknowledge and discuss a secret fear (secret even from himself, till he took a mindful look inside) that the new boyfriend might somehow usurp Greg's role as "the main man" in his daughter's life.

Getting clarity about the underpinnings of his irritation

through mindfulness helped Greg address his concerns productively. He listed even more of his concerns and then realized that a good next step would be to do the Zone of Control exercise. This prompted him to craft some healthy Thought Replacements around the topic of pride to use when he found himself starting to think of "zingers" to say around the new boyfriend or when he needed to have a semiproductive conversation with his ex about the alimony checks. It also helped him implement some creative ways to ensure he would have a presence in his daughter's mind even during her time at her mom's house. If Greg hadn't been practicing mindfulness to observe his thoughts in a nonjudgmental way, he would likely have languished in an ongoing struggle against a nagging urge to take ineffective swipes at his ex's new boyfriend, cheap shots that would have felt unsatisfying and potentially even embarrassing for him because he was painfully aware that such remarks actually only exposed his own insecurities. Good thing Greg built himself some mindfulness skills!

MINDFULNESS BENEFIT #6: YOU CAN EASILY UNDERSTAND WHICH TOOLS TO REACH FOR IN YOUR TOOLBOX.

Many high functioning clients are eager to learn a "toolbox" of skills they can use to better manage their energy. However, even the fanciest toolbox in the world is useless if you don't know *which* of its tools to use in a given situation. For example, an exercise designed to help you "put stressful things out of your mind" could be very *helpful* in a situation where further thought is clearly unproductive (for example, when you're agonizing over whether you should have reworded a text message that you've already sent, and you've already determined that there is absolutely no follow-up clarification text you could send after that imperfectly worded text message that would actually benefit you or serve any other positive purpose at this point). However, the *very same exercise* to "put stressful things out of your mind" could actually be *harmful* if you used it to avoid focusing on a situation where your attention could actually *help* you (such as considering your words carefully *before* you send an important and sensitive text message). Oftentimes, even if we *know* which tools are best intellectually, we can lose sight of that awareness in moments of distress; mindfulness helps with that, too. **Mindfulness trains you to take a breath (literally or figuratively),** to scan yourself and your situation to see what kind of tool would *really be* most helpful, so that you are not caught up in a momentary reaction to something getting on your nerves or making you feel insecure; yet it also takes your feelings into account. The simplest illustrations of this would be hitting your funny bone (also known as your ulnar nerve), having your foot fall asleep, or getting a paper cut at the tip of your finger where nerves are sensitive.[8] A person with no mindfulness skills would get totally absorbed in the immediate sting of physical pain, possibly experiencing panic over the sensations. Mindfulness skills are what help you say to yourself, "Yes, hitting my funny bone is certainly a strong and unpleasant physical sensation, but I know from awareness and experience that this will soon pass; and a handy thing that I can do to speed the process is to give myself a gentle squeeze on the affected area while I wait" (obviously you don't *say* this to yourself aloud, but it's part of your internal awareness and metacognition in this example).

The body-based example of hitting your funny bone is obviously very simple; but the "perspective is power" principle applies to complex social, emotional, professional, and cognitive challenges as well. There are plenty of personal and professional stories to illustrate this point throughout the book, especially in the upcoming chapter on the Three-Part Breath, so I'll refrain from providing more examples here just for the sake of space. But remember that **practicing**

mindfulness of your breath, or of your thoughts and emotions, helps you sharpen your powers of self-observation—and this helps you make great choices on which tools to use in most any situation.

Conclusion

The ability to step back and see an overview of your internal experience and your situational context *without* becoming reactionary is powerful: it facilitates awareness *and* the ability to strategize. This is simultaneously soothing and energizing. It is also an integral part of what a psychologist provides in many cases: thoughtful observations about your patterns that would be impossible to make if you got "caught up" in every moment-to-moment thought or emotion without considering its relevance to your broader tendencies and patterns.

Let me conclude with one final simile about mindfulness. Consider the painting style known as pointillism. It's the style in which, up close, a painting looks like it's just a bunch of little dots, but if you step back and view it from a slight distance you'll see a coherent image. In mindfulness and metacognition, a similar process occurs: instead of getting stuck and consumed in one "dot" of a moment, we're able to step back and see a broader context. This gives us greater insight and an increased ability to navigate the "bigger picture" of our lives, wisely choosing the most helpful tools for each particular situation.

6.

Special Considerations for High Functioning People Seeking Therapy

As you read, you may notice I sometimes mention therapy as a potential support. Of course, therapy is not always needed, but if you're considering it then I wanted to say that although I encourage therapy in many cases, I do feel that high functioning people may have unique needs when choosing a therapist. Variables like the therapist's intelligence and trait conscientiousness will likely matter; and variables like social class, education, or physical health may be an issue. Sometimes high functioning people can be very discriminating, which is great when choosing a therapist for a client whose life is relatively in order and who is just seeking to "fine-tune" themselves a bit, or "work through a bump" in life. In other cases, high functioning people, especially when feeling vulnerable or speaking to any sort of perceived expert or authority, can be people pleasers who assume that anyone with a degree to practice psychotherapy must have special intrapersonal or interpersonal knowledge beyond their own. This assumption is not always accurate.

If you are a high functioning person who is voluntarily going to therapy (rather than, for example, being mandated to attend therapy because of a court case or a psychiatric hospitalization), then it is important to remember that *you* are fully in charge of this decision; and if you don't feel rapport with a therapist, then you should shop around.[1] In fact, I encourage people to shop around even if they *do* like their therapist; especially if they're having their first experience in therapy.[2] As a *consumer* of therapy, I can tell you firsthand that not all therapists are "qualified," regardless of what the sheet of paper hanging on their wall says. As a high functioning person, feel empowered to trust your basic "smell test" of whether or not someone seems like they will be able to help you. **Here's a personal example to show you what I mean,** followed by a simple **scientific explanation** of why a high-functioning person's instincts are actually important information when choosing a therapist.

Personal Experience of Seeking Therapy

In my early twenties, I visited a therapist in Chelsea, one of my favorite neighborhoods of New York City. She was near my tiny shared room at a women's rooming house on Gramercy Park. I was new in town, rather young, and awed by New York (okay, I'm *still* awed by New York and hope I always will be!), and I was definitely prone to give added weight to the words of a New Yorker who was clearly older and well educated. I guess I viewed such people as "authority figures" on a certain level. I was seeking help with a very sensitive personal issue. I may share more in future books about what that issue was, but those details aren't important at this moment. The point now is just that I was extremely vulnerable. I was dealing with an overwhelming issue for which I knew I needed help. I not only needed a therapist with expertise, I needed a therapist that I could trust on a basic, fundamental level so that I could feel comfortable opening up in session to tell her about my problem and let her teach me the skills I needed.

I arrived at her office for my first appointment and sat down in the waiting area with a sense of optimistic expectancy. I knew it wouldn't be easy, and I was painfully aware that it wouldn't be cheap, but I was still eager to engage in therapy and finally deal with the problem that was plaguing me. Because I had experienced nothing but positive therapy relationships since my first visit as a teenager, it hadn't occurred to me that we might not be a good fit. When she opened the door to her therapy office, I was in complete shock by what I saw, but a combination of my midwestern manners and the context of being young, more inexperienced than I realized, and automatically thinking of her as an authority figure caused me to reserve judgment and try to look beyond the startling scene: her office was *filled* with *hundreds and hundreds* of old newspapers stacked and stuffed randomly all over the office (on side tables, the floor, bookshelves, her desk, and so on) and her teeth were all a disturbing shade of gray (think: the color of dark storm clouds—for real). I'm not saying that she couldn't have had an unusual dental condition and still been a great therapist, or even have been an active hoarder and still been a great therapist—but, as a first impression, she appeared to have a compromised ability or willingness to care for both her office and her body, and she also apparently hadn't considered the impression this might make on a new client seeking professional support when feeling vulnerable. She acknowledged neither the issue of her teeth nor her office to normalize or explain them in any way, so I couldn't tell if she was unaware of them or perhaps just wasn't bothered by them.

You can imagine why all of this made it hard for me to view her as someone who could "show me the way" to navigate some complex, sensitive tangles that were causing me distress. After all, my visceral first impression was that I was functioning better than she was. Both her teeth and her space suggested that she was functioning far outside of cultural norms of self-care for sophisticated professionals in New York City with access to resources such as wastepaper baskets and dental hygienists; and her failure to offer any explanation suggested that she lacked either the skills or the awareness to mitigate this first impression (or the skills and awareness to address these issues before they became visible to clients in the first place). I needed someone to help me bolster my own ability for self-care, and based on my initial impression, I didn't have confidence she could help me to do that—so I just sat through our initial consultation, politely answered some basic questions, paid her fee, and never returned.

Whether or not the therapist I've described had the skills to help me with my issue was almost irrelevant, because I wasn't feeling enough natural rapport to open up with her and absorb whatever input she may have shared. I went on to find another therapist with whom I connected almost immediately and who helped me tremendously. As I look back, I thank my younger self for being high functioning enough to *walk away* from the Chelsea therapist.

The Scientific Explanation

In psychotherapy parlance, the Chelsea therapist and I struggled to form what is called a "therapeutic alliance" (Zetzel, 1956). Research has shown that for high functioning people, a therapeutic alliance may be an even greater predictor of therapeutic success than the style of therapy being used (for example, Martin,

Garske, and Davis, 2000). The therapeutic alliance is important for all therapy clients, but it may be especially important for high functioning people—so let me unpack this for you. In layman's terms, the therapeutic alliance consists of the therapist and the client having the same goals for treatment, mutual belief in each other's ability to use therapy sessions to achieve those goals, and the presence of rapport between the therapist and client. There's a lot of overlap between these three components, as we'll soon see, but each one is important in its own way. Let's dive just a little bit deeper so you can really understand this—and let me assure you that most good therapists will be aware of the term "therapeutic alliance," so feel free to discuss any of this material with any potential therapists you interview if you feel it may be helpful in your selection process.

Mutual Goals

This might sound obvious, but you and the therapist absolutely must be on the same page about your therapy goals as being healthy and desirable. For example, a high functioning person might come to therapy seeking stress management skills because their need for achievement is driving them to get excellent grades in graduate school while working full-time, and they need a way to manage the extra demands of their situation. Or they might seek a therapist to help them manage inevitable moments of rejection as they climb the ladder of success to become a Broadway star. I have encountered clients in both of these situations and similar situations, whose previous therapist refused to partner with them in these goals. Instead, the therapist insisted on helping the clients develop an "insight" that the clients needed to "learn to sit with failure" or "drop their unreasonable expectations" (these clients did not need to learn to lower their unreasonable expectations, evidenced by the fact that they did achieve these goals and led happy, fulfilling lives, which they partially attribute to their work with me as someone who was willing and able to therapeutically partner with them on their goals).

While it is true that sometimes high functioning people can get on a "hamster wheel" of achievement where nothing is ever good enough—and it is essential that a therapist be able to help clients avoid this pitfall—it is also important that a therapist be able to recognize a client's potential and help them develop skills to reach that potential. High functioning clients, whose potential for achievement is generally greater than that of lower functioning clients on an objective scale of achievement, might struggle to find a therapist who is able to fully grasp and support that client's therapy goals. So please—be clear about your therapy goals, and make sure your therapist is really "on board" with them. I personally would not want to work with a therapist who regarded my goals as a manifestation of some "problem," such as wanting to achieve "too much." Of course I'd want a therapist who was able to help me see when I was being too hard on myself or trying for a goal that wasn't actually good for me; and I have had situations where I needed to explain to clients that their goal wasn't even actually desirable from a mental health standpoint (for example, clients whose goal is to have "no anxiety"—anxiety is actually a *healthy* feeling in measured doses). It is essential that the therapist and client can have transparent discussions about what exactly is being labeled as "overboard" by the therapist and/or the client, and that the client understands if the therapist is casting the client's goals as problematic in any way. Otherwise, you essentially have a ship on which all the oars aren't rowing in the same direction, which is counterproductive for everyone. So please—confirm that what you want for yourself is the same thing as what your therapist wants for you.

Mutual Belief in Each Other's Ability to Achieve Those Goals

Remember I said there was a lot of overlap in the three components of the therapeutic alliance? Well, here we go: just like you and your therapist need to have agreement that your goals are healthy, it stands to reason that if your therapist doesn't think your goals are reasonable, then that therapist *may* not believe in your *ability* to achieve those goals. However, just because a therapist doesn't think a goal is achievable for you, this does *not* necessarily mean the goal is unachievable! It may just mean that you need to seek a therapist who is used to working with higher functioning people.

In a similar sense, if you appraise your therapist as somewhat lower functioning than you, then you may (very legitimately) question whether that therapist is *equipped* with the skills, grit, intelligence, sophistication, self-awareness, or whatever else is needed to help *you* attain your goals. For example, although your therapist may agree with your goal of increasing your confidence and developing the skills to navigate complex social and business situations more effectively, you might question if a therapist whose own business appears clunky (website difficult to use, dingy office with cheesy sayings framed on the walls, person takes days to return calls) and/or who presents as socially awkward or a little slow (frequently asks you to repeat information you've already shared, appears slightly rumpled, doesn't seem to "get you") is *really* equipped to help you achieve your goals. It would almost be like seeing a college admissions counselor who had never been accepted to college. You'd think twice, right? Not that all therapists must have personally accomplished every goal their clients are targeting, but it helps if a therapist can display markers of significant achievement in terms of work, social dynamics, or whatever general domain the client wishes to develop.

Rapport

Obviously, if you and the therapist can't agree on appropriate goals, or if you don't believe your therapist is capable of helping you achieve those goals, then it will be difficult to establish a genuine therapeutic rapport. I've met with many new clients who explained that their previous therapist "seemed like a really nice person" but just didn't seem to have the skills, drive, or intelligence to help the client achieve the complex and sophisticated goals that the client was targeting. High functioning people are generally quick on their feet and able to "size up" a person or space quickly. If you start feeling like you're in "romper room" around a therapist who seems very nice and well-intentioned but who just doesn't seem to have the tools to help you improve upon your existing skill set, then of *course* it will be hard (and maybe even inappropriate) for you to become vulnerable with that therapist. In other cases, a therapist can be defensive or cover for their own feelings of inadequacy by becoming critical of a client's goals (such as an underachieving therapist who suggests that a client who wants a promotion may be "chasing achievement," or a therapist who is unable to succeed in dating might suggest that a client seeking support to find a desirable husband is "caught up in external validation"). Whatever the reason (except in cases when the client has problems forming rapport in general, even outside of the therapy room; or in cases when a client is unable to manage their life in basic terms), if you don't feel rapport with a therapist, please feel free to consider the possibility that the problem is with the therapist rather than with yourself—and keep shopping for the right fit.

For lower functioning people, who may struggle to provide their own food and housing or maintain a small circle of healthy relationships, the simple existence of a reliable and somewhat friendly person who meets with them every week and models basic self-care skills is likely to have therapeutic value, and forming rapport will typically be easy. The client has the chance to connect with someone whose level of intelligence, education, or general life skills and social skills are likely a step above the client's, so the client can learn from the therapist's overall modeling of skills as well as specific techniques the therapist might teach. In contrast, higher functioning people are able to meet their own basic needs in life; and they generally have at least a few friends to call if they just feel like a nice heart-to-heart with a sympathetic ear. They are generally able to mask their struggles (if they wish) from others because they have enough skills to keep life moving on a basic level, even during challenges. For them, opening up and seeking therapeutic help is more of a *choice* than a necessity. Since higher functioning people have more of a choice about whether to open up, and they have a broad base of social and cognitive skills already, they are often more discerning about who will be the right person to help them— and rightfully so. High functioning people are often seeking a therapist who has the skills and training to unlock even higher levels of functioning for the client, and they usually need to see this potential in order to develop a therapeutic rapport.

The moral of the story is that even if the therapist's appearance, manner, or office aren't screaming "lower functioning," like the therapist I encountered in my early twenties, you should still feel empowered to shop around if you feel unsure about whether you have a strong sense of *rapport* and interpersonal connection with a therapist or if you have concerns about whether that therapist is willing and able to support your goals. Of course, if you've seen ten therapists in a row and they all seem "off" in some way, then it's *possible* that you're being hypercritical or you just have a very hard time trusting. The general idea is just that in most cases, a high functioning person's positive gut-level feeling about a therapist is often an important predictor of therapeutic success.

If you start out with a positive feeling but it fades over time as you start to feel you've gotten into a rut, or if it seems the therapist has lost focus or made a misstep, or some other issue arises that makes you question the fit between you and the therapist, then I encourage you to discuss it in session. While discussing issues of fit may be less important with a new therapist (in those cases you might want to just try other therapists—no need to cram a square peg into a round hole), discussing problems with a therapist you did at one point feel very positively about can be a good opportunity to see if you and that therapist can course-correct together. Having candid talks to reclarify your therapy goals, or making an adjustment in the therapist's approach to your situation, or reviewing issues that have left you feeling dissatisfied with the therapist can actually be very illuminating. You may even find that by hearing your trusted therapist's perspective you'll come to realize ways you had been unknowingly sending mixed signals about what you wanted from therapy. But if you and the therapist never really had a strong "therapeutic alliance" in the first place, then shopping around without investing much (if any) time and money into therapy sessions just to discuss a lack of fit may be your wisest move.

In conclusion: while you may notice that I sometimes urge readers to consider therapy, I also encourage you to pay attention to your "inner antennae" about whether or not the person seems truly qualified to help *you*. Academic credentials and licensing are necessary but not sufficient for a good, helpful therapy relationship to take place. **Don't underestimate the importance of your natural sense of whether or not you feel rapport with the therapist and a sense of confidence about their overall abilities, intelligence, and level of conscientiousness.**[3] Even though you may not feel qualified to assess a therapist's clinical skills, remember that their clinical skills hinge at least partly on their ability to help you feel comfortable to open up and share yourself.

PART II

The Techniques

7.

The Three-Part Breath

No problem can be solved by the same level of
consciousness that created it.

—ALBERT EINSTEIN

The good news about the Three-Part Breath is that you can basically never go wrong doing it. The Three-Part Breath is a great starting point to **ground yourself, interrupt a negative internal monologue, treat your brain to some extra oxygen, improve your self-esteem with a moment of self-care, and practice mindfulness,** all while getting valuable information about which next steps of cognitive-behavioral-based techniques or other self-care might be helpful to you in any particular moment.[1] Sound good? Read on!

Use the Three-Part Breath when you want to do the following:

1. **Ground yourself.** As a yoga teacher, I was amazed at how students would always tell me how "grounded" they felt after doing the Three-Part Breath. As a clinical psychologist, I'd hear the same things from my clients. **What exactly do they mean by "feeling grounded"? The simplest way I know to answer is that it's the opposite of feeling scattered.** In a world of constantly chiming smartphones, twenty-four-hour news cycles, video conference calls, virtual reality, and social media, it's actually rather easy for us to lose touch with what's literally, physically, tangibly in front of us, and it's even easier to lose touch with the nuanced cognitive-emotional experience that is happening inside of us. Instead, we feel scattered, numb, frazzled, or "all over the place." The Three-Part Breath gently guides you to "tune in" to yourself in a simple, immediate, and fully present manner.

2. **Interrupt a negative internal monologue.** Have you ever noticed yourself stuck in a way of talking to yourself that you suspect isn't exactly healthy and might even be really unhealthy (such as being hypercritical of yourself, or running worst-case scenarios that are just freaking you out rather than helping you to prepare)— yet you felt unable to stop? In psychology, that's what we call a "negative internal monologue." The Three-Part Breath is simple enough that you can master it with a relatively modest investment of time to learn the steps, but it's complex enough that it will require your attention to actually *do* the steps. The attention it requires is a perfect antidote to a negative internal monologue: by handing your brain something *else* to focus on, you will be unable to sustain your negative internal monologue,

or at least you'll give the negative monologue some real competition while you focus on mentally guiding yourself through the breath. Even once you've mastered the Three-Part Breath to the point where it doesn't take as much of your cognitive energy to perform, it will *still* help interrupt a negative internal monologue because it still takes *some* mental energy to do it. And as you master the steps through practice, you will be simultaneously increasing your ability to redirect your attention and concentration wherever you choose because the Three-Part Breath is actually also a mindfulness exercise.

3. **Treat your brain to some extra oxygen.** The Three-Part Breath guides you to breathe deeply and hold the oxygen in your lungs for a moment before exhaling. This gives your brain and body an extra boost of oxygen, which helps improve overall functioning and decreases stress. I'm sure you're well aware of the benefits of oxygen, so I'll leave this one to speak mostly for itself!

4. **Improve your self-esteem with a moment of self-care.** By taking a moment to focus on yourself in an observant, nonjudgmental way and to practice a healthy habit that increases your mental clarity and self-awareness as well as your physical capacity for full, healthy breaths, you are demonstrating to yourself that you value yourself. If you practice the Three-Part Breath in moments of downtime as well as in moments of stress, you're also giving yourself permission to recognize and rejuvenate from the energy output required to manage stressors. You will also be showing yourself that you're willing to "go the extra mile" to provide yourself with a reservoir of energy and relaxation skills for use in challenging times.

5. **Practice mindfulness and get clarity about which techniques will be most helpful to use next.** I've saved the best for last. The Three-Part Breath is actually a mindfulness exercise. If you read the section on the benefits of mindfulness, then you know that practicing mindfulness is an amazing favor to yourself because it helps you take a "thirty-thousand-foot view" of yourself at any given moment to determine what's *really* going on with you. **Once you have more perspective on yourself, you will be much better equipped to know which technique from this book or other form of self-care would really serve you best at any given moment.** For example, if you do the Three-Part Breath and realize you're feeling mixed up and don't know why, this awareness would guide you to select a different follow-up technique (possibly Mind Mapping or even just more mindfulness exercises) than if you did the Three-Part Breath and realized you were stressed because of a big overwhelming task (perhaps you'd then do the Zone of Control).

When I lead clients in the Three-Part Breath for the first time, they often tell me that it has "worked" because they feel relaxed and their mind is peaceful. I then explain that the relaxation is actually just a *side benefit* that may happen sometimes when we practice this tool. **The Three-Part Breath offers the advantage of being a tool that provides relaxation and health benefits, but its primary purpose here is to increase mindfulness and act as a "scanning device" that helps you to realize which *additional* tools might be helpful to you. It can also help you recognize which types of strategies you actually want to *avoid* in certain circumstances.**

Buddhism and Breath

Pranayama is the Sanskrit word for breathing techniques, which are known as "breathwork" in Western English-speaking terminology. Sanskrit is the literal ancient Indian language of Buddhism; it is considered a sacred language in scholarly, theological, and yogic literature. The word *pranayama* is based on the Sanskrit word *prana,* which means "life force." The Buddhists believe (and Western science is proving) that by controlling our breath, we control energy to a life-changing degree.

How to Do the Three-Part Breath

Okay, let me start with a disclaimer: I know it seems ridiculous to have so many steps for something as simple as taking a breath. The good news is that once you've understood these steps and tried them a couple of times, they really will seem as natural to you as, well, breathing. Please try to remember that even something as simple as using a fork and knife to cut a bite of food and bring it to your mouth could seem cumbersome if it was broken down into small step-by-step instructions. However, just like using a fork and knife or doing a relatively simple breathing exercise, I'm confident that these steps are well within easy striking distance for you (with a bit of practice). If by chance you're more of a visual learner (some things are much easier shown than written), you can always check www.NervousEnergyBook.com/breathe for a video of yours truly offering a walk-through of this wonderful exercise.

Step 0: Locate the three parts of the Three-Part Breath. I've called this "Step Zero" because you won't have to do this step every time—but it's important to do it at least once so that you actually know which parts of the body are included in the Three-Part Breath. They are as follows:

a. **Your belly.** Put your hand over your belly and feel it expand like an inflating balloon as you inhale. This is the first "part" you'll use in the Three-Part Breath.

b. **Your middle chest.** Put your hands on the sides of your rib cage, approximately four inches directly beneath your underarms. For women, this is usually the place on your body that the sides of your bra covers. Feel your hands getting pushed slightly wider apart horizontally from each other as your chest expands with your inhalation. This is the second "part" you'll use in the Three-Part Breath.

c. **Your upper chest.** Put your hand at the center of your collarbone, the front base of your neck, or where a small locket on a short necklace might sit. Move your hand about three inches lower. Feel your hand rising vertically as you inhale. This is the third "part" you'll use in the Three-Part Breath.

Step 1: Breathe normally. Don't try to do anything to change your breath, just observe it in a nonjudgmental (that is, in a neutral and fact-based) manner. Your observations can and should be simple: for example, you might notice the temperature of the air as it hits your nostrils, or notice how deeply or shallowly you are breathing. Or you might notice how your clothing contacts and pulls away from your chest and belly from each inhalation and exhalation. Stay at step 1 for as few as ten seconds or as long as you like. Just FYI, you can skip this step in situations when you need to "cut to the chase" quickly, like in the example a little later on where I describe using the Three-Part Breath to center myself quickly after making a mini-blunder on national television.

A little trick to help you make sure you stick to simple, non-judgmental observations in this step is to imagine that a newspaper reporter has asked for five factual observations about your breath. (In my youth, newspaper reporters were known for saying "Just the facts, ma'am.") So you simply need to provide five straightforward, plain facts about your natural breathing in order to comply with the reporter's request.

Step 2: Exhale to prepare. This step helps you prepare for an inhalation into your belly and can also be skipped during "go time" moments. You will naturally exhale before a mindful inhalation when you're in "automatic mode" once you've had even minimal practice. However, you might find that sometimes, even once you're an old pro, you actually find enjoyment, relaxation, or increased awareness by taking the time to do this step in a deliberate, mindful fashion.

Step 3: Inhale from the belly. This is where the rubber hits the road!

a. **Belly.** Inhale into the belly, feeling it expand in a half-sphere shape rounding outward. You can place your hand with your palm on your belly button to really feel this (sometimes tactile feedback helps increase awareness and relaxation).

b. **Middle chest.** Continue the same inhalation up into your middle chest, feeling it widen horizontally. If you like tactile feedback and you're in an appropriate setting, you might place your hands gently on the sides of your upper-middle rib cage before you do this step. You'll actually feel a slight pressure pushing your hands horizontally farther apart from each other as your rib cage expands during this part of the inhalation.

c. **Upper chest.** Continue the same inhalation into the upper chest, feeling it rise vertically. You can place your hand across your chest and over your heart, as if you were reciting the pledge of allegiance, and you'll literally feel your hand rise vertically as your inhalation causes your upper chest to rise.

Try to notice each of the three parts and pause briefly as you transition from the belly to the middle chest, and from the middle chest to the upper chest. I call this "segmenting" your breath, or "locating" each part.

Step 4: Pause. Hold your breath for a moment, as long or brief a moment as you like, really noticing what it feels like to be full of oxygen. This is often called "the top of the inhale" in meditation circles.

Step 5: Exhale. Exhale just the upper chest, noticing that it drops vertically as it empties. Next, continue your exhalation, noticing how the circumference of your rib cage seems to shrink slightly as you exhale (if you have your hands on the sides of your rib cage for this part, feel your rib cage pulling *away* from your hands as you exhale). Finally, continue your exhalation through your belly. Once you feel like you've fully exhaled, try pulling your belly button inward as if you were trying to fit into a tight-waisted pair of pants; you might be surprised to see that this helps you exhale even more of the air from your belly.

Step 6: Pause. Pause for a moment after you've completed your exhalation, noticing what the "bottom of the exhale" feels like.

Repeat steps 3 through 6 until you decide to stop. Try to notice as much as you can about whatever you're experiencing. To help "prime the pump" for your observations, here are some examples of common observations:

- How the air feels as it moves through your body with each inhalation and exhalation
- An initial desire for deeper breath as your attention focuses on breathing
- The feeling of your clothing seeming tighter on inhalations and looser after exhalations
- The temperature or dryness or moisture of the air in the room as it hits your nostrils.
- Feelings of insecurity about whether you're "doing it right"
- Feelings of relaxation
- Feelings of pride for taking a moment to practice or learn self-care
- A heightened sense of awareness about yourself or your current state
- Feeling like you're "already full" of air by the time you reach the middle chest.[2]

Step 7: Observe your normal breath. Conclude by repeating what you did in step 1, where you just let your breathing happen naturally without deliberately breathing into the three parts or controlling your breath in any way whatsoever. As in step 1, challenge yourself to make at least five neutral, fact-based observations about your natural, effortless, uncontrolled breath. In step 7, these fact-based observations can include how your breathing is different from how it was in step 1 (for example, "I notice that my breathing is deeper than it was a few minutes ago when I first observed my natural breaths today"). Comparing two objects is a great way to increase our powers of observation. Observing the breath before and after doing the Three-Part Breath helps us build our powers of neutral self-observation by giving us two "objects" to compare (our natural breath pre- and post-performance of the formal Three-Part Breath).

Pro Tip: Prize Fact-Based Observations Rather Than Unbounded Reflection in Mindfulness and the Three-Part Breath

Why is it so important that observations during the Three-Part Breath are fact-based? Because the *real goal* of the Three-Part Breath is to help us increase our ability to notice ourselves in a nonjudgmental way, without getting buffeted around by reactions *to* whatever we're observing. This skill of meta-awareness is a key component of mindfulness. Judgment and reactivity actually have a lot of value, but it's also good to be able to step back from them sometimes. Doing so helps you be more aware of the roles of judgment and reactivity in yourself and others and to be more clear-headed when you want to be. So please try to notice whatever you feel, without judgment—just for a few minutes—as part of the exercise.

To see some examples of the difference between letting your thoughts spiral versus just logging your observations when noticing that you're breathing in a shallow manner, see the following comparison chart:

Spiraling Thoughts versus Mindful Observations Regarding Shallow Breathing During the Three-Part Breath

I'm still breathing so shallowly; how could this still be happening after I've practiced this exercise several times now?	I'm still breathing in a shallow manner.
I wonder if this shallow breathing means that I'm not focusing enough?	Shallow breaths just seem to feel really natural to my body right now.
Will I ever be able to breathe deeply all the time?	With these shallow breaths, my chest rises and drops in a gentle, subtle manner that actually feels very pleasant.
Hmmm. . . . Should I even breathe deeply all the time?	Shallow breathing feels really familiar to how I felt while I was sitting waiting for my performance review.
Am I cut out for meditation and breath-work? Will this work for me?	I noticed that now, shortly after I became conscious of the shallow breathing, my belly seemed to feel hungry for a deeper breath and just pulled it in naturally on my next inhalation.

Building the skill of nonjudgmental self-observation in low-stakes situations like observing your breath will allow you to be able to become more steady and objective as you practice self-awareness in more challenging situations.

When you complete step 7, I encourage you to write your observations on paper or share them aloud with another person (a friend who can be your "breathing buddy," a yoga teacher, personal trainer, physical therapist, or psychotherapist are all good choices). **This sharpens your observation skills as well as your ability to put your experience into words.** This is so important in Buddhist tradition that one of the Three Jewels of Buddhism is called the *sangha*, which is Sanskrit for "community." Many people say they've tried mindfulness apps on their devices with mixed results, and I've always felt that one of the primary reasons those apps can fail is that if the user is relying solely on the app, the app doesn't typically stimulate you to **put your experience into *words*, which is a key part of increasing your observation skills as well as your ability to communicate that experience to other people**. Part of the reason mindfulness works is because it helps us know and feel connected to ourselves as well as to others, at least when we make sure to practice putting our observations into written or spoken words.

Whatever you observe during mindful Three-Part Breaths, please try to remain nonjudgmental of yourself. **The point is less to do the Three-Part Breath perfectly than it is to improve your breathing skills as well as your powers of neutral self-observation.** Even if you find that you're losing track of the parts of the breath, this is still a great observation in itself and an opportunity for you to practice nonjudgmental self-awareness as you gently return your focus to try anew. The Three-Part Breath is a tool to help you build your powers of nonjudgmental self-awareness (including the ability to practice nonjudgmental awareness of challenges) and ultimately of self-control.

If you notice that you're struggling to control your breath or sustain your focus during the exercise, try to regard that observation the same way you would if you were at the gym and observed that you were struggling to lift a heavy weight: bodybuilders know that they *only* strengthen their muscles by working with whatever weight will *challenge* them. So if you find yourself at the edge of your comfort zone or even squarely outside of it, that may just indicate that you're doing a great job challenging yourself—which is often the springboard for learning and growth.

Above and Beyond: Mindfulness of Thoughts and Feelings

Once you feel comfortable and somewhat skilled at observing your breath in an objective, fact-based manner, try the following "add on" technique. Just like you practiced making fact-based observations about your breath, only focusing on the breath you are having or just had, now you will **practice observing your own thoughts and feelings the same way.** Because it is challenging to observe thoughts and emotions since they are abstract, intangible objects, mindfulness meditators often practice the following technique.

Add-On Technique for Thoughts and Emotions: Passing Clouds

After you've warmed up your mindfulness skills with the Three-Part Breath, let your eyes close, if they aren't closed already. See a blue sky in your mind's eye. See one cloud passing from left to right in that sky till it goes out of the "sight" of your mental "view." See it followed by another cloud, passing left to right till it disappears, and see that second cloud followed by another cloud, and so on and so on. Now notice your own thoughts or emotions passing by in your mind while you continue to visualize the clouds passing. Attach each thought to a passing cloud.

The point of this exercise is *not* to "get rid" of your thoughts as they pass by. The point is to notice that every thought passes naturally and is automatically replaced by another thought and to observe those thoughts as a passing stream; this way you will not become reactive or "go down a rabbit hole" by getting consumed by any one particular thought. **Even if it seems that you're having the same thought over and over, please know that psychologically there's actually a difference: each time a thought seems to repeat, it takes on a slightly different quality**

because it is now a repetitive thought and therefore different than the previous time you experienced a similar one. Its repetition will bring about a new experience of the thought as repetitive; and this awareness will put the thought in a different context. For example, the first time you think of your ex it may feel innocuous; the third time you think of him you may notice that this thought is now part of a pattern in which he's on your mind a lot and you might become curious about why; or you might notice that the thoughts all cluster around certain aspects of that person. In other words, you may begin having thoughts *about* the repetitive thought. Here's another example: "Wow, I keep focusing on that annoying colleague; it's interesting that I'm doing that, since I certainly don't think of myself as *wanting* to focus on her; yet my mind does seem to be gravitating toward her pretty frequently, at least during this exercise."

The "trick" in this situation is to make sure you don't *follow* any of the thoughts. An example of "following your thoughts" would be if you got so consumed with thoughts of your colleague or ex that you started methodically trying to determine why the person was on your mind, or if you deliberately mentally replayed your interactions with the person rather than simply *noticing* that he or she was on your mind, or if you began actively trying to push the thoughts *out* of your mind. All of these would be what we call *reactions* to the thoughts. Instead of analyzing, developing, judging, or rejecting any individual thought, just keep focused on maintaining a nonreactive state in which you keep your focus on neutral observations of your stream of consciousness. For example, you might come to notice that your colleague *eventually* drifts out of your mind naturally and is replaced by thoughts about something deeper, then you might observe that your initial preoccupation with an annoying colleague was actually a way of avoiding something that felt harder to grapple with. Make sure you recognize these "metathoughts" about your thoughts as well, and attach those to a passing cloud.

Once you feel comfortable linking your thoughts with your visual mind through the cloud exercise, see if you can start categorizing the thoughts and attaching the thought's *category* rather than the thought itself to a passing cloud. For example: Christina notices that her ex's last words arise in her mind for a moment, so she categorizes that as a "boyfriend thought" as it passes; then she thinks of a filing deadline and categorizes it as a "work thought" as it passes; then she judges herself for thinking of work so much and categorizes it as a "self-critical thought" as it passes. **This extra step of categorizing our thoughts rather than reacting to them helps to strengthen our metacognition skills. Those skills are invaluable** when we need an extra boost of perspective on ourselves or are in danger of "spiraling" in reaction to upsetting situations.

If you do this exercise and notice that the majority of your thoughts are falling into a certain category, you can take that information as just a passing observation or as an indication that some type of action or self-care is needed. For example, William did this exercise when he was pondering a move to a new city for a potential job and realized that nearly all of his thoughts fell into the "potential problems" category. This helped him realize that he needed to spend some time deliberately considering the potential benefits in order to make a truly balanced evaluation of the opportunity. If he hadn't been practicing mindfulness, he would have gotten stuck in reaction to whatever initial concerns about the potential move happened to pop into his mind, and he would have spent hours (if not days) googling the past ten years of the city's crime statistics instead of being able to take a mental step back and realize that his overall approach to the question of a potential move was almost myopically focused on potential problems, to the point of excluding important information about potential benefits.

The Three-Part Breath is different from the other tools in this book in the sense that it is almost universally applicable to any situation. It is rarely the *only* step that is needed, but it is often the best starting point.

Here is an example of how the Three-Part Breath helped me connect to mindful observation and curiosity rather than judgment of myself or others.

Using the Three-Part Breath to Convert Feelings into Information

I was sitting in the comfortable leather armchair of my office, with a new client seated on the matching couch. I always feel an especially heightened awareness around new clients, partly due to the need to ensure I'm capturing all the necessary information as I try to orient myself to a new case. But I'll admit that some of the heightened feeling of "being on" around new clients is also probably due to what we call "impression management" in psychology, which is just a fancy way of saying that we want to make sure we're coming across in the way we'd like to be seen and known. However, with this particular client, I found myself feeling *extra* wired—and self-conscious.

My mindfulness training was foundational in mastering (or at least *trying* to master—I always have more to learn!) the part of psychologist training that involves learning to recognize which elements of yourself around a client are your "normal self" and would likely be present regardless of the client, and which elements are being *evoked specifically by the client.*[3] So it was part of my training in both mindfulness *and* psychology to notice in a nonjudgmental way that, with this client, I experienced a huge spike in self-consciousness beyond my normal "new client nerves."

I suddenly developed a strong sense of embarrassment about a small scratch on the wall that I'd never even noticed before; in that moment I felt as if that tiny scratch rendered my entire office embarrassingly dilapidated. I also observed myself having a similar anxiety about a scuff that seemed to materialize from thin air right on the tip of my shoe, and I felt as if that scuff rendered my overall appearance completely rumpled and unprofessional. I subsequently noticed myself using a slightly more tentative tone than I normally would. It wasn't a huge deal, in the sense that I was still totally able to focus on the client, and I don't think I came across as timid, but logging these little "stray reactions" was part of my training in psychology *and* in mindfulness. The awareness of those insecurities actually helped me assess the client on a deeper level. Here's how:

Rather than spiraling into a **reactive mode** (for example, starting to get distracted with mental notes to fix the wall and visit the shoe cobbler, crossing my ankles to try to hide the scuff, attempting to force a more confident vocal tone, launching into self-criticism for the presence of scuff and scratch, or feeling foolish or judgmental of myself for experiencing this irrational moment of extreme self-consciousness), **I simply let my observations and my ensuing insecurity sit in my mindful awareness without *reacting* to them. I just *noticed* the fact that these things were occurring to me and I let them accrue into the broader picture that my observations were painting.** That picture depicted me suddenly feeling unusually self-conscious about relatively little things that had not registered as problematic when I had seen a *different* new client earlier that very same day. I wasn't yet sure why I was feeling this way, but I knew I needed to center myself quickly *without* blocking my awareness of my feelings, and that my sudden insecurities might be indicative of an important context that I hadn't yet fully realized. So I started (very!) subtly doing some Three-Part Breaths in order to calm my nerves and center myself in mindful awareness as I listened to the client's story.[4]

Grounding myself in mindfulness through the Three-Part Breath allowed me to become *curious* **about my insecurities rather than** *address* **them.** This approach allowed me to take a step back and realize a potential connection between what I was feeling and what the client was saying, and the subtle ways in which he was behaving. This facilitated an important insight: part of his reason for seeking therapy was that he was quite lonely. He was a successful "Mr. Big from *Sex and the City*" type of man who had no trouble getting a date or surrounding himself with hangers-on. Yet he felt lonely. Very lonely. As we worked together, we came to understand that he struggled with a profound fear of rejection and often dealt with his fear by pretending not to care much about anyone or anything (sometimes even convincing himself, at least temporarily, that he really *didn't* care) and playing an unconscious, perpetual game of "let me reject you before you reject me" with dates, friends, and even family.

During the course of treatment, the client and I eventually came to see that this defensive facade was, ironically, *creating* the problem it was intended to *solve*: all of his defensive behaviors actually kept him trapped in loneliness because he was constantly pushing people away. He learned to open up to others and actually even to himself (plus he found a wonderful bride!). Discovering *his* insecurity over the course of the next few sessions put the sudden burst of insecurity *I* felt during that first session into a fresh and informative context. However, when I was initially experiencing a bout of insecurity at his first visit, of course I had not yet realized that this was actually somewhat by design on his part: he consciously and unconsciously focused his eyes or other forms of attention on people's flaws in order to maintain a sense of control and power and to keep them at arm's length. **Without the Three-Part Breath to ground me in mindfulness, I may have allowed myself to spiral into *reactions* to the insecurity I felt rather than simply** *noticing it in a nonjudgmental and curious manner* **and may have missed a pivotal insight into this client's way of relating to others.**

I confess—I also had my shoes polished and my wall fixed after that appointment!

Why Practice Is Key for Three-Part Breath Success

Remember that the Three-Part Breath is actually a form of meditation; and there's a reason that even the most experienced people who practice meditation refer to it as *practice*. Meditation, including mindful breathing techniques, is something that may feel slightly different each time you do it. Each experience will depend on what you were feeling or experiencing in the moments before you decided to practice at that particular time. Learning to notice and understand those differences represents great progress because it signifies that you're building your self-awareness; this is true regardless of whether each individual experience happens to feel positive or negative. The key is that you're *noticing it*.

In case you need more enticement to practice the Three-Part Breath even when you're not in a moment of distress, remember that the discussion of mindfulness benefits in part 1 of this book included the fact that you can better understand your "baseline." **By practicing the Three-Part Breath during times when you're not feeling particularly stressed, you'll give yourself the chance to develop a deeper appreciation of your baseline self as well as learn to notice how subtle nuances affect your cognitive, emotional, and physical states.** This knowledge offers you invaluable insight into yourself and how you respond to the world; that insight will be a powerful tool in moments of distress. The better you know your baseline state from practicing mindfulness even when you're feeling like your regular, everyday self, the more exquisitely you'll understand what's happening within yourself during moments of stress. This empowers you to know what tools to choose for self-care during moments when you're feeling anxious, blue, jittery, upset, frazzled, confused, or any of the other "negative valenced emotions" that exist in the universe of psychology.

There's an old saying among mindfulness teachers about the perils of learning to build a tepee during a thunderstorm: instead of learning how to build a tepee during a thunderstorm, we *practice* learning how to build a tepee during calm weather so that during a thunderstorm we can whip that tepee up without having to exert a great deal of cognitive struggle, trying to remember the steps of building it while we're simultaneously being pelted by raindrops and gusts of wind. The point of the metaphor is that **if we build mindfulness skills during calm moments of everyday practice, we'll be able to rely on well-developed skills during a "thunderstorm"** (which is actually when we need the skills the most). Don't make the mistake of turning to the Three-Part Breath only during "thunderstorm moments," when you're feeling overwhelmed, and before you've really learned the steps to the point that you can recall them with minimal effort. The steps are simple and can be learned in a short time (a half hour maximum, one minute minimum); and might require a few days of practicing two to three minutes per day. That small investment of practice will be a lifesaver during moments of peak stress. Here's an example from my own life.

The Three-Part Breath as a Practiced Rescue Skill: Oh No, Please, God—Not on Television!

It started out as a wonderful and exciting opportunity when I was called to CNN studios to provide comments for a news story. Although national television can sometimes feel a little intimidating, it also feels exciting and glamorous to me, and it represents a chance to connect with the world beyond my private office. I entered the studio eager to make a positive impression and get some great footage for my media presence, so the pressure was definitely on.

One of the challenges with television is that you need to think and speak quickly, while somehow also seeming natural and conversational. This can be hard to do gracefully sometimes; it's a skill I'm still building to this day. Because of said need to express oneself very quickly yet naturally on television, I had dutifully rehearsed my talking points before the segment. I sat in the studio as the show's host and her other guests discussed the news story. I was trying to remain attentive to everything being said, while also keeping my own talking points "front of mind" so I would be totally ready to animate myself and jump into the conversation whenever she pivoted to me. My nervous energy was so heightened that, in retrospect, I realize that I would have benefited greatly from doing some silent Three-Part Breaths while listening to the host instead of letting my body sit there in the jittery, overcaffeinated state that was about to lead to my most embarrassing TV moment ever.

When the host pivoted to me, I realized mid-sentence that I was unsure if I was pronouncing a word correctly. Rather than just taking my best guess and moving on, I became so self-conscious of this one word that I kept trying to use an easier-to-pronounce form of the word to rephrase my point. But my efforts were extremely counterproductive because instead of allowing me to move forward, these efforts actually kept me stuck on the sentence that was tripping me up. I knew I had to do something to "snap out of it," but instead of silently pinching myself under the table or taking a quick deep breath to reset myself, I actually *gave a bizarre, long and hard wink with my left eye.* Why? To this day, I do not know. Actually, in the process of writing this book, I think I may have figured it out: I was in a headspace where I was unwilling to tolerate anything short of perfection, because I desperately wanted that TV appearance to have a maximally positive effect on my career. My perfectionism ironically *prevented* me from confronting the problem and fixing it; instead I made the situation worse by remaining stuck until my body manifested the stress in its own skittish way. As soon as the problem became undeniable to me through that bizarro wink, I was **immediately able to use a mindful Three-Part Breath as a rescue technique.** Read on to see how I did it.

Even as I was actually in the nightmare moment of doing my weirdo wink, I realized what I was doing and how bizarre it was going to look on camera—yet I felt powerless to stop! It was the epitome of **nervous energy gone haywire,** exacerbated by an overdose of coffee and heightened anxiety due to this being one of my first times appearing on national television. Once it happened, there was a split-second choice I had to make: I could go completely to pieces and melt right there in embarrassment on national television, or I could (somehow) regain my composure *immediately.*

I finally, *finally* realized it was time to do the Three-Part Breath! It may have been a little overdue, but after the "winking disaster," I **immediately, almost automatically did a rapid, mini-version of the Three-Part Breath that was a total lifesaver.** I've watched the tape of this show more times than I care to admit, and if you watch this moment closely (which I hope you never will!), you can actually see my chest flowing through the Three-Part Breath during one quick second, and then my demeanor changes completely. That Three-Part Breath gave my brain a quick boost of oxygen and rescued me from the downward spiral I surely would have taken otherwise. It not only **reset my body out of an escalating sense of panic, it offered my mind an immediate comfort of something familiar that I knew was a "tried and true" centering technique, and it awak-**

ened my more mindful self that could *choose* to focus on moving forward rather than getting mired in a moment.

This story illustrates **how important it is to *practice*** the Three-Part Breath so that we can turn to it during moments of extreme stress when we don't have the cognitive resources to try to *recall* the steps. **If I hadn't practiced the Three-Part Breath to the point that I could do it almost automatically, it would not have been a viable tool in this extremely high-pressured, fast-moving situation.** Imagine how automatically you can tie your shoes: you probably don't have to think about it at all by this point in your life. But tying your shoes is actually a complex enough task that probably required a fair amount of thought and effort before it became automatic to you. The same principle applies to the Three-Part Breath: it's simple enough that, **with a little practice, it will become automatic and your friend for life.**

Troubleshooting

1. **I can't seem to get enough air.**

Ironically, this could mean you're doing it absolutely right and that you just need to keep practicing. Many people tend to take very shallow breaths that only use the upper portion of the chest. The Three-Part Breath forces you to locate certain muscles that facilitate deeper breaths (namely, the intercostal muscles) and control your primary breathing muscle (the diaphragm) in a deliberate manner. This can feel awkward or difficult at first. The key word here is "muscles," meaning that muscles can be trained; in fact they *must* be trained to function at their peak. Similarly, the capacity and efficiency of your lungs will increase with deliberate practice. This increased capacity, efficiency, and muscle control will be helpful in moments of stress when we tend to automatically drop into even *more* shallow breaths as part of a vestige of the caveman "fight, flight, or freeze" response to threats (even a modern-day "threat" like a biting email can trigger this response). In these situations, a few rounds of Three-Part Breathing can literally and figuratively help us to "catch our breath," bathe our brains in oxygen, make better decisions for present-day stressors, and help us come across as more relaxed in group situations.

2. I just get sleepy.

This could mean several things, all of which suggest you should keep practicing. Your reaction could suggest that you're not sleeping enough, in which case the best remedy is to allow the Three-Part Breath to guide you into a peaceful nap, or simply practice it at bedtime. Another possibility is that you might be confusing sleepiness for deep inner quiet and the trancelike feeling that can sometimes arise if you haven't experienced deep inner quiet very often before; this is actually a very special mental state wherein the mind often experiences profound healing and growth. If you think this may be the case, I urge you to keep practicing and allowing yourself to "drift" a bit before you naturally return to full consciousness, then write or speak your recollections of whatever was on your mind during your drift. In situations like these, the sleeplike feeling will generally decrease each time you practice, until your body and mind finally feel like they've "caught up" on deep downtime in that special state. Another related possibility is that you might just be someone who hasn't previously known of any tools that can stimulate relaxation, and you're just experiencing a healthy urge to "play" or explore the boundaries of how such techniques can affect your body and mind.

It is also possible that the Three-Part Breath is guiding you to awareness of thoughts or feelings you've previously avoided acknowledging, and you're using sleepiness as a way to avoid letting that awareness develop further. If you think this might be the case, I urge you to remember that the Three-Part Breath is not *creating* those thoughts or feelings; it's simply bringing them to your awareness so that you can determine how you want to address them rather than have them "running in the background" of your mind. In situations like this, it's often especially helpful to consider writing down or sharing the material you think you've been suppressing so that you can address it with the full power and resources of your conscious mind, and then move forward.

3. It's hard to remember the steps.

Congratulations, you're totally normal in this regard! Almost no one is able to recall the steps with ease after a first introduction, especially if you've really allowed yourself to just focus on the sensations and observations rather than memorizing steps. You might be someone who expects perfection from yourself, or you might be someone prone to self-criticism, or you might have a low tolerance for mild frustration. Either way, this actually represents a great opportunity for you to learn how to encounter a moment of imperfection with a nonjudgmental attitude as you may experience a normal, expectable process of minor grappling during the learning process.

Fret not: I can practically guarantee that after a few days of practicing for several minutes per day, the idea of inhaling in three steps, holding a moment, and then exhaling in three steps will be well within your grasp of memory. Give yourself a break: remember that you're not just learning the steps, you're also learning to use certain muscles you may not have used before, and you're simultaneously stimulating your cognitive and emotional awareness in ways you may not have experienced before. It's totally normal to need to *practice* this a few times over a few different days before you expect to perform a new task without deliberate recollection or reminders of the steps. Practice the art of self-compassionate self-discipline and keep trying. Soon it will be second nature to you!

Obviously, if you experience significant dizziness or if you have any medical concerns, by all means please do see your primary care physician. And remember the disclaimer located in the front of this book on the copyright page. Otherwise, please give yourself at least five opportunities spread over three different days to practice before you really start asking if you might be struggling more than others in your efforts to learn something new. Remember: if you need or want extra help (or just like watching videos), you can access a video of me doing the Three-Part Breath online at www.NervousEnergyBook.com/breathe. Otherwise, be patient and give yourself some breathing room!

Mindful Breath and Relaxation: Not Always Hand in Hand

Many high functioning people sometimes struggle to slow down and relax, so I wanted to address the topic of mindfulness, relaxation, and breathing. As discussed in the first of the "Six Benefits of Mindfulness" list in chapter 5, mindfulness and relaxation are not the same, even though relaxation is sometimes a benefit of mindfulness. Mindfulness is about increasing your self-awareness, which can involve slowing down your thought process—but the purpose of that slowdown is to facilitate greater powers of observation and awareness, rather than simply to promote relaxation. The practice of mindful breathing can certainly *be* relaxing sometimes, because it often signals to yourself that you're taking a moment for self-care and considering how to best meet your needs. This process, combined with the extra oxygen and physical control experienced via the Three-Part Breath, often creates a sense of reassurance that many people find relaxing and calming. But **the relaxing effects people sometimes experience through mindful Three-Part Breaths are really just side benefits of the primary benefits, which are increased capacities for nonreactive, nonjudgmental self-observation and self-awareness.**

To illustrate how mindful breathing can sometimes be used for purposes that have absolutely *nothing* to do with "just relaxing and letting things go," consider the following example.

How the Three-Part Breath Helped Christina Win in Workplace Warfare

Christina was accidentally copied on an email revealing that a colleague was spreading embarrassing falsehoods about her to management. The falsehoods not only spread negative misinformation about her work performance on a recent case; they included references to her painful breakup, with comments suggesting that perhaps she had been distracted at work "because I know her boyfriend recently left her; maybe that's part of the problems with distraction and focus she seems to be having lately." She and the colleague who sent the poison-pen email were both being considered for the same promotion, so it seemed likely that this was part of the colleague's effort to increase his own chances of success by sabotaging Christina's. The promotion would come with a salary raise big enough to pay off the remaining mortgage on her mother's modest home to thank her for all the sacrifices she made while Christina was growing up. In other words, this promotion mattered to Christina's pride in her work, her healthy sense of competition, and her fierce desire to honor her mother.

The moment Christina saw the email, her blood seemed to run both hot and cold simultaneously. Her mind immediately began rapid-firing through all sorts of potential responses to the situation. As a high functioning person with significant cognitive resources,

Christina was able to imagine a host of potential reactions within just a few seconds—ranging from forwarding the email to an ally in upper management immediately and copying the culprit so she could simultaneously address the lies and put him on the defensive, to marching over to the colleague's desk and asking him about the email in a loud voice in order to shame him and expose him in front of the entire office. She also considered saying absolutely nothing to anyone and instead sending immediate responses to the many recruiters who constantly tried to poach her for other firms, since the idea of drawing attention to her breakup in any way whatsoever, especially in the workplace, felt worse than appearing naked in public or just escaping to another firm. The references to her breakup were so humiliating that a part of her just wanted to hide forever, while another part of her wanted to clobber the culprit; still yet another part of her was focused on how to salvage her chances of getting the promotion. All of these parts were vigorously active *at the same time, and they all wanted her to take action immediately.*

Thankfully, Christina had the mindful awareness to realize that she was feeling *extremely* triggered (justifiably so), and that **the wisest action to take before committing to *any* further action was to do a few rounds of the Three-Part Breath,** including the important steps of observing herself before and after breathing deliberately into her belly, middle chest, and upper chest. The point was ***definitely not* to "relax and let go," but to take a careful survey of herself and then spring into action with a fully informed perspective.** The first thing she noticed was that it was unusually difficult to get air into her belly, and that her skin had become so hot that the air felt cool as she inhaled, and that a little lump seemed to be forming in her throat as if she were about to cry. She also noticed that she actually felt a touch of the spins.

Thanks to her mindfulness skills, Christina didn't become *alarmed* about these observations—she simply logged them into her awareness. Taking the time to notice these physical sensations in a nonreactive manner helped Christina step back and get some perspective on exactly how disoriented and overwhelmed she was feeling. By realizing this from a bird's-eye view of herself rather than just *being* disoriented and overwhelmed, Christina was then able to realize the best next step: to practice a few minutes of mindfulness of her thoughts and feelings (using the "passing clouds" technique described earlier in this chapter as an add-on technique for the Three-Part Breath), rather than just focusing on mindfulness of her breath. This allowed her to fully recognize *all* the pieces of herself that had become activated by the email to the point of causing such a profound physical reaction.

Christina was better able to slow down and scan herself in a nonreactive way after having done the Three-Part Breath, since the extra oxygen and slowed breathing had interrupted the "fight, flight, or freeze" reaction she initially experienced. As she delved into her next step of practicing mindfulness of her thoughts and feelings, she noticed she was experiencing a mix of anger, betrayal, fear, and even shame due to the embarrassing nature of the falsehoods and their potential impact on her goal of a promotion. She also noticed that she was experiencing a spike in sadness and insecurity just from having had her ex-boyfriend's name called to mind by reading the email, and she realized that she would have felt some of these feelings by encountering his name independent of any workplace drama. Interestingly, she also observed that she was feeling jealousy toward the colleague. The colleague seemed to come from a background of privilege, and Christina always thought he seemed to have such an easy life in comparison to her own. She realized that this incident reminded her of having been made fun of by "rich kids" on the playground for her secondhand clothes as a little girl, and that this current incident was also triggering parts of her childhood self that had always felt fearful of deprivation.

Once Christina was aware of all the reactions and the "subre-actions" she was having, she was able to identify the wisest next moves. She spent a few minutes practicing Anchoring Statements, assuring herself that she was now a perfectly safe adult who was no longer in danger of deprivation, so that whatever reaction she chose in response to the email would not be guided by old fears from child-hood. She also deliberately focused her attention on the reasons for the breakup in order to keep a sense of perspective on the sadness, so that she would be able to address this "low blow" from the colleague without becoming consumed or overpowered by sadness from the breakup. She knew that coming to tears over the "boyfriend re-mark" in front of management may have garnered sympathy, but it would also have been humiliating. Moreover, crying could have endangered the promotion by potentially bolstering the colleague's suggestion that Christina was "off" because of unmanageable feel-ings about the breakup. She was also able to consider her feelings of jealousy in an objective manner and remind herself that she actually didn't know anything about the colleague's personal life; she realized that he probably had private struggles of his own or he wouldn't be sinking to such unprofessional lows. This insight helped alleviate her jealousy and allowed her to (eventually) dis-cuss his behavior with management in an objective way that was not colored by a tone of jealousy; she knew that coming across as jealous or appearing to have an extraneous personal issue with the colleague would have weakened her position in a complaint. The law firm's partners were actually quite impressed with how she handled the situation, and she eventually accepted the promotion—in fact, she now *manages* the poison-pen emailer—and secretly admits to a bit of schadenfreude-fueled pleasure in having him report to her.

Christina's example illustrates that **while the Three-Part Breath can certainly feel relaxing sometimes, its usefulness is absolutely not limited to times when you're just trying to relax.** If you practice the Three-Part Breath as a way to build skills of observing yourself in a nonjudgmental, fact-based way, it will aid in situations when you need to **galvanize and synergize your mental resources** rather than just relax yourself.

When You Really Want to Use Breathing as a Way to "Just Relax"

If you've already done the Three-Part Breath and realized that actually the best next step is to find ways to cultivate relaxation, here are a couple of breathing techniques to try!

Modify the Three-Part Breath: S-L-O-W

One simple way to modify the Three-Part Breath so that its focus will be more on a mindful awareness of relaxation feelings rather than functioning as a general mindfulness "scanning tool" is to silently spell the word "slow" as you move through the three parts and the holds at the top and bottom of the breath. So when you inhale into the belly, silently say "S." As you continue up to the middle chest, silently say "L." When you reach the upper chest, silently say "O." When you hold for a moment at the top of the inhale, silently say "W." When you exhale the upper chest, silently say "S," then "L" as you exhale the middle chest, "O" as you exhale the belly, and "W" as you take a moment at the bottom of the exhale. Then start with "S" again as you inhale into the belly. This simple change helps adapt the Three-Part Breath into a bit more of a relaxation tool than a mindfulness tool; you may be surprised how the simple cognitive challenge of linking each part of the breath with a letter of the word "slow" requires just enough of your cognitive efforts to prevent your mind from spinning out into other topics, while simultaneously keeping your focus upon slowing down through a simple repetitive body-and-mind-linked suggestion.

Try a Purely Relaxing Breath with
No Connection to Mindfulness Whatsoever

When you're looking for a breathing technique that centers around pure relaxation rather than increased awareness, you might enjoy a breathing technique that I have termed "Cocoon Breathing." I call it Cocoon Breathing because it is designed to create a peaceful, private feeling of safety and relaxation deep within, as if there were a layer of protection surrounding you and buffering you from the rest of the world. It's best to be in a place where it's safe for you to close your eyes, at least the first couple of times you do it. Here's how you do it:

STEP 1: WARM UP

It is often helpful to start with a round or two of mindful breathing, the Three-Part Breath, or whatever other breathing technique helps give you a nice boost of oxygen and warms up your awareness of your breath.

STEP 2: LET GO

When you feel ready to start Cocoon Breathing, stop doing *anything* to control your breathing. No counting breaths, no trying to deliberately move your breath into certain parts of your body, no effort to control whether you're breathing through your nose or your mouth, and no focus on "breathing deeply" unless your body is just doing so naturally. Let your body decide when and how deeply or shallowly to inhale and exhale, and let it do so at its own pace.

STEP 3: FOCUS ON YOUR EXHALATIONS

Without trying to control your exhalations, just focus your attention on feeling or noticing them. Our heart rates actually decrease during exhalations; exhalations are part of our bodies' natural slowdown mechanism (also known as the parasympathetic nervous system). This is why we have expressions like "waiting to exhale" or "stop holding your breath." We know innately that our exhalations are geared toward relaxation. Let your eyelids drop closed as you exhale. Keep them closed if you feel comfortable, but also *imagine your eyelids closing again, or "mentally close them"* again on your next exhalation. You may be surprised how this sends a "double signal" of relaxation to your body and mind.

STEP 4: LINK YOUR MIND DEEPER INTO THE EXHALATION

With each exhalation, imagine your feet connecting down into the floor. If you're sitting, you can imagine the connection going down through your heels and/or the balls of your feet. With each exhalation, you can also focus on feeling the weight of your body supported by a couch or chair if you're sitting, starting with the trunk of your body and also your back. You might even start imagining that each exhalation is moving down through your body and into your feet, trunk, or back, and then going down deeper into whatever is supporting your body. You may also start noticing that with each exhalation, your jaw relaxes a bit, and your tongue may possibly even relax, too. You may also invite yourself to notice your shoulders dropping with each exhalation as they relax.

STEP 5: ENJOY YOUR PRIVATE INTERNAL SANCTUARY

With each exhalation, imagine again your eyelids closing even though you're keeping them closed, just like you did in step 3. Once you've done this a couple of times, use each exhalation to imagine a shade being drawn down on a window, creating privacy. Imagine this a couple of times. Imagine with each exhalation that the shade is coming down, or that your eyelids are closing again, or that you are spinning yourself into a safe and warm cocoon. This is your private inner sanctuary of relaxation. You may wish to press your thumb and forefinger together to "lock in" this connection with your relaxation sanctuary. You may find that pressing your thumb and forefinger together like this again in the future helps your body to "snap back" into this state more quickly if needed.

ADAPTATION FOR OPEN EYES

Although the Cocoon Breathing exercise includes closing your eyes, you can modify it to keep your eyes open if needed. The key is just to focus on your exhalations and give your mind easy ways to participate in the body's process of relaxation, by guiding your mind to notice it happening—and to notice how exhalations can create inner peace.

8.

The Zone of Control

*Start by doing what's necessary; then do what's possible;
and suddenly you are doing the impossible.*
—FRANCIS OF ASSISI

Sean arrived at my office with a worn, haggard expression on his otherwise handsome face. An analyst for a well-known hedge fund, he seemed to be carrying the weight of the world on his shoulders. As we talked, I learned that Sean had been putting his analyst skills to work studying his chances of getting an important promotion. He'd been spending hours carefully considering everything from whether his suits had the right cut to rumors that the hiring committee favored certain alumni affiliations that he unfortunately didn't have to concerns about his good-but-imperfect job performance. While it is generally helpful to consider the components of a problem carefully, Sean found himself constantly analyzing and reanalyzing to the point where he began to feel like he was just spinning his wheels and exhausting himself.

Sean had reached a state of "analysis paralysis," often described by my clients, whether they're professional analysts or not: they get so consumed with *studying* or *analyzing* a situation that they struggle to take any action because they get stuck in "what ifs" or "yes, buts"; or they get so fixated on parts of a problem that are beyond their control that they end up feeling defeated before they've really given their best shot at successfully managing the components they *can* control. There is a great deal of value in thoughtful and thorough consideration of life's dilemmas before taking action. I certainly have clients who struggle to manage impulsivity; these clients *wish* they had the problem of overanalyzing sometimes. However, there is a tipping point where we *know* that we're stuck on a mental hamster wheel and we need to start taking tangible action steps rather than continue to analyze ad nauseam. Sean needed help crossing certain dead-end items off his "worry list" so that he could free his energy and focus his efforts on the aspects of his bid for promotion, where he could be most effective. The Zone of Control[1] is perfect for this type of situation.

In session, Sean and I constructed a list of all the factors relevant to this potential promotion that he'd been analyzing. In addition to the items already mentioned, Sean's list included concern about a significant error he'd made on the job several months earlier; hope that his current performance was at a standout level; awareness of a few gaps in his knowledge of the ever-changing landscape of hedge-fund regulations; and general anxiety about what he'd heard was a grueling interview process, one with senior executives who prided themselves on how many candidates they'd been able to recognize as unsuitable after putting them through something rather scarily termed a "stress interview."

Once we had our list, the next step was to divide the list in two: one list for the things Sean could control, and one list for the things he could not control. These lists were called the Zone of Control and the Zone of Non-Control, respectively. Clearly, Sean couldn't do anything about his alumni affiliations, so that one had to go in the Zone of Non-Control. Likewise, he couldn't change the past and undo the mistake he'd made several months earlier, so the mistake went into the Zone of Non-Control as well. But as we discussed the other items on his list, he was able to locate actionable steps he could take to address his worry:

- Although his budget didn't allow for new suits, he was able to make an appointment with a tailor to make sure the ones he had fit him perfectly, and at least get a new tie and cuff links—so this went into the Zone of Control.

- He was able to ask his boss to review his current performance and suggest areas Sean could target for improvement, so his concern about his current performance went into the Zone of Control as well.

- He was able to schedule mock interviews with several friends and mentors to sharpen his interview skills so he would be prepared for the dreaded "stress interview." He also realized he could use these mock interviews to get practice discussing the big mistake from several months back in a simulated interview environment. Although he couldn't change the mistake, he could at least practice "spinning" it, should the topic arise in an interview, as he feared it would. So he placed interviews into the Zone of Control.

- He also found a couple of books that would help fill the gaps in his knowledge. Clearly within the Zone of Control!

Ironically, the process of putting items into the Zone of Non-Control often stimulates ideas about what actually *can* be done about those items. **Perhaps making the definitive statement "There's *nothing* that can be done about this" provokes a positive mental challenge for many high functioning people to see if maybe in fact there is actually *something that can be done, even if it seems small.*** In Sean's case, he had a realization that although he couldn't change his alumni affiliation, he could at least check LinkedIn to see if he had any close connections from favorable alumni groups that could potentially "put in a good word" for him. This enabled him to relocate the alumni issue from the Zone of Non-Control into the Zone of Control. We don't need to be able to solve an issue completely in order to place it into the Zone of Control; we just need to know that there's at least *something* we can do about that particular issue.

Once Sean could see which items truly belonged in the Zone of Non-Control and were therefore "dead ends" for him to keep ruminating about, he had a much easier time choosing to quit focusing his mental beams of attention upon on those topics and choosing instead to focus those beams where they belonged: in areas where he could actually be helpful to himself. In mindfulness meditation, we often compare the concept of "mental attention" to the beams of headlights on an automobile: wherever we point those beams is where our focus will be. The same concept applies for the Zone of Control: **once we can identify where the focus of our beams of mental attention will be the most illuminating and productive, then our mental journey starts to feel more "on track" and, in fact, it is more on track when we are focused on a plan of actionable steps.** The haggard look on Sean's face began changing to an expression of focus and determination once he quit his Sisyphean worrying about items in the Zone of Non-Control.

Identifying logical steps to address the items in the Zone of Control enhanced Sean's ability to feel motivated and energized, because he had a clear path of action to increase his odds of meeting his goal. Whenever he felt anxiety about the promotion, he simply consulted his list and got to work on everything from seeing a tailor to reaching out to arrange potential mock interviewers. **Each time he crossed an action step off his list, he felt an energy boost and pride in himself for his mini-accomplishment.** Plus, he was **decreasing his stress around the promotion by methodically and proactively whittling away at the stressful components of this goal.** The Zone of Control helped Sean realize that his anxiety about the promotion was actually a **valuable source of energy** and that he simply needed to **give that energy a *productive* target so that his nervous energy could work to his benefit.**

It's a well-documented fact (as well as common sense) that focusing on things that we can't control often leads to feelings of helplessness and depression, as well as a lot of wasted mental energy. No wonder Sean was looking haggard before he started focusing on the Zone of Control!

How I Used the Principles of the Zone of Control in Business

You may recall from chapter 1 of this book that I had a lot of nervous energy when I was first starting my practice, and one of the ways I coped was to make long lists of things I could do to help ensure success, and that I would turn to that list whenever I was at the office but not with a client. Having a list of things I could do to build my practice not only helped increase my productivity and efficiency, it kept me from staring at an empty office and getting flooded with feelings of worry during the start-up phase, when clients were less plentiful. In other words, the list kept me focused on the Zone of Control.

(Continued)

Have you ever had a boss that always let you know exactly what you needed to be doing, as well as why you needed to be doing it, without micromanaging you? That's what the Zone of Control approach did for me: it gave me plenty to do with a clear sense of why it had to be done, yet it also afforded me the latitude to choose which types of things I felt most inclined to do at any particular moment. When I was feeling social, I'd do things like call nearby doctors to see if I could visit their office and discuss how we could be referral partners. For example, I built relationships with elite cardiologists who were treating patients for high blood pressure; these patients are often high functioning people who also need to learn stress management skills. On other days, when I was feeling more introverted, I'd sit quietly and design brochures to take along on those future visits to potential referral sources (I did *everything* myself back in those days). The beauty of the Zone of Control is that it keeps you so focused on all the things you can do that you almost don't have time to sit stewing about things in the Zone of Non-Control.

Did my Zone of Control list block my awareness that, despite my best efforts, it was still possible that my dream of a successful private practice might not come to fruition? Did it neutralize my underlying fear that failure at this venture might ultimately lead to financial heartache? Of course not. The Zone of Control is not intended to block awareness of factual truths; it is intended to **help us harness our emotional and cognitive energy toward efforts that will increase our likelihood of success.** Putting my fear that my practice might not succeed despite my best efforts into the Zone of Non-Control *did* help me avoid getting stuck on that fear, which was very helpful. **Ruminating on that fear would have served no productive purpose** for me; and, in fact, it would have been a *counterproductive* waste of valuable time and energy.

The Zone of Control gave me something that was simultaneously both productive and soothing to *do* with my nervous energy. Whenever fear of failure popped up for me during the early phases of my practice (fear popped up rather often back then, since my practice had actually *not* yet been proven viable), I would **take the little boost of adrenaline that often appears during moments of fear and use its accompanying energy to tackle items in the action steps**

of the Zone of Control instead of using that energy to fuel a frenzied worry-fest about something I could do nothing to change. I'm proud to say that this approach was successful to the point where my practice became so full that I actually had to hire other therapists very soon in order to accommodate the volume of business that arose from my relentless efforts at attracting clients. In fact, I teach a course for therapists seeking to build their own successful practices. Thank goodness for nervous energy!

DIY: How to Put the Zone of Control to Use in Your Life

Before you read the DIY steps on how to *do* the Zone of Control technique, I urge you to grab a pen and paper first! A tangible record of your work will give you something to focus on during moments of stress, when you might otherwise be prone to mentally bundle all of the little items in your Zone of Control (and possibly even the Zone of Non-Control) into one big, overwhelming package rather than *enjoy* the fact that you have broken your stressor down into manageable pieces with clear and helpful action steps. An organized list will keep you from getting buffeted around between anxiety or concerns about each little component of your goal. Since each component typically relates to other components, it's easy for each component to *ping* you into thinking of other components, and next thing you know, your head is spinning. Having all of the pieces accounted for on a single sheet of paper will increase your overall ability to be strategic. Plus, each time you cross off an item from your written action list and literally *see* a record of your progress, you will feel a boost of dopamine (in laymen's terms, this is one of the brain's naturally occurring "feel good chemicals"), as well as a sense of productive control over whatever concern prompted you to list that action step!

So please do yourself a favor and complete the Zone of Control on paper, or at least type your responses in an email to yourself. It is a little bit more effort for a few minutes while you complete the exercise, but it will save you tons of time and mental energy in the long run. You can also go to www.NervousEnergyBook.com for a worksheet if you wish, but a simple sheet of paper used according to the directions below will work just fine!

The Zone of Control Step-by-Step

STEP 1: TAKE INVENTORY

During step 1, simply write the overall goal or issue at the top of a sheet of paper and then list underneath as many components to that goal as you can. For example, Sean wrote "GET A PROMOTION" at the top of his paper and then he listed things like doing well at the interview, mastering certain skills, and so on beneath his heading. During this step, don't worry about how to manage the components or try to decide whether they'll wind up in the Zone of Control or the Zone of Non-Control. Just challenge yourself to list as many components of the issue as you can. Don't worry if the components seem very big or very small. The idea here is just to take an inventory of all the things that are "in the back of your mind" as well as the clear "front of mind" factors that are relevant to your goal or issue. Remember, no component is too big or too small to include in your inventory.

STEP 2: DIVIDE AND CONQUER

Your next step is to divide the inventory into two lists: the Zone of Control and the Zone of Non-Control. One simple way to do this is to fold a sheet of notebook paper in half; then list the Zone of Control items on the left side of the fold, and the Zone of Non-Control items on the right side of the fold. It's important not to rush this step. One at a time, carefully consider each item on your inventory list. Ask yourself whether or not there is anything you can do about that item. If there is nothing you can do about the item (for example, William acknowledging that he couldn't grow taller when he reviewed his inventory of factors around his overall anxiety about whether his date would like him), then it must go into the Zone of Non-Control. If there *is* something you can do to mitigate the concern (such as Sean recognizing that although he couldn't afford new interview suits, he could at least get sharp tailoring), then the item goes in the Zone of Control.

STEP 3: PROACTIVE PROGRESS

As soon as you've divided your list of factors into the Zones of Control and Non-Control, the next step is to jot down the *specific* actions you can take on the controllable items. If they're in the "controllable" column, then by definition there is *something* you can do about them. Write that "something" down in clear, actionable language next to each item in the Zone of Control column. Whenever you're feeling anxious or eager to work on whatever goal prompted you to make a Zone of Control list, choose an action item and put your nervous energy to good use!

VARIATION

As an alternative to focusing on whichever Zone of Control task seems best based on your natural rhythm, current mood, and energy levels, some clients have done the following: choose one or two tasks in the Zone of Control that they've identified as the highest priority or most time sensitive, and work on those tasks till they feel their stamina fading; then pivot to other tasks on the list. This type of strategy can be useful if you know that, left to your own devices, you might never feel naturally drawn to certain essential tasks, or if you have certain very important tasks that require almost endless persistence.

For example, I worked with a recently divorced mother of two young children whose divorce settlement provided a limited amount of financial "runway" before she absolutely *had* to be earning money. Her goal was to become a successful financial advisor as quickly as possible. She knew she would have a tendency to spend days designing the perfect brochure yet neglect actually ever reaching out to any prospects. So she decided to focus exclusively on the items in the Zone of Control that were directly relevant to making money whenever she had the time or energy to build her financial planning business and then use the other tasks, such as perfecting her brochure, as "treats" when she felt she'd genuinely expended her best efforts toward the Zone of Control items that were most clearly tied to actual income.

SAMPLE ZONE OF CONTROL WORKSHEET

Feel free to use a blank sheet of paper to complete this exercise, write directly in this book, or go to www.NervousEnergyBook.com for a worksheet if you wish—but all you really need is a blank sheet of paper!

1. What is your big goal or general concern?
2. What are all of the components of this goal or concern? List them in writing, rather than just keeping them in your head. For example, if your goal or concern is to get into an MBA program, you might list things like GMAT scores, letters of recommendation, good interview skills, tough ratios of applicants to spots available, and the application deadlines bumping against competing deadlines at work. If your goal is to get in better shape, you might list things like enrolling in a gym, getting some exercise clothes, finding a type of exercise you enjoy (or dislike the least), carving out time for an exercise schedule, getting social support, improving your diet, creating a timeline to

your desired fitness level, and finding new ways to cope with stress that don't involve emotional eating.

3. Consider each item from the list you've made as you complete the blank chart shown after step 5. Transfer each item from your list into the chart, listing the things you cannot control in the "Zone of Non-Control," and the things you have some capacity to change in the "Zone of Control." Please note that the chart shown after step 5 is just a sample; your chart can have as many (or as few!) rows as you need, based on your exact situation.

4. In the "Action for Zone of Control" column in the chart, list the actions you can take to create a favorable result for the items in the "Zone of Control." Feel free to add as many actions as you like.

5. Whenever you feel worried or tense or stuck (or just feel like taking action) regarding your big goal or general concern, work on the action items.

ZONE OF NON-CONTROL	ZONE OF CONTROL	ACTION FOR ZONE OF CONTROL

Troubleshooting

1. **I feel overwhelmed by all the items in my Zone of Control, and there's practically nothing in my Zone of Non-Control!**

Don't worry if your Zone of Control ends up being really huge and you discover that there's actually very little in your Zone of Non-Control. Some people get worried if they see that there's a lot in the Zone of Control, because they feel daunted by all the tasks. If this happens to you, let me reframe the situation by suggesting that **having a lot of things you can do to facilitate your goals is actually a good thing.** Your Zone of Control's long list of action items is giving you a variety of choices on how to spend your time, and all of those choices will help you to feel empowered and productive because they're all prescreened activities that were specifically identified as things that would help advance you toward your goal. My list of things I can do to help grow my practice and my brand is *still* practically endless, and I actually like it this way. It's much more anxiety-provoking to be in a situation that makes you feel powerless to help yourself than to be surrounded by potential ideas and action steps.

Try choosing just one item on the list, whichever one feels the least intimidating or the most fun, and see if you can use it to help yourself get moving. If you still feel overwhelmed by your Zone of Control list, consider the To-Do List with Emotions exercise in chapter 9 of this book; or, of course, there's always the option of asking a therapist or coach to review the list with you as well to see if adding some self-care might be helpful. Depending on the material in your Zone of Control action list, you might also be able to delegate some of the material. For example, Sean gave his assistant a list of all the people he wanted to ask for help with mock interviews and had the assistant do the legwork of creating draft emails for him to send requesting their support. Even this small relief of "admin burden" helped him a lot, since he can sometimes get bottlenecked on "little things," like composing relatively simple emails if those emails pertain to a broader topic that carries emotional weight.[2] Even if you don't have an assistant, you may be able to get a friend to help or barter with you on certain tasks—asking for help when needed is a high functioning thing to do!

2. My Zone of Control seems tiny, and my Zone of Non-Control seems huge.

If you complete the exercise and find that your Zone of Non-Control is actually very large, and you're worried that there may not be enough material in your Zone of Control for you to be effective at meeting your goal, I suggest that you consider asking a trusted friend or therapist to review the list with you. Sometimes just having a brainstorming session with someone who has good problem-solving skills, a creative mind, or a supportive presence can help stimulate ideas that can move items from the Zone of Non-Control into the Zone of Control.

However, if you've exhausted every possible way to gain more agency over an issue and realize that it *is* really beyond your control, then this insight may help free you to focus your attention on other issues in your life where you can be more effective. If the issue is too important to disregard while you focus on other things, yet you're still realizing that you're ultimately powerless over it, then this, too, is a valuable insight; so please remember to take a deep breath and thank yourself for beginning to face this quandary squarely. You might want to save your Zone of Control worksheet so you can show it to a trusted friend or therapist and get emotional support around the experience of being powerless over something that feels so important to you. If you think about it, the act of getting clarity about your limited ability to be effective on an issue may provide you with a sense of liberation or healthy detachment; at the very least, it may stimulate you to learn coping skills or increase your support network in a difficult situation.

3. I can't seem to get the stuff in the Zone of Non-Control "out of my head."

Take refuge in knowing that there's a big difference between "getting something out of your head" and choosing strategically to avoid focusing on it. The goal here is the latter. We don't want to block our awareness of the facts; we just want to avoid *focusing* on certain facts if there's nothing we can do about them. It's important to note that there is a big difference between deliberately choosing not to focus on things we cannot control, and being "in denial." When we're in denial, we block our awareness of things that cause distress to the point of pushing that awareness out of our conscious mind and into our unconscious mind. Blocking awareness of facts can be counterproductive because it deprives us of the chance to address our emotions around the material we're denying, and it deprives us of the knowledge that material may be able to provide.

For example, although Sean couldn't fix the mistake he made in the past, it was actually very helpful for him to be conscious of his disappointment over it. This fueled him to really understand the factors that led to the mistake, thereby helping him decrease the likelihood of repeating it. Coming to terms in this manner allowed him to genuinely forgive himself and move forward. Although he wanted to forgive, his goal was *not* to forget. Remembering the mistake not only helped him avoid repeating it, but also demonstrated to his managers that he fully understood the mistake and was ready to take ownership whenever reference or discussion of it arose. If he had been in denial and tried to pretend the mistake was "no big deal" and he "wasn't upset at all," he would have run the risk of appearing cavalier, repeating the mistake, harboring feelings of regret or self-criticism that he couldn't quite understand, or possibly taking out his frustrations by becoming unnecessarily critical of the mistakes of others. Similarly, if William had tried to pretend that his height couldn't possibly be a factor for him in dating—rather than facing the fact that his height might be an issue for some women but that it was still beyond his control—he would have run the risk of assuming women were rejecting him for reasons based on his personality rather than potentially for height preferences, or he may have potentially found himself feeling nervous and insecure for reasons he didn't understand.

The good news is that putting something into the Zone of Non-Control inherently prevents us from being in denial about it: we have actually put it down on paper and literally *recognized* it. By facing the fact and being *aware of it* yet also not *overfocusing on it*, **we get the benefit of awareness without the baggage of brooding.** If you find yourself ruminating on things in your Zone of Non-Control rather than just having a mindful awareness of them, you might try the following potential remedies:

- Ask a trusted friend, mentor, or therapist (whichever person seems most appropriate to the material) to review your Zone of Non-Control with you to make sure there's *really* nothing you can do about the items in that list. Sometimes our minds keep wanting to revisit the list because we have an unconscious awareness that maybe there's actually something we *can* do if we think about the list again in a productive and creative mindset.

- Accept that *urges* to think about the material on the list might be just old cognitive habits that you developed before you created your wonderful Zone of Control list. When someone who has slouched for a long time decides to sit up straight with the shoulders back, it initially feels awkward; he or she feels naturally drawn to the old position. The person must constantly choose to adopt the new behavior (sitting straight with shoulders back) till it becomes the "new normal." This is why having a tangible, written Zone of Control action list is so important: in times of stress or vulnerability when you might be prone to ruminate on things you can't control, try just focusing your eyeballs on your Zone of Control list and getting to work. Or perhaps try the Mental Shortlist technique (coming up in the next chapter). Practicing the Three-Part Breath and other mindfulness techniques has also been shown to help people have more control over where they *choose to focus* their mental attention, even in the face of strong urges toward tempting distractors or "dead ends" like the Zone of Non-Control.

- You may need emotional support around the material you have listed in the Zone of Non-Control. For example, Sean benefited from talking through the past mistake and being guided into a process of productive review of the mistake as well as a process of self-forgiveness. He also benefited from role-playing conversations about it so that he was prepared for occasions when the mistake might be discussed in the workplace. Another example is that William benefited from therapeutic challenging of distorted and inaccurate thoughts he harbored about the unchangeable fact of his height, such as a belief that he was irretrievably challenged in dating because of his height. Addressing these beliefs rather than just labeling the concern as "overwhelming" and pushing it into his unconscious helped him accept that although *some* women might have an issue with his height, many women couldn't care less (and some petite women even *prefer* men closer to their own height!). If you feel "stuck" on letting go of an item in the Zone of Non-Control, that can be a clue that you need some support addressing that item. If this is the case, please thank yourself for going through the Zone of Non-Control process so you could develop the valuable insight that you'd like some support coming to terms with certain items in your list.

9.

Mental Shortlist

Tell me what you pay attention to
and I will tell you who you are.
—JOSÉ ORTEGA Y GASSET

Stephen was a talented, driven, and successful entrepreneur with a tenacious mind. He came across as affable and easygoing, but everyone in his life knew he was churning with energy. It's part of how he got to be so successful, turning a startup in his basement into an eight-figure multimillion-dollar business in just five years. He often joked that part of the reason he did so well was because "giving up isn't in my DNA." I have to agree that he was an exceptionally focused, persistent person. Once he set his sights on an idea, his mind was focused there like a laser beam—his energy sometimes seemed to take on a drive of its own that made it appear almost effortless for him to sustain his focus. He was the proverbial "dog with a bone" once his mind got fixed on something, and this was a point of pride for him—generally speaking. While this feature of his mind was an advantage in many situations, it was a liability in others.

Even if your mind isn't *always* tenacious like Stephen's, you've probably had situations in which your cognitive and emotional energy seemed attached to a person or situation in a manner that felt almost automatic and intractable, or even a little "obsessive." This can be incredibly favorable when you're feeling naturally drawn to ponder an issue or challenge for which your energy is yielding desirable results and feeling constructive; but the same tenacity can be equally *unfavorable* when your mind seems to keep tracking on a topic that you'd really prefer to "put on the shelf." Examples of the latter can include anything from a breakup to an embarrassing incident that keeps replaying in your mind, or a workplace situation in which there's nothing you can do but wait—yet you keep thinking about it obsessively to the point that it feels like you're "spinning your wheels."

In Stephen's case, his tenacity became a liability rather than an asset when he had an extremely high-stakes meeting with investors scheduled to occur in two weeks and he could *not* stop thinking about it. To a certain degree, this was helpful—at least at first: his focus on the meeting had stimulated him to prepare for it *very* thoroughly. He had done everything from crafting and rehearsing the perfect pitch; to researching business connections he had in common with the investors so he could get his colleagues to "just happen to mention" something positive about him to the investors; to personally meeting with the manager of the private club where the event was scheduled in order to put a very fine point on his message to the manager that *everything* had to be absolutely *flawless* for this extremely important meeting. (I'm afraid Stephen may have traumatized that poor manager, and I'm only half joking.)

"Doctor, you have to help me," he said. "It's like I have a one-track mind on this friggin' meeting. It's getting to the point where I'm worried that if I can't stop thinking about this meeting I'll end up doing something stupid like sending the guys yet another email to say how much I'm looking forward to the meeting, just because it somehow feels better to be doing *anything* for this meeting than to just leave it alone for now—even though I know at this point anything further I do is going to be overkill, over the top—I'd look desperate, neurotic, or worse. But I can't seem to turn it off in my mind. And the more I tell myself to quit thinking about it, the more I think about it! I'm actually getting on my *own* nerves here, but the harder I try to stop, the worse it seems to get. It's like when someone tells you not to think about pink elephants and then all you can think about is pink elephants. My persistence has always been one of my greatest assets, but now it's like it's gone haywire and turned against me. What can I do?"

Before I go any further, let me say that I don't mean to suggest that the Mental Shortlist is the *only* way I worked with Stephen to unpack and manage his obsession with this meeting. We explored it on multiple levels, including nuanced issues related to his individual history. But I won't detail that part here, since the technique that actually seemed most helpful to him—and which has also been most helpful in many other cases involving a high functioning person's exceptional powers of focus latching on to something in a way that has become counterproductive or unpleasant—was the Mental Shortlist technique. Here's how Stephen and I used the Mental Shortlist to great success.

I explained to Stephen that the human mind often develops habits in order to save energy and thereby increase available mental bandwidth. **This process of efficiency generally serves us very well, except when our mind has an old habit that is no longer productive.** In Stephen's case, he had developed a habit of thinking about this meeting to the point that it had become automatic. This meeting was on the top of his Mental Shortlist of "go-to" topics, and in fact it seemed to have become the *only* item on that list. Moreover, as he had also noticed, the irony is that when we try to tell ourselves *not* to think about something, we often inadvertently reinforce our habit of thinking about that very topic, since we actually need to think about the topic in order to "remember" not to think about it: it's a catch-22 situation.

The simple, elegant solution to this dilemma is to deliberately create a *new* Mental Shortlist of juicy, productive, or otherwise enticing topics to dangle in front of your mind when you start veering automatically over to the topic you'd actually rather leave alone. I suggest you come up with at least five topics to have on this list, and that the topics cover a variety of domains in your life. The list should also be diverse in terms of how much cognitive energy its items require: you want things on your list that will be meaty enough to satisfy you if you have an hour to kill in front of a computer, and also things that are light enough to consider briefly while waiting in line at a store. You need a list that will cover you whenever and wherever your "thought monster" strikes. In Stephen's case, his new Mental Shortlist included the following items:

STEPHEN'S MENTAL SHORTLIST

1. Thinking of ideas for birthday and holiday gifts for his wife and kids, then writing down the ideas and browsing or acquiring the gifts online. (Stephen was often underprepared with gift ideas for loved ones on special occasions, and really wanted to change this.)
2. Researching African safari companies and travel agents to plan the lifelong "dream trip" he'd always wanted to take but never had time to explore (till now).

3. Playing really loud music on his headphones so he couldn't think about anything besides the music, and running on the treadmill while doing so if a treadmill was available and he had the energy. A treadmill wasn't always available, of course, but at the very least he could pop on the music and blast away, even if just during his commute.[1]

4. Writing letters of praise to his top-performing employees, or at least mentally reviewing and building lists of what performance highlights he wanted to feature whenever he had time to write the letters. (Stephen was big on increasing employee loyalty and engagement through personal recognition, plus it made him feel good on a personal level.)

5. Checking out the websites of his competitors (Stephen had a very strong competitive nature, and staying on top of the competition always piqued his interest); and building a list of changes to his own website or business offerings to implement if his investigations stimulated ideas on how to keep his business at the top of the market.

Whenever Stephen's mind started to autofocus on the topic of his investor meeting, he would turn his eyeballs to his shortlist and concentrate on those items instead. Was it easy? Actually, sometimes, it was. He was rather surprised that, often, all he needed was a list of good alternatives that had previously "slipped his mind" when he was getting stuck on the topic of the investor meeting. Other times, switching focus was a little harder—but it was still easier than if he hadn't done himself the favor of creating a hot list of alternative topics. Sometimes, he would just try to quickly mentally recall all five items on his Mental Shortlist; that activity in itself sometimes gave him enough of a mental challenge to divert his focus away from obsessing about the meeting.

While the Mental Shortlist technique *seems* simple, I'll admit it is *deceptively* simple. There is a very important step that is essential in order for this technique to work: you absolutely, positively, *must* write your list down and keep it with you at all times if you want it to really be there as a resource when the old tempting topic is singing its siren song. While your shortlist may seem perfectly simple, straightforward, and easy to remember when you're in your rational mind, calmly and creatively putting together a clever list of enticing new go-to topics, beware that when the "thought monster" strikes you may actually have a very hard time remembering your list, much less holding your focus on it—so please, write it down and/or at least commit it to memory with a clever acronym. For example, Stephen organized his into "GAME C" (G for gifts, A for Africa, M for Music, E for Employees, and C for Changes). The "C" stood for "changer" in his mind, so GAME C signified "game-changer" to him (Stephen didn't get stuck on the technicalities of whether "GAME C" was technically an acronym—he just found it to be an easy and inspiring way to organize his list). Having things organized helped Stephen to feel confident when he needed to recall his list during a moment when he was unable to check his paper copy.

Having a tangible list you can use to literally control your focus just by pointing your eyeballs at it will be a lifeline in your hour of need. I sometimes compare it to the idea of having delicious, attractive, premade healthy snacks in your refrigerator so that you'll be less vulnerable to wild, random cravings after a long day when your mind is tired and you're feeling stressed. In those moments, we're actually less equipped to *think of* a healthy snack even though we'd be perfectly willing to *eat one* if someone presented us with something easy and we didn't have to do anything but relax and enjoy it.

The same thing applies to choices in our "thought diet": **when we have a premade list of attractive topics handy, it's much easier to just focus on that list during vulnerable moments than having to scramble for ideas *during* a strong mental craving to ruminate on a topic that we know is best left alone.** If your high functioning mind is feeling tempted to try and keep your new Mental Shortlist "all in your head" because you're usually pretty good at just remembering things, please humor me and write your list down anyway. Please. Your future self will thank you!

Other great uses of the Mental Shortlist include when you're trying to avoid ruminating about your ex after a breakup, or trying not to overthink a first date. I've also worked with clients who used the Mental Shortlist technique after sending in their applications to MBA programs, or other **situations when there's *suddenly* nothing more you can do toward a goal:** After having spent months investing huge amounts of cognitive and emotional energy in the application, the essays, the letters of recommendation, and all of the other application hurdles to clear, many people understandably have a hard time just "turning it off" when the application process is complete. **The Mental Shortlist helps them ease into the process of changing an automatic habit that was once useful** (devoting any moments of mental downtime to thinking about the application and how to improve it) but has lost its utility since the applications have now been submitted and there is nothing to do but wait. Basically, anytime you realize you'd like to break a habit of focusing on almost any topic in your personal or professional life, the Mental Shortlist is a technique to consider.

It is important *not* to use the Mental Shortlist technique to distract yourself from topics where your focus is actually *needed*. For example, when Christina discovered that a colleague was actively working to sabotage her chances of promotion, using the Mental Shortlist as a first line of defense to escape her discomfort would have been a terrible idea: although confronting the problem of sabotage was painful, ignoring the problem and diverting her focus to other things just to avoid the discomfort would have made things even worse. Christina *needed* to address that situation.

Once Christina had successfully addressed the issue with management, she was free to use the Mental Shortlist to help "reset" her mind's newly developed cognitive habit of focusing on the culprit and on how to manage the situation. For several days, she had focused on the sabotage rather frequently in service of a healthy goal to fully consider the best way to respond to the problem. Focusing on the sabotage had actually provided her with a fair amount of almost *pleasurable* feelings because thinking of constructive ways to deal with it had stoked feelings of pride in her willingness and ability to defend her boundaries, and her focus helped generate new ideas to manage the situation. However, once she took action and met with management, she knew she had reached the point where further focus on the issue would be rumination rather than productive focus—so at *that* point, the Mental Shortlist became an appropriate technique to use whenever her mind seemed to "default" to the topic of her sabotaging colleague.

DIY: How to Put the Mental Shortlist to Use in Your Life

The goal is to create a list of at least five enticing topics you will focus on whenever a certain "dead-end" topic" enters your mind. A topic is a "dead end" if there's really no upside to continuing to focus on it, and in fact, there may even be a downside to continued focus. Common examples include exes, job interviews for which you've already done your follow-up and no further action would be appropriate, past arguments that are totally pointless to continue reviewing, embarrassing incidents that are stuck on replay in your mind, obsessive health concerns when you've already gotten medical reassurance that you're fine, or **any topic where you realize you're prone to overthinking to the point of your own detriment.**

Some people like to put the list in their phone, because they always have their phone with them. Others like to put the list on paper and keep it in their wallet or purse. Personally, I'm a fan of seeing things in your own handwriting. Handwriting is very personal, and sometimes reading your Mental Shortlist in your own handwriting connects you back to the moment of calmness and clarity you were experiencing when you created it, more so than an impersonal digital font might. However, I truly recognize that each person is different, and some people feel so "at home" on their phone these days that putting the shortlist there actually makes the most sense. Choose whatever writing method is best for you, but definitely make sure you have a written list rather than trying to keep the list in your head. Aim for at least five items on your list so that you'll have a variety of options. The idea is to have a list that will be so full of interesting, enjoyable, or productive topics that switching your focus will be almost *fun* when the old topic calls your name. For a worksheet to stimulate you with more ideas for your mental shortlist, see www.NervousEnergyBook.com.

Troubleshooting

1. **Focusing on my new Mental Shortlist doesn't feel natural.**

This is totally normal. If focusing on these items were natural, you wouldn't need the list in the first place, because you'd be focusing on these things already. You're doing this exercise because you want to develop *new* habits. The good news is that if you stick with it, thinking about the topics on your Mental Shortlist will become your "new normal" cognitive habits over time, and thinking about the old topic you're trying to forget will come to feel unfamiliar.

However, if you're really struggling, make sure you double-check that there's *really* nothing you can do about the old topic. If your mind is resisting diversion, it could be because there's actually something more you need to do about the topic you're trying to leave behind. Also, make sure you have done all you can to create a truly enticing list of topics as options on your shortlist: this will make the process of changing your focus as easy as possible.

2. I can't think of enough items for my Mental Shortlist.

This is proof that you *really* need to be doing this exercise. If you are struggling to think of alternatives to your dead-end topic even when you're in a calm, rational mindset, then it is understandable you're having a hard time letting that topic go. There may be a shortage of other areas of focus in your life. Ask a friend, family member, or therapist to help you think of some fruitful topics for your list. Or take a look at your calendar and notice what's on your horizon to see if that stimulates ideas about happenings in your life that could benefit from a little planning or mental preparation. If your calendar is woefully empty or you can't think of any supportive people to help with your list, perhaps you can add "finding ways to meet new people" to the top of your list! Another item that is almost always good to have on your Mental Shortlist is the Three-Part Breath or any other breathing or meditative technique you'd like to practice.

10.

To-Do List with Emotions

Human behavior flows from three main sources:
desire, emotion, and knowledge.
—PLATO

Sarah was a cardiothoracic surgical fellow. As I'm sure you can imagine, the path to becoming a cardiothoracic surgical fellow is *not* an easy one. After a decade of rigorous medical education received through multiple hypercompetitive admissions processes as she advanced through various trainings in this highly specialized field, Sarah was able to do things that most of us could never imagine (seriously—just *try* to imagine breaking someone's breastbone on purpose, slicing that person's heart open, *fixing* it, and then sewing him or her back up again as part of your normal day-to-day). Personally, I'll admit that part of the reason I chose psychology over psychiatry, and chose to limit my practice to low-risk, high functioning people is because, frankly, I would struggle profoundly if I had to wrestle with a patient's death as a potential consequence of making a mistake.

In addition to clearing these Herculean educational and professional hurdles, she had done them even as her mother passed away in an auto accident caused by a drunk driver. Even in that extremely vulnerable moment, Sarah had not allowed herself the luxury of a break from school, because it would have derailed certain steps that had taken years to arrange, and she could not financially afford to set the entire process of becoming a cardiothoracic surgeon back by waiting a year to resume training with next year's cohort after taking time off to grieve. (If she waited less than a year, she couldn't rejoin her original cohort because the participants would be too advanced—therefore her only real options were either to take off an entire year or continue without any significant break.) However, even if she could have found a way to absorb the financial cost of a yearlong break, she knew that such a lengthy break might cause her to lose some of the delicate manual skills she was building in the cardiothoracic surgical suite; it would have been unrealistic to take a year off from surgical training and expect to just "pick up where she left off" the following year. Perhaps most importantly, she knew that her mother, who had been extremely proud of Sarah's accomplishments, would never have wanted to be the reason, in any way, shape, or form, for her daughter to jeopardize her career. So Sarah soldiered on through twenty-four-hour hospital training shifts and dealt with her grief as best she could. This was several years before I met her, and I still struggle to fathom how she did this. What I'm trying to say is that Sarah was tougher than many of us, even the highest functioning among us, can truly comprehend.

Sarah came to see me because, for the first time in her life, she felt her nerves of steel beginning to fray. She was completing her final year of fellowship, after which point life would get much easier when she could take a position as an elite surgeon rather than a disposable fellow. Medical fellows, especially those in highly competitive fields, experience a process that is almost akin to hazing: the senior surgeons have paid their dues and often tend to place the brunt of any gruntwork upon their fellows, and they are *not* known for delivering feedback in a kind, constructive manner. Sarah's attending surgeon was known as a particularly difficult personality. It is a well-known dynamic in hospitals that the more prestigious a surgeon is, the more license he or she often feels to ride roughshod over the training fellows, as if there is an inverse relationship between "soft skills" and surgical skills. (Have you ever heard the joke: "What's the difference between God and a cardiothoracic surgeon?" Answer: "God doesn't think he's a cardiothoracic surgeon." It's a common joke in hospitals, and there's a reason why.) I remember experiencing these types of dynamics when I was a graduate student training in psychiatric emergency rooms and inpatient units working under senior physicians and psychologists, and I can only imagine how these dynamics would feel "on steroids" for cardiothoracic surgeons and their fellows.

If these issues had been the extent of her challenges, I actually don't think Sarah would have come to see me. Somehow, she had been able to carry on with a stiff upper lip, undeterred by a multitude of challenges throughout her life, and she had navigated with great success. The factor that was throwing Sarah for a loop was her three-year-old son. (Yes, she had also been doing much of her training work while pregnant! She worked right up till her delivery, and she was proud of this fact. This woman was a *soldier.*) Specifically, her toddler's new habit was pulling on her heartstrings in a way that she'd never experienced before: he would wrap his arms around her ankle and plead, "Mommy, stay here—my heart needs help, too!" as she marched out the front door after a brief respite from the mind-numbing twenty-four-hour hospital shifts.

Maybe the goodbyes were just hard because of natural maternal bonding; maybe they were harder because the boy's father wasn't there to offer support; maybe they were hard because she was leaving him with her mother-in-law, who undermined Sarah in subtle ways with the guise of "helping" . . . or maybe the goodbyes struck a particularly painful chord because of her relatively fresh grief for her own mother. Sarah had no idea why they were so painful, because she hadn't unpacked any of her feelings or considered any of these factors. In fact, I didn't even learn about this concern of hers until I had interviewed her very closely; it wasn't till she told me the story of her painful goodbyes, in response to my very specific questions about her daily routine, that she began to break down in tears and get in touch with the pain she was feeling. Prior to that moment in therapy, I think Sarah believed she just needed to "toughen up" a bit more, and she couldn't understand why she was having trouble doing so. What she would come to understand was that learning to acknowledge her pain would empower her to address it, and she would thereby become even more capable of reaching *all* of her goals, including her goal of feeling confident about herself as a mom.

When she first arrived at my office, Sarah knew only that her normal ability to function with nerves of steel appeared to be faltering, and she wanted help to stay on track. Her hours were long, and she had an enormous amount of work to do between shifts for her final presentation to conclude her fellowship. Sarah was carrying an enormous emotional load of job stress, grief over her mother's death, and a variety of other factors (her mother-in-law was living with her in a tiny New York City apartment to help care for the toddler, while Sarah's husband was living and working in the state where they would normally reside together except for this fellowship year).

Despite all of these extraordinary stressors, Sarah simply arrived at my office and said she was frustrated *with herself* for being "lazy." She cited her struggles to discipline herself to do things like clean her apartment or work on her final presentation as evidence of this "laziness." Sarah sought help because she thought maybe something was *wrong with her*; she thought she needed to learn how to push her emotions aside and get things done. **Ironically, what Sarah needed in order to get things done was actually to get *in touch* with her emotions.** This concept is often new for high functioning people, who may have accomplished a great deal by learning how to put their emotions aside.

Sarah was actually unusually adept at putting her feelings aside; doing so is practically a job requirement for surgeons (slicing into people's bodies the first few times usually requires some high-level emotional gymnastics, as I'm sure you can imagine). Like many high functioning people, Sarah was actually *so* good at putting her emotions on the shelf that she had forgotten how to take them back down from the shelf and deal with them. This was leading to a backlog of unaddressed feelings that were lurking in the back of her mind, outside of her immediate awareness, and manifesting in her conscious experience as a general lack of motivation and sense of depletion when attempting her to-do list.

In psychology, we sometimes call the act of putting your feelings aside in order to get things done "compartmentalization." The ability to compartmentalize is certainly very helpful when we're dealing with circumstances where there is literally or figuratively no room for feelings. Whether you're slicing into a patient or managing a boardroom crisis, we can all understand that there are certain strategic moments when it's best to have a "stiff upper lip" and not get sidetracked by your personal emotional reactions. But these moments of putting our feelings aside *must* be accompanied by a period of reconnection with our feelings; otherwise those feelings may fester and come back with a vengeance, or they may manifest as a low-grade feeling of numbness, lack of fulfillment, or procrastination.

As Sarah and I looked at the to-do list about which she was so self-critical for not having the energy to complete, I asked her to talk about the emotions associated with each item. She looked at me like I was speaking Greek. "There's not a lot of *feelings*," she said. "I just need to *do* these things," she explained to me as if I were a small child. I asked her to humor me, and so we went through her to-do list together, talking about each item and the feelings it stimulated.

What Sarah's To-Do List with Emotions Revealed

1. "Finish my final presentation." The first thing on Sarah's list was to work on her final presentation for her surgical fellowship. In case you aren't aware, many surgical fellowships conclude with a final presentation. These presentations are special because it's the last time the presenter will be speaking as anything but a fully trained surgeon; they're sort of a rite of passage. Sarah wasn't sure why, but every time she thought about this topic she had a heavy feeling in the pit of her stomach, and she seemed to feel a sense of procrastination that was surprisingly hard to overcome (especially surprising for a woman like Sarah, who didn't typically struggle to make herself do *whatever* needed to be done). Up until now, the primary feeling had been irritation with herself for "dragging her feet" on getting this presentation ready.

I asked Sarah to discuss the presentation and what it meant to her on a personal level. She began to reply in a tone of voice that conveyed a forced calm, almost as if she were being asked to explain to a fully capable adult how to tie his shoes. "Well, *obviously* what this presentation means is that I'm finishing my surgical fellowship, and what that means to me on a personal level is—" Her voice seemed to catch in her throat for moment, and her tone softened. She said quietly, with her eyes growing moist, "It means I'll be finishing everything, all my training, and I know my . . . my . . . my . . . my *mom* would be so proud when that happens but she won't be able to see it."

Sarah's incredible workload, combined with her being a new mom to a young toddler, sharing a small space with her mother-in-law, and enduring a prolonged distance from her husband meant that she simply hadn't had time to process why this final presentation brought about such a heavy feeling-state for her. Once we connected with the (deeply heartfelt, albeit painful, and totally understandable) feelings that this final presentation stimulated for her, Sarah was at least able to *understand* herself better and stop berating herself for being "lazy." This newfound insight allowed us to create plans for ways that Sarah could honor her mother during her fellowship completion.

Even something as simple as including a final slide in the presentation to recognize her mother's pivotal role in helping Sarah reach this point helped her to *gain rather than lose* energy and awareness as she addressed the simple truth that this presentation marked an incredible milestone that she yearned to share with her mom. In addition to realizing that she wanted to recognize her mother in some way during the presentation, Sarah also came to realize that she needed to give herself more space for quiet reflection and self-care when memories of her mother arose as she worked on the presentation, rather than pushing those feelings aside and fostering feelings of numbness. I'm not saying the presentation became *easy* at that point, but I can say that Sarah regained her focus and momentum on her preparations and did very well on the actual live presentation—plus she said it was very fulfilling on an emotional level to share the last slide honoring her mother's contributions to her career.

2. "Clean my apartment." Sarah seemed a little embarrassed even to bring this one up, but since I asked for specifics on what she meant regarding her concern that her general energy and focus were slipping, her struggle to stay on top of domestic chores came up for discussion. I was actually rather surprised that Sarah was even doing her own cleaning. For goodness' sake, she was a *cardiothoracic surgical fellow*, as well as a mom to a young toddler, not to mention that she was married to a very successful lawyer back home. Moreover, her mother-in-law was living with Sarah and her son to *help support* Sarah during this difficult final year of training. Sarah had accepted a fellowship position in New York City because it was an incredible opportunity to complete her training under a world-class surgeon at a premier hospital and thereby increase her earning power for the rest of her life. . . . So why was house cleaning even an issue? I asked this question as gently as I could.

"Well," Sarah responded, "I don't really know, to be honest. If it were up to me, I would just hire someone. But my mother-in-law says she doesn't like having strangers in the apartment." I responded, "Um, okay, is there a reason she doesn't clean the apartment herself, then? Since she has no other job, her entire reason for being there is to *support you* in the extremely challenging final stretch of your surgical training, as you simultaneously adjust to motherhood while dealing with temporary geographical distance from your husband, and she is declining your offer to provide a professional cleaning service?"

"Honestly, that's a good question," Sarah replied. "I guess that it just feels like she's doing us such a huge favor by being here that I don't want to ask for anything more. It's not like I have a general problem with the idea of doing housework; I don't mean to come across as *entitled* or anything. I'm just sharing this because you asked about what stuff on my to-do list seems to be weighing me down or just not getting done."

I was still a little stunned by the idea that this mother-in-law, who was presumably there to *support* this fledgling family, would somehow think that the best way to do that would be to require Sarah to do all of the cleaning herself, and by the idea that Sarah thought it could seem entitled that she wanted to hire a housekeeper to ease her burden after grueling twenty-four-hour surgical shifts and to free some time to work on her presentation. But I held my tongue and simply asked more questions.

"Sarah, when you think about doing the housework, can you tell me what comes to mind for you on a personal level?"

Once again, Sarah's eyes grew a bit misty. "Well," she said, "the worst part is knowing that I'm home but I still can't really focus on my son. He's too small to be in the bathroom with me when I'm scrubbing with bleach, and he likes to get into all the kitchen stuff so much that when I'm really tired from work, it seems to be best if I just focus on powering through the cleaning quickly by myself, and maybe at least spend a little quiet undistracted time together cuddling or reading later before he goes to bed. But by that point, honestly, I feel so tired, and I'm afraid he feels like our time together is an afterthought or not very high on my list."

I quietly asked, "And where is your son during those moments when you're cleaning the kitchen or bathroom?"

"He's with my mother-in-law," she responded with notes of exasperation and sadness. "And, honestly, that makes me really upset, because she's been around him all day while I've been at work, missing him! Why can't she just let me be with him for those moments? I feel so bad literally shutting the door on him while I'm cleaning after I've been gone for the past twenty-four hours, and then she's sitting there acting like she's doing me a favor by laughing and having fun together with him, or comforting him if he's having a hard day, or just whatever they're doing, while I'm sitting there cleaning by myself in another room." I nodded affirmatively, and told Sarah those feelings made perfect sense.

"I have to say, it actually feels really good to tell you this," she continued. "I hadn't really thought about it this way till now. Saying it aloud and realizing how it sounds when I actually stop and think about it is really helpful: I can see I'm not avoiding housework because I'm lazy; I'm avoiding it because I want to be with my son during my 'downtime' from becoming a fucking[1] cardiothoracic surgeon, which, by the way, I'm doing so I can make a bunch of money and help support my family—probably including *her* one day! I'm angry that she doesn't seem to notice why this might be important to me. But, in fairness to her, I guess I haven't really talked about this much, because somehow all of my feelings weren't really super clear to me till now. And, actually, as we talk about all this, I realize how much I wish my husband were here to see what I'm going through and be a shoulder for me to lean on. I don't even think he knows about this whole housecleaning thing." Sarah's voice conveyed a combination of anger and sadness as she painted this woeful picture for me. No wonder she didn't want to do housework! **This was *not* a problem of laziness or entitlement; this was a problem of emotional disconnection from the *context* around her to-do list.**

That disconnect between Sarah's to-do list item of housecleaning and the deeper emotions around it had stopped Sarah from developing the insight and confidence to take corrective action around the problematic dynamic of being barred from her son while she accommodated her mother-in-law's preference of Sarah doing all the housework herself—an arrangement that was actually *counterproductive* to the mother-in-law's ostensible goal of *supporting* the family during a difficult time. Once Sarah got fully in touch with the reasons why she didn't want to spend *any* of the precious few hours she had available for time with her son on housework, she became empowered to enlist her husband to join her in having a clear conversation with her mother-in-law about the fact that, although they appreciated her mother-in-law's desire to be helpful, they needed her to understand that the current housecleaning situation was *not* helpful and had to change.

Sarah's mother-in-law actually understood quite easily when the young couple explained the factors in plain, honest language; and Sarah's husband was actually very thankful to learn about the situation so he could "come to the rescue" and help contain his mother's quirks. The distance had been hard on him, too, and he was yearning for a way to be more supportive; Sarah just had never let him know how. Let's just say that housecleaning was no longer on Sarah's to-do list after that conversation!

3. "Go to the gym." I'm not a medical doctor, but part of my clinical qualifications include being able to make general assessments of whether someone is height-weight proportionate, and to make general assessments of the person's self-care based on objective factors about his or her appearance. Sarah was an attractive woman who clearly took care of her appearance. She also looked like she was carrying about twenty pounds of extra weight on her slight frame, and, of course, she was working a very stressful job. So I could understand why she was at least

trying to get to the gym as a way to take care of her body and potentially relieve some stress. I asked her to talk about the feelings that arose for her when she thought about actually *doing* this item on her to-do list.

"Well," she said, "I don't mean to sound like a broken record, but actually part of the issue is that I know my mother-in-law sometimes gives my son foods that my husband and I don't want him to have, if she thinks we won't find out; and so I actually feel really bad when I'm not there if I have any actual choice about being nearby. I can't stay home from the hospital, of course, but the gym is something where I'd be *choosing* to leave him with her, even though I know she's feeding him things I don't think are good for him. Honestly, I don't know why I'm making such a big deal about it—it's little stuff like cookies, but we just don't want him eating that stuff right now.

"Also," she continued, "I really don't want to sound like I'm complaining, because I do feel superprivileged to be at my fellowship, but honestly, even aside from her—sometimes I just feel so drained that it's really hard to discipline myself to go to the gym and do a yoga class. Yoga classes have always been the only thing that worked for me, but because my schedule is so weird and always fluctuating, I just can't seem to get into a groove around their normal class times—plus you have to sign up for the classes online and I just—"

Sarah stopped here to put both hands up with her palms and wrists facing out, a gesture that seemed to blend traffic stopping with surrender, and she combined this with a hyperbolic shrug and headshake that seemed to say, "I don't know what to do." During this gesture, she also looked down. Her downcast eyes seemed to signal defeat, yet they also focused upon her belly and thighs, where she dropped her hands with a sigh. She grasped her thighs and looked at her belly with quiet frustration.

"I actually love to work out," she said after a moment, in a voice that sounded as if she was trying to convince me of who she really was. "I took regular ballet classes till college, and even then I'd still visit a class when I could find time. I really like feeling connected with my body—I'm a doctor, for goodness' sake. I'm *all about* the body—and I really do *want* to be at the gym; I used to go and take yoga classes and I loved it—but now it's just so hard to get into a groove because my schedule changes so frequently, and for the first time lately I just feel like I *can't*. It's like I've hit a wall or something."

The emotions that Sarah came to realize she was having around this to-do list item were a sense of vigilance about her son's food and insecurity about herself as a mother for not being more proactive about his diet; shame for feeling ungrateful to her mother-in-law; fear of causing conflict with her mother-in-law if she were to make an issue about the sugar; powerlessness over her inability to adhere to a fixed group fitness schedule; and fear of becoming obese if her current lack of exercise continued.

Once we unpacked these emotions, Sarah was able to see that the most constructive thing to do was to enlist her husband to join her in a conversation with the mother-in-law again, where they explained that although they appreciated her willingness to help, it would actually be most helpful for them (and best for the baby, too!) to have a clear set of rules that was observed reliably by everyone, and that the healthiest dynamic for the child would be that the rules would come from his parents. They explained that if a new program of having a professional house cleaner and respecting a no-sugar rule felt too cumbersome for the mother-in-law, they would certainly understand if she needed to do what was best for her and choose to reconsider her decision to "help," but they wanted her to know that her *desire* to help was appreciated.

I'll be honest: it wasn't an easy conversation, according to Sarah's report. The mother-in-law took the first "sit-down" about housework rather easily, but she bristled at this second "family talk." She began to feel that "her way of doing things" wasn't going to be accepted because it was at odds with Sarah's (and Sarah's husband's, too, actually, since he wanted Sarah and himself to be in charge of their son's rules rather than having the mother-in-law create her own rules). Sarah and her husband had to agree with the mother-in-law that, in fact, she was correct: her way of doing things, at least in certain regards, such as giving sugar to their son, actually *wasn't* okay with Sarah. Her husband was in agreement, but since he wasn't there finding empty Oreo wrappers and dealing with the toddler's plea that "Grammy lets me have them; why not now?" her husband's sense of immediacy around these issues was less clear. And that was part of Sarah's *burden*. She was dealing with all of this *without* the physical presence of her husband (and without the presence of her *own* mother to act as a counterbalance to the mother-in-law). Once again, her husband was actually *eager* to step up and offer support once Sarah let him know about her struggle.

Although some hard conversations were involved, Sarah finally did get her mother-in-law to *really* adhere to respecting Sarah as the "woman of the house" and take accountability for the fact that she had moved into the home with a stated wish to *support Sarah* as a new and very busy working mother, and this meant respecting Sarah's rules for her son. Sarah also required a bit of cajoling from me to hire a personal trainer to animate her at the gym once per week. As a linear thinker, she was able to understand that this actually cost less in the long run than the medical and emotional drain of obesity, which is where she was headed if she didn't get support.

You may notice that some of the solutions for the gym were actually similar to the solutions for the housecleaning issue (boundaries with mother-in-law, support from husband, and hiring external support). This is not uncommon: oftentimes, a few stubborn issues in our lives will start bottlenecking our progress or well-being in a variety of areas. Sometimes this is not the case, but don't be surprised if it is. It doesn't make you a broken record; it just means you may have located an important, recurring chord that needs some fine tuning! Frequently, for high functioning people, the common themes that are bottlenecking multiple items on a to-do list are things like asking for help, overaccommodating people because we're afraid of conflict or are addicted to people-pleasing, or being willing to contract a little extra support (such as a housekeeper, trainer, therapist, or other "helpers").

High-functioning people are often so good at doing things by themselves that they feel guilty or lazy asking for help, but then they wonder why they seem to feel stuck or unable to "get to the next level." The reason is that there's a natural limit on how much any one person can do in any given day. As high functioning people take on more in life as they get promoted, build a social life, and get involved in more activities, it's only natural that certain things will fall by the wayside unless they get a bit of support to match the growing list of responsibilities they have accrued as a high functioning person.

Similarly, high functioning people are often so good at "powering through" their to-do list without getting "bogged down" by emotions that they often disconnect from the emotions entirely; this can lead to procrastination, a sense of depletion, or just an avoidant attitude around certain things on their to-do list for reasons they don't understand. This may turn into a negative spiral if they start getting down on themselves for not accomplishing certain things on their list, when the reason they're not doing those things in the first place is because they actually need *support* rather than self-criticism. So if you're feeling anything less than energized around your to-do list, try checking out the To-Do List with Emotions exercise yourself!

DIY: How to Put the To-Do List with Emotions to Use in Your Life

1. **Create a list of tasks.** This part is pretty straightforward. I'm sure you've created a to-do list before, so I won't go into much detail here beyond the obvious direction to list your tasks, but I will encourage you to break tasks down into small steps as much as possible. This allows you to enjoy a sense of momentum as you cross each item off your list, and it allows you to see if there are certain *parts* of tasks that are carrying emotional baggage for you. For example, if you're struggling to get to the gym on your way home from work, don't just put "Go to the gym" on your list. Instead, you might include each step, like putting "Pack and bring gym bag to work" separate on the list from "Sign up for class in gym's app the day before," and "Attend the gym class."

2. **Notice the emotions that accompany each task.** Like Sarah, you might initially think there *are no* emotions around your tasks. This is a telltale sign that you may be disconnected from feelings about a task. Perhaps I'm just being a psychologist here, but I believe we have emotions about almost everything. So give yourself a moment to think about each item on your list. If you're feeling stuck, maybe try the Three-Part Breath as a warm-up to awaken your mindfulness skills, then ponder the task to see if you can notice any "background" thoughts and feelings about the topic coming to the fore. Note this

information in the "emotions" column as shown in Christina's example chart following these instructions.

3. **Plan a dose of self-care.** Once you are aware of the emotions around your tasks, you are much better positioned to deal with them in a healthy way. This not only feels good, it tends to help free your energy to work on the task at hand, since you're no longer sandbagged by unaddressed emotions.

While the example of Sarah's situation had a lot of heaviness, since she was dealing with grief over her mom, sometimes the issues on your list may seem smaller. But, as a psychologist, I can tell you that even feelings about "little things" can add up over time. Here is another example, using the same worksheet format that you'll use when you make your own to-do list. It's a sample To-Do List with Emotions from Christina, the lawyer who was grappling with a painful breakup and a colleague who wanted to sabotage her chances of a promotion.

As you can see from Christina's list, a self-care plan can take many forms. The idea is just to notice your feelings around your to-do list and then treat yourself to a self-care plan that addresses those feelings productively. Some might feel that Christina's plan for how to respond to Marc is catty, while others might feel it's actually a great way for her to hold him accountable and set clear boundaries. The point is just that having created a plan that fully addresses her emotions in a way that works *for her* causes Christina to be more empowered about her upcoming briefing than if she just tried to pretend that "everything's fine" and offered herself no extra support. Deep down, Christina knew that incident had rattled her (understandably, I think!), and her self-care plan reflects the things that make *her* feel supported—and that's what matters, since it's *her* meeting at stake.

Christina's To-Do List with Emotions

TASK	EMOTIONS	SELF-CARE PLAN
Host Mom's birthday.	Afraid because I'm predicting embarrassment. Everyone will ask me how I'm doing re: breakup, and I don't want to talk about it.	Craft preset responses to have ready for inevitable awkward questions.
Drop off ex's keys.	Scared because I'm predicting sadness. This feels so final.	Plan a brunch date with supportive friend, and drop off the keys on my way to the brunch date so that I'll have an extra dose of support to look forward to right after the drop-off.
Attend briefing with Marc, the coworker who tried to sabotage my chances of a promotion.	Furious that I even have to be in a room with him. Also afraid I'll feel small and victim-y, like I did back in grade school when rich kids used to pick on me. And that makes me angry, to think that he could possibly make me feel that way; or, even worse, that I would *let* him make me feel that way!	1. I know it sounds crazy, but I actually think booking a hair blowout the morning of the briefing will boost my confidence and make me feel poised/polished. When I have a fresh blowout, I look and feel my best! 2. Triple-check my notes on the briefing so there'll be zero chance of him "one-upping" me at the briefing. 3. Put it in my calendar to hit the gym afterward so I'll have a good outlet for all the extra adrenaline that might hit me when I see him. 4. Prepare a frosty response to say if he has the gall to attempt small talk with me—maybe something like, "Marc, based on your email, I think it's best if we keep our relationship strictly professional." I know it may seem immature, but I can't help it—I want to put him in his place in a clear yet HR-approved way if he tries to brush this whole thing under the rug and act all friendly. Feeling prepared with a preset way to respond to any personal small talk will help me avoid the nightmare scenario of getting stuck feeling like I have to smile and chat with him like everything's fine.

VARIATION: TO-DO LIST WITH EMOTIONS FOR BIG GOALS

There is a variation on the To-Do List with Emotions that you can use, if you like, for big goals: same setup, but each item is an objective toward that goal, rather than a general to-do list of your week ahead. For example, if you wanted to apply to graduate school but you were feeling daunted by the overall process, you might make a list like the one here. The idea is to break down the larger goal into smaller pieces. Taking the time to do this not only helps with organization (which tends to increase efficiency, decrease anxiety, and improve mood all by itself); it also helps you understand the emotions you're having around each step so that you can plan for a smoother path to progress!

To-Do List with Emotions for Grad-School Application

TASK	EMOTIONS	SELF-CARE PLAN
Write personal statement (PS).	Totally nervous! Is there anything interesting about my life?! How does anything about me actually fit into a personal statement for graduate school?	Start *really* early on this one. First, I'll spend 10 mins. a day for a week just listing random things that are cool/interesting about me that might be good to include, without even trying to create a PS. I'll also reach out to a few friends who have gone to grad school and ask them for copies of their PSs. This will at least help me to get started.
Take GMAT (or GRE) test.	Uh, nervous again. I have really bad test anxiety.	Enroll in a test-prep course so I can at least have community with others who are going through the same thing, while also learning some good test-taking tips and brushing up on the subject matter.

Fill out the long and tedious online application programs for 15 schools.	*Bored* and *lazy*. I'm *so bad* with admin. And I get so *mad* at myself for dropping the ball on basic stuff like this, but I also *hate* doing this type of admin.	Take my laptop to a restaurant/bar I like and do my applications over dinner/drinks so at least I'll be pleasantly distracted by a nice atmosphere while I fill out those mind-numbing forms. I don't need to be super focused to type out my name and address, etc. 15 times! Maybe I'll aim for 5 applications per outing.
Ace my interviews.	Confident, but also a little tense. If I'm getting called for an interview, it will mean they liked my application and at least on paper I have the right qualifications. A lot is riding on these interviews, and I want to make sure I give it my best shot.	Check with my undergraduate center for career education to see if there are any mock-interview workshops, or maybe check LinkedIn to see if I have connections with people who went to my programs of choice, and ask if they might be willing to give me a mock interview with feedback. That extra layer of preparation might help me feel at ease, as I'll have really done my due diligence!

Troubleshooting

1. **I've tried the To-Do List with Emotions, and I'm just not noticing any emotions around my tasks.**

You might be someone like Sarah, who is so good at compartmentalizing that you've actually (temporarily!) lost your ability to reconnect with your feelings. Ask someone who is "good at feelings" (such as a therapist, friend, or family member, who seems to draw you out) to review your list with you. Maybe talking it through with another person will help you to find the emotions that are currently stuck in the back of your mind. As a psychologist, I can tell you that it is a fact that we have emotions about everything, even if they're hard to locate—the same way that people who don't remember their dreams still *have them.* Another way to stimulate emotional awareness if you are drawing an emotional blank is to ask yourself, "If I *did* have emotions about this item, *what would they likely be?*" Sometimes this question at least helps you to think logically about connecting emotions with activities if you want a nudge in the process. One final tip is to try looking at a chart of emotions; I call these "emotional vocabulary stimulators." You can find them by searching online, or access a few of my favorites at www.NervousEnergyBook.com.

2. I've tried lots of self-care plans, but I'm still feeling stuck.

You might be creating self-care plans for the emotions you're listing, but perhaps you're not listing certain emotions because they're hard to face or they feel taboo. For example, Greg the single dad had a hard time admitting that one of the emotions he felt around picking up his daughter was shame that stemmed from having to face his wife's new boyfriend during the pickup—a man with whom she'd had an affair during her marriage to Greg. Therefore, self-care plans like "set an alarm to remind me when to head out for the pickup" to address emotions like "nervous I'll be late" were not helpful, because they didn't address the *real* emotion of shame that he was feeling.

Obviously, there's no quick fix for the pain Greg felt, but once he got clear about how the pain was driving his pattern of being late for the pickups, he was able to implement a more effective self-care plan of planning a speakerphone call with a supportive friend to occur during his drive to pick up his daughter. Sometimes he'd talk with the friend about how he was feeling regarding the pain, but often he'd just shoot the breeze and chat casually. The idea was just that Greg needed to feel like someone was "in his corner" as he prepared for even a momentary face-to-face with his wife's new boyfriend.

If you find that your self-care plans aren't helping, check in with yourself to ensure you're listing the real emotions around your to-do list. If you are definitely listing accurate emotions but you're still struggling to complete your tasks, see the troubleshooting tips below.

3. **I notice lots of emotions, but I can't think of any self-care plans that feel sufficiently helpful.**

There are several possibilities here:

- It's possible that you might need to confirm if you're actually addressing your true emotions, like in Greg's example. Maybe the plans don't feel helpful because they're not addressing the deeper emotions around your task list.

- It's also possible that you are totally in touch with some very overwhelming emotions, and that because these emotions are so strong you might benefit from having a supportive friend or therapist help you brainstorm more ideas for self-care. You may even find that you experience talking things over with a friend in a self-care brainstorm session as an extra act of self-care in itself!

- It's also possible that you're not fully invested in the *reasons* why these items are stagnating on your to-do list. If you're struggling to write a report for work because you actually hate your job, then reflection about the emotions might cue you to realize that you'll actually benefit from focusing *less* on acing your report and focusing *more* on a job search. Obviously you probably still need to do the report, since you don't want to totally neglect your current job, but having clarity about *why* you don't want to write the report and then taking corrective action around the broader topic of your career would likely help to stop negative feelings about your job from bottlenecking your progress on the report.

- It's possible that you're in danger of overextending yourself. You may need to learn when the most high-functioning, accountable thing to do is to recognize that you have overextended yourself. High functioning people sometimes take on way too much. When I started my practice, I had a motto: "I don't say no to work." This was great, till I found myself overbooked and spread too thin. Admitting this to myself was hard at first, but it was ultimately what prompted me to start raising my fees and hiring other therapists, which turned out wonderfully both personally and professionally.

If you think something like being overextended may be the reason you're feeling stuck, congratulate yourself for having taken the time to reflect and fully realize the situation. Review your list to see how you can strategically delegate or postpone certain items, give yourself permission to bow out of whatever is not giving you a good enough return on the investment of your time, or find other creative ways to rethink your task list. Don't hesitate to ask a supportive friend or therapist to review the list and help you think things through; sometimes when we're overwhelmed it's hard to see even potentially obvious (or creative!) ways to free up our time and energy.

- It is possible that you're depressed and experiencing lethargy as a symptom of depression, or for some other medical reason. As always, please don't hesitate to seek professional help if self-help doesn't seem to be working.

11.

Mind Mapping

Take a bird's-eye view of the situation before choosing to react.
A change in position can change everything.

—ARIELLE FORD

You don't need me to tell you that our minds are jam-packed with complex connections, but you may want a tool to help you navigate that complexity. Mind Maps are a great tool for high functioning people because they help illuminate the myriad connections and associations happening within their high functioning neural networks. A "neural network" is the term psychologists use to describe the literal, physical pathways between neurons (brain cells) that represent memories, feelings, thoughts, and even bodily sensations. A classic example of a neural network in action is that when you smell apple pie, you may feel instantly transported in time and place back to childhood memories from grandma's kitchen (if your grandma happened to make apple pie, of course). Your present-day olfactory neurons are literally connecting with old memories stored in other parts of your brain. These connections were made early in childhood but they still function; somewhat like an old back road that hasn't been used in a while but still connects two places just the same as when it was brand-new.

You may be surprised to know that some studies suggest that intelligent people tend to have *fewer* neural pathways than less intelligent people. That may sound counterintuitive at first, but some scientists suggest that having fewer pathways is part of what allows intelligent people to access information quickly: their brains don't have to spend tons of time and energy sorting through a bunch of "dead ends" to get the information they need; instead, their brains identify the most helpful pathways and then exploit those "short-cuts" for speed and efficiency. This approach is great for rapid, comprehensive processing of information and stimuli, but it does increase the importance for high functioning people to ensure they really understand the landmarks their minds are using to process information, since a "wrong turn" or a "missed stop" could pose a greater vulnerability if they're in the high functioning mental "fast lane."

This is admittedly an oversimplification, but neural networks function similarly to a chain of standing dominoes: when one domino is tripped, it "triggers" the domino next to it, and a chain reaction for all the other connected dominoes will ensue. Some of the "domino reactions" are fully within our conscious awareness (for example, I see a waiter in a restaurant during lunch and I prepare to order food), and some are more outside of our awareness, either because certain domino connections have *so many other dominoes* between them that it's hard to realize *which* domino will eventually lead to a particular reaction, or because we're just so busy with other things demanding our immediate attention at any given moment that it's hard to pay attention to "background dominoes" getting triggered. Also, sometimes we might be deliberately push-ing certain thoughts, feelings, or memories out of our conscious awareness—but they may still be happening "in the back of the head." All of this can make it hard for us to know why we think or feel the way we do about certain things or situations: we may not be aware of the total neural network being activated at any given time.

For an example of how some mental domino effects might be harder to discern than others due to the competing demands for our attention in day-to-day life, consider the following set of thoughts and feelings activated during a business lunch. **Some of the thoughts and feelings described here were conscious, and some of them were happening "in the background" while the diner focused on the client during the business lunch.** As you read, un-derstand that the "dominoes" in the unconscious mind don't have a sense of time: if the unconscious mind is reminded of an old hurt or wound, it can experience the emotions from that event as if it were happening currently. The unconscious can also have dominoes that connect associations between concepts that don't *seem* to have a logical connection. The unconscious can even make associations that affect the conscious experience based on multiple meanings of words (such as the word "fire" in the upcoming example), words that rhyme, or words that for some reason connect back to an early childhood memory.

Example of Conscious and Unconscious Neural Networks Being Activated

Tameka came to my office and shared that although an important business luncheon went well, she felt surprisingly unsettled. As we unpacked the details of the meeting, we discovered some unconscious associations that were happening in the background of her mind. Her sense of feeling unsettled made much more sense after we brought some of the unconscious associations into awareness. For the sake of clarity, I've added the unconscious context to the beginning of the story in italics—but please understand the italicized material wasn't actually spoken by Tameka, or even in her full consciousness, till after we had done some digging to understand what part of the context was previously escaping her direct consciousness.

"The waiter at my important business lunch looked vaguely like my old friend Joe, who cheated on my sister when they dated many years ago. I haven't thought of him in years. I felt guilty for her pain because I was the one who originally introduced them, though she was always prettier, and some secret part of me felt relieved to know that I wasn't the only one who had been cheated on, and then my sister grew distant and moved to California. . . . I love California. I'd like to meet someone special myself. I wonder how the California wildfires are doing now. . . . I really don't know why, but for some reason after my important business lunch meeting today, which actually went very well because I was super quick-witted (practically on fire!) and totally focused on what the client was saying (and emphasizing to him how fidelity is key in our business, and how we treat our customers like family!), I somehow found myself experiencing a strange feeling of guilt and insecurity during my walk back to the office, as I tried to focus on the best way to follow up with the client after our lunch. I wonder why. I wasn't really thinking about anything except the client, and the meeting went very well!"

As you can imagine, much of the mental activity related to a vague resemblance of the waiter to an old friend named Joe was happening largely *outside* of Tameka's conscious awareness, because Tameka was devoting all of her conscious energy to acing the lunch meeting. She didn't know *why* metaphors like "being on fire" and phrases like "we're all about fidelity" and "we'll treat you like family" seemed to be at the tip of her tongue during the meeting, but something as random as a waiter's resemblance to someone from her past could have actually triggered a variety of neural-network chain reactions. Such chain reactions can eventually affect our conscious thoughts and feelings as well. The fact that we're often having all these cognitive and emotional processes happening outside of our conscious awareness isn't necessarily a problem, and obviously we can still function just fine; my client's lunchtime meeting went very well. But **when it comes to certain situations, it's worthwhile to pause and check "under the hood" to see what neural networks might be active for you.**

Tameka's Mind Map

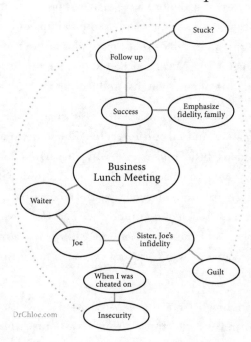

Mind Maps can help when you want a fun and interesting way to explore your neural networks around certain topics. There are instructions on how to do a mind map for yourself later in this chapter. In the meantime, here are some specific examples of when Mind Maps can be useful:

1. **Big events.** You have a big life event or just something that has a lot of layers happening, and you want to be sure you really understand the full meaning, concerns, and feelings (even positive ones!) related to the event. Things like weddings (your own wedding or the wedding of someone close to you whose wedding affects you in some way—like the wedding of an adult child, an ex, or even a best friend), funerals, graduations, starting a new job, beginning (or even contemplating!) graduate school, learning you or your partner is pregnant, buying a house, contemplating a potential breakup or divorce, or moving to a new city are all examples of big life events for which Mind Maps can help us understand the *complete* picture of our thoughts and feelings.

2. **Feeling stuck.** Mind Maps are also great when you're feeling stuck, numb, or overwhelmed by something, even if you don't fully understand why (the Mind Map can actually *help* you understand why). Examples include feeling surprisingly nervous around a certain colleague or work situation, feeling unmotivated at work, struggling with physical fitness or emotional eating, or feeling irritable or shy with someone (or everyone!) for no apparent reason.

3. **Daily debrief.** Creating a Mind Map can also be an interesting way to unpack your day. Some high func-

tioning people are so focused on hitting their to-do lists throughout the day that they lose touch with their "background" thoughts and feelings. This can lead to a "hamster wheel" feeling in which they don't really feel connected to *why* they're doing what they're doing or don't really understand *why* they feel (or don't feel) certain things. Using Mind Maps can be an alternative to traditional journaling, in which you need to compose sentences and potentially feel like you need to explain why or how certain concepts connect. In Mind Mapping, you don't need to do any of that; you're just exploring and observing the connections within yourself.

What Are the Benefits of Mind Maps?

The benefits of getting a clear view of all the "background stuff" happening in your mind are myriad. High functioning people are usually very quick to recognize that having information and context, especially about key decision-makers (that is, themselves!), is valuable. Although the benefits of better understanding your own mind are hopefully at least somewhat self-evident, I'd still like to highlight some of the big ones:

1. **Distress or eustress[1] are less likely to sneak up on you for big (or small!) life events when you've made a Mind Map.** This point is especially helpful for high functioning people whose default response is often, "This is great, everything's fine, I'm handling it!" Many high functioning people tend to broadcast this message to the world so strongly (and even sometimes compulsively) that they lose touch with their own needs or vulnerabilities; this pattern ends up costing them in the long term because they were caught off guard on big emotions that

seemed to "pop up out of nowhere." Mind Maps help you to locate those vulnerabilities *in advance* so that you can plan good self-care for maximal well-being, productivity, or whatever is *your* desired reaction to life's events. Examples of this preplanning include:

* Booking a massage at a local place or a phone date with your best friend during that four-day holiday trip to your in-laws' house so that you'll have some built-in "me time" to decompress during a potentially stressful trip

* Making a brunch date with your friend directly after your scheduled key drop-off with your ex so that you'll have a planned "hard stop" and dependable source of post-drop-off emotional support

* Planning a vacation that will commence hours after submitting your graduate school applications to celebrate and give yourself a well-deserved mental release

* Deliberately doing the legwork of selecting and ordering or queuing up a great new movie ahead of time in order to ensure you'll have an easy, quiet evening and go to bed early the night before a big presentation at work

* Scheduling an organizer or friend to help with sorting through "sentimental objects" a few days after your child moves out for college

The idea is that Mind Maps can **help us forecast our feelings and create targeted self-care plans.**

2. **Making a Mind Map can help you understand if certain "false factors" are shaping your decision-making process.** For example, I had a female client who struggled

with a tendency to keep chasing "cool guys" that played games and seemed evasive, despite her wish to focus upon reliable, emotionally available men who would make a good potential husband and father. When we did a Mind Map around dating, she was able to see that her history of having immigrated to the United States from an impoverished country when she was just six years old and barely spoke English, and having subsequently felt like an outsider who struggled with feeling "less than" her peers during her first few years in the affluent school system where her parents relocated, was now causing her to approach dating from a historical, childlike part of her past identity that was seeking men with a "prom king" type of persona. The Mind Map helped her see that a part of her believed that by attaining the "coolest guy in the room" as an adult, she could somehow appease or vindicate the shy, insecure, and oft-rejected girl from the past who yearned for acceptance and social status through popularity. Gaining clarity around this dynamic through Mind Mapping helped her find compassionate ways of giving her inner child some much-needed comfort, while still approaching her marital search from a perspective that addressed the needs of her current adult self.

3. **Making a Mind Map is like practicing a written form of mindfulness meditation: you're literally just observing and noting the associations that come to mind, without feeling like you have to immediately understand or justify or explain the connections.** This means you get all of the benefits of mindfulness meditation, but the one I'd like to highlight here is that this is an act of self-esteem: by taking a moment to notice and explore how the differ-

ent "dominoes" of your brain connect, you're sending a behavioral signal to yourself that you are worthy of attention and recognition.

4. **Creating a Mind Map is a way to practice observing yourself and translating your observations into short words and phrases on paper in a quick and casual manner.** This helps you know yourself better and learn how to find words and phrases to narrate your experience in real-time conversations. (In case you didn't know, "narrating your experience" is just a fancy psychology way of saying "tell other people what's going on inside.")

Caroline's Quarter-Life Inventory

Caroline was a polished, attractive young woman working at a publishing firm in Manhattan's Flatiron district, historically a home to many of New York's most storied publishing houses. Part of my training as a psychologist includes observing how a person's physical appearance (in psychology jargon, her "presentation") conveys information about that person in terms of identity, lifestyle, and how she is perceived by the world. Caroline presented as poised, early in her career, polite, diligent, and capable. I could see how, in the workplace, terms like "fresh-faced," "green," and "eager" might be applied to her, generally in a positive sense, albeit also a sense that implies there is still considerable room for professional growth and development. Not surprisingly (because of my fees and the low salaries normally paid to entry-level employees), Caroline's parents were paying for her session with me. I'll admit that when taking a new client whose parents are paying for an adult child's sessions, I am sometimes cautious that the "child" may have an attitude of entitlement, struggle to take ownership of responsibility to make changes, or exhibit a lack of accountability. This was *not* the case with Caroline.

When I came to greet Caroline from my lobby for her first visit, she jumped up and thanked me effusively for meeting with her. She enunciated clearly, spoke in a nice easy-to-hear volume, and made good eye contact, which signaled confidence; yet her voice and manner were still markedly deferential. She tilted her head to one side and beamed at me as she shook my hand, drawing out the word "you" as she said, "It is *so* nice to meet *youuuuuu,* Dr. Carmichael. Thank you *so much* for taking the time to meet with me today. I *love* your blogs, by the way!" She was going above and beyond an amiable greeting, and she seemed to be doing so consciously. It wasn't terribly "over the top" or anything, but the impression she made seemed deliberately constructed to broadcast that she was energetic, polite, and agreeable. She appeared to be trying to win my positive regard in the same way one might when greeting a professor for a graduate school admissions interview. She was so solicitous that she almost seemed to erase the context that *she* was in fact the client and it was actually *my* role to try and make *her* feel welcome and comfortable, and to demonstrate whether or not *I* could prove useful to *her.* Caroline was taking responsibility for *my* comfort, even though *she* was actually the client.

Many clients, especially younger ones, will often relate to me in a slightly deferential manner, especially during the first meeting. I understand this may be partly because of age differences and partly because they are trying to convey respect for my expertise, and I can relate. I would actually probably make an extra effort to be congenial if I were meeting a specialist doctor for help with something very important to me and I wanted to do all I could to ensure that I quickly established a strong sense of rapport so she would "go the extra mile" for me if needed. But Caroline's greeting still stood out as a little "extra," to the point of suggesting that she might be shortchanging herself socially or professionally if she were constantly this obsequious when meeting new people whom she viewed as potential authority figures, experts, decision-makers, clients, first dates, big crushes, or anyone who might trigger a need to please. I'm not saying this to imply anything inherently bad about Caroline; in fact I liked her very much. I'm just sharing this context so you'll get a richer picture of who she is and how she comes across. Or at least, how she *came* across prior to our work together!

To her credit, part of Caroline's reason for seeking therapy was that she was self-aware enough to realize that her perfectionist, people-pleasing style might start to pigeonhole her socially and professionally if she didn't learn how to move beyond her "eager beaver" persona. True to her "one step ahead" form, Caroline was already aware that this "teacher's pet" communication style may have worked very well for her as a college student whose primary goal was to get A's on her report cards and glowing letters of recommendation from her professors; and it had certainly served her well as an early-career office darling ("of *course* I don't mind getting your coffee; I actually *love* going to that cafe!"). But now her experiences in the sophisticated, nuanced, and ultracompetitive world of New York City's publishing industry, where the ability to *wield social influence (at least a little!) and navigate complex social interactions* matters at least as much as merely *pleasing people,* had made Caroline see that she would need to mature a bit if she was going to be taken seriously for potential leadership or client-facing roles. Similarly, in her personal life she was realizing that she would need to do more than just people-pleasing if she wanted her wish to be in an exclusive dating relationship that would at least *eventually, ostensibly, possibly* lead to marriage and children to be taken seriously in New York City's dizzying dating scene.

Once she was seated on my sofa and had paid me more compliments ("Your office is so beautiful! Oh yes, thank you, I'd like a glass of water, thank you *so much!*"), Caroline carefully tucked an imaginary loose strand of hair behind her ear and earnestly began to explain that her primary reason for coming to therapy was what I have come to call a "quarter life check-in." These types of "taking stock of my life so far and mapping out my future" visits are very popular with high functioning people around Caroline's age, but high functioning people of all ages are often interested in this type of proactive, goal-oriented approach.

Caroline had recently turned twenty-five years old, and she wanted to make sure she didn't let this milestone pass without performing "due diligence." Specifically, she wanted to think about her next five years so that she didn't find herself suddenly "terrified" (her word, not mine) about turning thirty if she'd let those five years pass without being deliberate about how she wanted to use (or *not* use) them. It was all I could do to hold myself back from giving her a standing ovation. Caroline's people-pleasing and perfectionist tendencies definitely needed some reining in (for her *own* benefit, and by her *own* description), but the high level of conscientiousness and forethought that marks many people with these tendencies was also clearly working to her advantage in many ways, including by stimulating her to seek support with her "quarter life check-in."

Taking stock of your past twenty-five years and charting out a tentative course for success over the impactful years of twenty-five to thirty is no easy task, especially if you're someone who is blessed with an active mind that likes to "follow up" on things. It's almost par for the course that you'll jump around a bit as you try to organize, explore, and find words to describe your current situation and your future goals. If you already had it all organized, you wouldn't need to do a check-in in the first place, right? But as we talked about her professional life and her dating life, Caroline kept making verbal asides like "I know I'm all over the place" and "I don't even know why this matters." She seemed to be undermining herself for mentioning what she called "random" things that came to mind as we discussed her goals—things that she was labeling as "non sequiturs," which actually were very relevant, as she came to see after taking a few therapeutic moments to connect the dots. During this process, she recalled things such as an early memory of a first-grade teacher impressing upon her the importance of following directions, a popular high school boy whose memory still stung as she remembered "chasing him shamelessly," her parents' emphasis on respecting authority figures ("They said it would get me far in life, and you know I have to say they were right—it actually has!"), or her first boss's decision to fondly nickname her "My girl Friday" ("I remember actually feeling really proud of that nickname, even though I know that must sound totally weird—but I actually liked it!").

As Caroline reflected on my questions about her early attitudes regarding careers and her seemingly automatic tendency toward people-pleasing, she also revealed that her father had experienced a period of unemployment after being laid off from his job during her early childhood. She acknowledged that perhaps it was around this time that she began to avoid asking for new clothes, money for class trips, or other "extras" that she feared might stress him. During this time, she began to hide her needs from her parents because she felt a poignant sense of guilt for whatever money her parents spent to feed, clothe, and house her during this difficult financial chapter of their lives. Caroline came to see that during this time in her life she'd begun to take responsibility for others' feelings in a way that she still seemed to be doing in her current life. Examples included everything from hiding her disagreement with her boss on even minor editorial points (which, ironically, may have led to negative feedback on her performance review about her boss's *wish* for Caroline to demonstrate more proactive, independent thought) to her difficulty expressing her wish for a committed relationship with a man with whom she was currently settling for a casual relationship ("I wouldn't want to make him uncomfortable or feel overwhelmed, you know, by, like, cornering him with a big 'relationship talk' or something").

All the while, as Caroline shared what she kept referring to as her "random thoughts," I made notes of key words, key events, and what appeared to be connectors between them. These notes were the beginning of our Mind Map.

Enter: The Mind Map

To help Caroline literally and figuratively "connect the dots" on her past and present selves and her aspirational future self, which is important to most "quarter life check-in" clients as well as other clients who just wish to take stock of their "place in time," we decided to do a Mind Map. The Mind Map helped Caroline see that her past identity was constructed around being a "good girl" who found safety and worth by her ability to follow directions and please others to the point of losing touch with her own needs, and that some of this identity was actually different from the identity she wished to create in the future. It also helped her see that she felt intimidated by her goal of marriage because it connected to the topic of dating, which was strongly associated with a fear of rejection based on some very painful memories from high school dating; and with an idea that the best way to support a man is to hide your needs from him. The Mind Map also helped her see that her shame around those memories had prevented her from really *dealing* with them, because she preferred to pretend they were no longer an issue for her, and that this denial was actually bottlenecking her ability to heal from the past and date in a confident, unfettered manner.

Once we got all of this "on the table," literally and figuratively, it was much easier for Caroline to have insight and perspective about herself, including being able to recognize that there were certain parts of herself that might *seem* to bring her safety, and in fact *had* brought her safety in the past, but that needed to *grow and change* if she wanted to move beyond her current place in life. For example, she saw that the part of her that had buried itself completely in work rather than venturing into dating had served a purpose in high school and college as well as in the first year or two of establishing herself in the working world, but it would almost certainly stand in the way of her marital goals if she didn't learn how to find balance. She saw that the "good girl" part of herself that made a great editorial assistant and always made the "teacher's pet" list had helped her to feel safe, but that this very same "safe zone" would be a *barrier* in her desired identity as a sophisticated senior editor who could hold her own with big-name authors.

As you will see, Mind Maps help when you have a lot of complex pieces to hold at once—and high functioning people *do* tend to have a lot of complex pieces to hold at once! They tend to be aware of *many* factors, thinking on multiple levels (past, present, future; or dating, social, family, career; or self-esteem, fitness, and so on), and they want to think about *all* these factors at once because these factors *do* often intersect in ways that are important to understand if we want to make an integrated, whole-self assessment of a situation. However, because even people with the best working memories struggle to keep more than a few things in mind at once, it's hard to keep these multiple, complex factors and all of their relevant connections in mind all at the same time. Mind Maps help take the pressure off us to keep too many things in our working memory at once, and they help us better see the connections between different parts of ourselves.

Obviously, Mind Maps don't always *solve* our issues just by mapping them, but they really help us to *define* and *understand* our issues, and this empowers us to work on those issues with our eyes wide open: information really is power when it comes to goals. If I had just pushed Caroline to start taking career risks without having a deep appreciation for how her "good girl roots" mattered to her and had actually *helped* her in many ways up to this point, my interventions would have fallen flat, because they would have disregarded an important part of her historical strengths. Similarly, when Caroline had previously tried to "white-knuckle" her way through dating without pausing to understand her vulnerabilities, she found herself constantly afraid to express her own needs because of her stifled fears from the past. Because she had never fully understood her past, she kept repeating it (ironically!) by chasing men around (basically continuing to go for "popular boys," being super available, and trying to mold herself into whomever she thought *they* wanted her to be instead of considering whether *they* were actually good candidates for *her* goal of getting married and having children).

Seeing a map of her mind helped Caroline "see herself" more clearly in her day-to-day life. She started to use the "good girl" as a shorthand label to notice when she was "feeling small" (and then *acting small*) in dating or at work; and she was better able to recognize when outdated parts of herself were coming into play (for example, the part of herself that thought being agreeable would be a great way to win points at work, even in conversations geared toward critical thinking). This literal sense of perspective (the Mind Map *literally* gives you perspective, since it is an *actual* overview of the major landmarks of your mental landscape!) on how the way she was feeling at any particular moment fit into broader patterns of her lifelong sense of identity was very helpful to Caroline.

Sometimes, just having insight is enough to change a pattern— and sometimes simply *realizing* through insight from Mind Maps that she was falling into the old patterns was enough to stimulate her to revise herself in the moment. Other times, Caroline needed to introduce extra interventions to deliberately channel the new approaches she wanted to pilot. But having a *map* of where she was coming from and where she wanted to go gave her the insight and confidence to try new behaviors because she knew her efforts were part of a well-informed, self-aware strategy rather than just momentary impulses. Each person's Mind Map is different, and there are many different ways to use them—but Caroline's is a good example of how we can take something as complex as our *identity* and sketch it out into basic concepts so we can start noticing connections.

Before you look at the directions for doing your own Mind Map, you may want to take a look at Caroline's. I think Mind Maps really may be something we understand better intuitively or visually than by reading step-by-step instructions (though instructions certainly help, too). Have a quick look at Caroline's Mind Map, then try your own!

Caroline's Mind Map

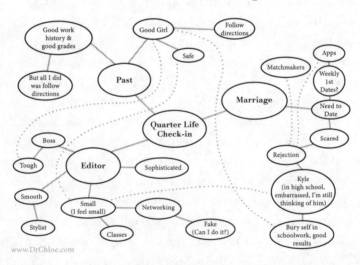

DIY: Put Mind Maps to
Work in Your Life

Please note that you'll ideally have an actual sheet of paper for this one, and a pen or pencil. If a sheet of paper isn't handy, the back of an envelope or a cocktail napkin will work fine. Try to write freehand rather than using your phone or computer, unless you have a special software program that makes it really quick and easy to draw circles and lines. Many computer programs seem to make basic exercises like this one more complicated than a simple pen and paper. Too much complication can impede your intellectual and creative process, so unless you have a computer drawing program you absolutely love, I urge you to go "low-tech" on this one!

1. **Define your starting point.** Choose any issue or topic that you'd like to explore—the issue can be large (remember that Caroline's topic was actually *her entire life*) or seemingly "small" (example: "Feel guilty for using my vacation time") or anywhere in between (examples like "Dating" or "Job searching" or "Budgeting" or "Healthy diet" also lend themselves well to Mind Mapping). The topic can be as broad or as specific as you want, but I suggest you try to limit yourself to an absolute maximum of seven words to describe your topic when you're choosing the initial keyword or phrase for step 1. Write the keyword or phrase down on the center of your sheet of paper and put a little circle around it.

2. **Start your map.** When you look at the starting point, what is the first word, feeling, or phrase that comes to mind? This is your "first reaction." Draw a little line from the starting-point circle and write whatever key-

word or phrase captures your first reaction, then draw a little circle around your first reaction.

3. **Keep going.** You will do a and b as you make your Mind Map, but you can do them in whatever order feels best to you. You can also toggle back and forth between them if you want. The idea is just to keep noticing the items you write, along with your associations or reactions to those items, until you feel like your Mind Map really captures all of the important items that are directly or indirectly connected to the item in your starting point.

   a. Look at your starting point and draw additional lines from it, connecting to circles where you'll note additional reactions you have to the item in your starting point. This is basically just repeating step 2, but with additional reactions besides the first reaction. We'll call these items "additional reactions" for the sake of simplicity. The first reaction and additional reactions each have a connector line going directly from the starting point, meaning that the starting point directly made you think of these items.

   b. Look at the item in your first reaction circle and any additional reaction circles, and draw lines connecting to *new* circles, noting your reactions to *these* "subconnection" items. Feel free to draw additional lines out from the subconnection items if those items are making you think of additional concepts, thoughts, or feelings that feel like they might be relevant, even if indirectly. If you have strong thoughts or feelings about the subconnection items that don't seem relevant to the starting point, but they still feel like very strong reactions it's totally fine (and even encouraged!) to note them anyway. Sometimes we don't always understand *how* things are relevant until we have time to see the whole map and reflect.

Keep doing a and b until your Mind Map seems to capture the total picture of your thoughts and feelings about the item in your starting point.

4. Once you've got all the "data points" on your map, you may notice that certain items in certain circles connect, resonate, or overlap, even if there isn't a line directly connecting them on your map. Draw a dotted line connecting any such circles. For example, Caroline noticed that "I feel small" appeared originally on her map as a reaction to the idea of becoming an editor; but as she reviewed her map, she realized that same feeling connected to her past history of feeling like she needed to be a "good girl" to feel safe through approval and acceptance and to a painful early dating experience when she felt rejected. The dotted lines on her map reflect these connections.

What to Do with Your Mind Map

The Mind Map will help you gain insight about yourself. The question of what to *do* with that insight is different for every situation. You may find that simply gaining clarity about yourself and the underpinnings of some of your initial reactions to certain topics helps reduce anxiety, increases motivation, or helps you make better choices that take your *whole self* into consideration. Here is another example, quite different from Caroline's, of how I've seen clients use the insights they've gained from Mind Maps.

Locating Matt's Sense of Purpose

Matt was a stressed-out lawyer with a wife and three kids who was suffering from a lack of motivation at work. He did a Mind Map with a starting point of "My job" and quickly saw that thinking of his job conjured up a fear that his job was trapping him into a lifestyle that would cause him to end up overweight and with no life outside of work, which was in stark contrast to the glamorous life his younger self from law school had envisioned when planning a career as a partner-track attorney. The whole *point* of this job to his younger self was to wear great suits, have disposable income for travel, and live a lifestyle akin to James Bond, at least in terms of style and sophistication. The Mind Map also demonstrated that he feared not really knowing his kids because of all the time he spent at the office; yet it also captured the fact that his job was a ticket to provide for his wife and children—and this connected to early memories of feeling "not good enough" when his father's presence in his life decreased dramatically during Matt's preteen years when his parents divorced.

Gaining insight around all of these "background" items connected to his job helped Matt make peace with the part of himself that felt he was "failing" because his life wasn't as glamorous as his law school self had planned.

"That part of me didn't know the joy that my wife and kids would bring me, so comparing my life against that old standard doesn't actually make sense—and it feels really good to know that I'm not 'failing,' that I've just changed my goals," he said as he reflected on the map. He also came to see that his slowly but surely increasing waistline had been bothering him more than he'd cared to admit; and that a part of him (very logically) *did* blame the increase on his frequent focus at work. This insight nudged him to splurge on a trainer to meet him at the office come rain or shine so that he wouldn't harbor quiet resentments toward his job over a false choice between health and work. Removing the option to blame his job for a lack of physical exercise significantly improved his feelings about his work, and of course was also very helpful for his health.

Realizing how *good* it felt to provide for his kids in *contrast* to what his father had done helped Matt reconnect with a sense of purpose in his work and realize that becoming a father himself had stirred some old childhood memories that he needed to unpack. It also helped him realize that providing for his kids was actually a very important way of supporting them, and that he wanted to ask his wife to help communicate to the kids more often that his reason for working long hours was to *support his family.* He also realized that he wanted to start planning short pockets of travel to places no one in the family had ever been. This offered him a way to connect with his wife and kids on a deeper level while also giving a little nod to the part of himself that chose this career partly as a way to afford travel. These insights and ensuing actions helped Matt feel emotionally lighter, more connected with his *reasons* for work, and less stressed about family and health. All of this combined to produce greater motivation at work, which was his original concern at the starting point.

Troubleshooting

1. **When I look at my starting point, I feel a bunch of different reactions simultaneously. Which one should I use for my first reaction?**

First of all, congratulations—you definitely picked the right exercise when you chose Mind Mapping! Mind Mapping is perfect for situations in which you are thinking or feeling multiple things at once, because it helps you to separate the issues and thereby make them more manageable. Don't worry about which reaction you choose to write down first. The point of terming the material you write on your map as "First reactions" and "additional reactions" in steps 2 and 3 for Mind Maps is more for the sake of trying to explain the exercise logistically. If you have multiple simultaneous thoughts and feelings from your starting point (or from any subsequent points on your map), just write each one down with a circle and arrow, as explained in step 3. It won't make any difference which one you write down first; the point is just to make sure you get all the data points out of your head and onto your map!

2. **How do I know when I'm done?**

This is a good question. While there's no litmus test for knowing exactly when to consider your Mind Map complete (since your neural network is obviously much more vast and rife with connections than could be captured on a simple sheet of paper), a good rule of thumb is to stop when you feel like your Mind Map captures the thoughts and feelings that seem relevant to your starting point, and when you don't have any additional strong thoughts or feelings to add when you glance at any of the items on your map. Many people feel a mental sense of "exhaling" when their Mind Map reaches this point. It's almost like making a to-do list: yes, you probably *could* keep building a to-do list that was *infinitely* long, but once you have a list that captures the important stuff, you usually have a natural feeling of awareness that your list is complete.

Most Mind Maps can be completed in five to twenty minutes. If you feel like you might be going "overboard," it can be helpful to pause with whatever you have and just work on understanding your insights about the material you do have, knowing that you can always return to add more material or even do an additional Mind Map about another topic, if you wish, at a later time.

3. My Mind Map basically just shows me that I'm feeling stuck and overwhelmed. What now?

First of all, I'm sorry you're feeling stuck and overwhelmed. As you face the way you're feeling, it's important to remember that the Mind Map did not *create* this state: the Mind Map is merely a tool that is literally reflecting and showing you on paper some of the dynamics that are happening in your mind. This means that even if your situation seems hard to face, you still did yourself a big favor by getting a clear picture (literally) of some of the issues you're confronting right now.

To locate the best way forward, you might consider looking at *one circle at a time* and asking yourself if there are ways you can impact or get support with each issue. You might also check in with yourself to confirm that you're not allowing perfectionist tendencies to create outsized feelings of guilt, shame, or being overwhelmed around your situation. It's also possible that your Mind Map is ringing a helpful alarm bell to signal that in fact some very "heavy lifting" changes need to be made in your life, if your current dynamics are truly as unmanageable as they seem. Sometimes it helps to take your Mind Map as a "visual aid" to acclimate a trusted friend or therapist to all the obstacles you're facing, and get some support figuring out the best way to navigate a challenging map. At the very least, you'll stop being "stuck in your head" about the problems, because you'll be gaining a fresh perspective from someone you trust.

Again, I'm sorry that you're feeling stuck and overwhelmed. Kudos to you for taking the important first step of mapping out the factors in this situation so that you can get whatever support you need to deal with them as proactively as possible. When we have a clear and accurate map, it is at least a little easier to better understand how to put one foot in front of the other and move forward.

12.

Worry Time

Let our advance worrying become
advance thinking and planning.
—SIR WINSTON CHURCHILL

Kate immediately stood out on my client list for the day not only because she was a new client, but because the notes for her visit indicated that she was another therapist seeking business consultation for her private practice.[1] Moreover, Kate had flown in from Tennessee (most clients located outside of New York just see me by video), so I was conscious of the extra investment of time and energy she had made in order to make this meeting happen. I had also been BCC'd on my receptionist's email responding to Kate's requests to confirm the appointment; in those emails she had earnestly expressed to the receptionist how excited she was for this meeting. It was rather endearing, and of course it was also flattering.

Although I was "feeling open" based on what I knew about Kate's efforts and enthusiasm regarding this meeting, I was also somewhat cautious: I'll admit that some people in my own profession can sometimes be a little kooky (see chapter 6 on Special Considerations for High Functioning People Seeking Therapy), so I approached the lobby to greet her with a mix of optimism and watchfulness.

Kate's nose was buried in a beautiful caramel-colored leather folio containing tabbed, highlighted notes when I spotted her in the lobby—a woman after my own heart! Despite the July heat and her travel, she appeared poised, fresh, and cool in a casual belted linen dress and stylish strappy sandals with a modest kitten heel, perfect for strolling New York City streets. Her glossy black hair was pulled back from her face, which rose with a sense of expectation as I approached.

One of the first things Kate did upon entering my office was to present me with an elegantly wrapped gift, which was a small silver pen from Tiffany & Co. She explained with an interesting mix of deference and pride that although she was from Tennessee, she was very connected with her Chinese heritage and hoped tha would accept this gift as an expression of her cultural tradition of giving a gift at the start of a new and special business relationship. As a lifelong lover of culture, etiquette, and business, I was aware of this tradition—but I had never experienced it personally. I was at once charmed, intrigued, and impressed.[2] But I was also still a little cautious. Kate was so polished that I'll admit I experienced a momentary sense of insecurity: I was hoping I would meet her standards!

Kate turned to her beautiful leather folio as she settled into my sofa, explaining that she had already watched *all* of my training videos for therapists in private practice and had completed the videos' accompanying worksheets as well (she'd brought her completed worksheets for reference). She'd also brought a list of questions so well organized that some of them were based on direct quotes from my training videos; she had even noted the exact times the quotes appeared in the videos for greater reference!

"I just wanted to make sure I use my time with you wisely," she said with a smile and a faux-sheepish shrug as I leafed through her annotated list of notes and questions, only half trying to disguise my incredulity. Kate knew her preparation was a little overboard, but she seemed a bit proud of this—and why shouldn't she be? Her preparation was stellar, and it evidenced her willingness to invest herself in building a successful private practice.

Many therapists who want to establish a private practice focused on high functioning people have a lot of questions and concerns. To a certain degree, this illustrates a desirable level of conscientiousness and cognitive activity around their goal of creating a successful practice. Kate took these concerns to a whole new level: she worried about everything, from not having enough clients, to having *too* many clients; from worrying she looked too young to worrying she looked too stuffy; she even once asked me if I had an opinion about the right level of *humidity* for a therapy office. I wasn't surprised when Kate confided in me that she was driving herself crazy with all of her worry, to the point where she was missing out on the joy of building a practice.

I was concerned that in addition to driving herself crazy, Kate might be inadvertently repelling the very same clients she was seeking to engage. Excessive worry about the self (or one's business, home, or other extensions of the self) is a form of hyper-self-consciousness, and it is also a form of self-absorption. Self-absorption is generally *not* a good thing when you're in a business that focuses on *others*, such as the business of therapy. The irony was that Kate *knew* she was going into "worry overdrive" sometimes, but she felt powerless to stop . . . and so, like many high functioning people, she sometimes worried about whether she was worrying too much! There was a part of Kate that felt a sense of safety from worrying, because it meant she was focused on warding off problems—yet she also knew that her worrying was actually *becoming* a problem.

Since Kate was a therapist, one might assume she knew all about techniques like Worry Time, which is a pretty common cognitive-behavioral therapy technique. But I'll let you in on a little secret: sometimes therapists are so close to the forest that we can't see the trees. I finally decided to introduce Worry Time when Kate confessed that she sometimes struggled to pay full attention to what a client was saying during session because her inner "worry monologue" was so loud that it distracted her from the client. While she knew this was problematic, she feared it would be irresponsible to push her worries aside: she was (true to form) worried about dropping any important concerns. As soon as I began to ask Kate if she had ever considered trying Worry Time, she laughed knowingly as she playfully raised her hands to cover her blushing face.

"Oh no," she moaned with pseudo-mortification. "I think you might be right. But I have to say I'm afraid it won't really *work* for me. My worry habit can be pretty tenacious! I'm a lifelong worry aficionado! I've tried telling my inner worry monologue to just *shut up* sometimes, but I can't seem to do it."

I assured her I felt it was worth a try, and emphasized that Worry Time works best when we recognize the *value* of worry rather than looking at worrying as just a bad habit that we're trying to limit. I reminded her that it was partly her "worry habit" that stimulated her to be so prepared for our first visit, and I recognized this as a clear upside of her capacity for consternation. The idea, I explained, was to *harness* the worry by giving it the right format, one where it could manifest as strategic planning rather than skittish fretting.

Kate was worried that Worry Time wouldn't work for her (of course she was!), but she decided to give it a shot. She had already defined the hours of operation for her private practice as part of her homework from my video training program; now she decided to allocate two hours of each scheduled workday for worrying about the business.[3] She did this with the understanding that if she booked a client during her "worry hours" then she could reschedule her worry session—as long as she averaged two hours per day at the end of each week, she knew she would have enough time to devote to her worries. Whenever she found herself furrowing her brow while waiting in line at the supermarket or other random places, she simply pulled out her phone and added event details to the "Worry About Business" event she had created in her calendar.

To her pleasant surprise, Kate found that Worry Time helped her enjoy the same sense of accomplishment she had previously felt when worrying on a whim, plus it ensured she would use her energy strategically: **She could sit down and give these worries her undivided, guilt-free attention, rather than try to field them extemporaneously.** Reviewing her list in a clear state of mind helped her see which items were legitimate (making sure she had professional stationery) and which items were wheel-spinning time wasters (whether that stationery should be on twenty-five-pound or twenty-seven-pound paper). Another benefit was that by writing down the worry topics in her calendar as they arose, she no longer had to waste cognitive energy trying to keep track of them mentally; and she no longer had to stay constantly focused on stressful topics just to keep them "front of mind." Consolidating her focus also saved resources of time and energy on what psychologists call "task switching," which is the time and energy it takes the brain to change its focus. Of course, another added benefit was that Kate was finally free to **relax and enjoy idle time** (which is essential to the mind's ability to recharge and think creatively, by the way!), instead of polluting it with compulsive, unbounded worrying.

DIY: Put Worry Time to Work in Your Life!

This one is super simple! But it can be deceptively simple. The trick is to make sure you actually block the time in your calendar, enter every worry item into your list as soon as it starts gnawing at you, and dutifully arrive ready to worry at your appointed time (or at least reschedule it if something urgent interrupts your worry plans).

1. **Decide how much time you need to worry.** Every situation is different, but common choices for clients in my practice range from ten minutes per day to a single sixty-minute session per week. Kate went far above this amount, but she had a very practical reason for this. The point is just to assess the overall quantity and importance of your worry material and then reverse-engineer how much time makes sense for you to spend on it.

2. **Plan the time into your calendar.** This step is crucial! If you're really someone who loses time and energy to "wheel spinning" worry, then take this opportunity for change. Please don't say to yourself, "I can ballpark this—I need to spend about fifteen minutes per day, so I'll just aim for that and trust it will pan out." The whole reason that Worry Time works is that the part of your brain that *needs* confirmation and detail *will not rest* till it knows that *for certain* there is a *specific* time that is *totally dedicated* to uninterrupted worrying about whatever material tends to get stuck on your mind. At the very least, try it for a week and see how you feel!

3. **Build your worry agenda.** Throughout the week, add to your agenda of worry-worthy items whenever you feel the need. No item is too big or too small. (If an item truly requires *urgent* attention, then of course you should address it as soon as possible rather than postponing it till Worry Time.) Don't get stuck trying to evaluate whether or not

something is worthwhile; if it's on your mind, just deposit it onto the worry list and be done with it till Worry Time!

4. **Sit down and worry.** I mean it—sit down at your appointed time with a pen and paper, and write/think/research about your worries. If you discover you *really* need more time to explore a particular topic, add more time for that issue into your calendar at the end of your session. But oftentimes, clients find that the simple act of sitting down to review whatever random issues have popped into their minds and onto their worry lists throughout the week seem quite manageable at best (and maybe a little silly at worst—which is actually good news, too, if you think about it) when they actually focus on those issues in a rational, focused state of mind. This step can also pave the way for increases in mindfulness and metacognition: for example, reviewing your list in aggregate may guide you to notice that your worries all tend to cluster around certain themes or occur in certain patterns.

Troubleshooting

1. **What if there are problems I can't solve?**

Let me reframe this as a helpful insight: congratulations to you for getting clarity about this rather than engaging in Sisyphean worry about problems you cannot solve. Please see the Zone of Control technique! You are better off focusing your energy on problems you *can* solve than problems you cannot solve. If there are worries that you cannot solve but which *must* be solved, it is still an accomplishment that you've realized the need for help. Talk your situation over with trusted friends, family, or professionals to see if you can get some support solving the problem.

2. **What if my worries seem silly when I actually review the list during my Worry Time?**

That would be great news! Enjoy a good self-compassionate chuckle as you thank yourself for using the Worry Time technique instead of spinning your wheels on those "nonissues" at the moment when they initially *seemed* like such a big deal. For extra points, practice mindfulness to see if you can figure out *why* they seemed like such a big deal at the time. Were you under stress? Were you talking to someone who makes you feel insecure? Don't force yourself to worry about the "why factor" too much, though; it's fine to just have a good chuckle and move forward!

3. **What if it's hard to redirect my attention away from the worry once I've written it into my worry list?— like, if I still keep thinking about it.**

You can either try the Mental Shortlist technique or see the very next item in this troubleshooting list.

4. **What if I have a genuine "worry emergency" that can't wait until my next scheduled Worry Time?**

Good awareness on your part! Worry Time helps you put boundaries around worries that are mere "mental chatter" draining your moment-to-moment energy. If you have an awareness that one of your worries is *not* in this category but is a legitimate issue that needs your immediate attention, then please—by all means go ahead and focus on it right away!

13.

Response Prevention

*He who controls others may be powerful, but he
who has mastered himself is mightier still.*

—LAO TZU

Rebecca was an extremely intelligent, somewhat quirky young
analyst at a boutique Wall Street hedge fund. She had overcome
many challenges in life, starting when she was born to a teenage
mother who married her father (ten years her senior) at a shotgun
wedding. Her father was frequently absent, partly due to his occupation as a truck driver and partly due to what Rebecca described as
"major problems" with women and gambling. Although he earned
a decent living driving a truck, the family often faced angry bill
collectors due to the financial strain of her father's extracurricular
activities. She recalled one particularly painful memory of her parents having to sell their dining room table in order to pay the rent.
Her mother was practically a child herself when she married, and

she grew into a meek, somewhat codependent woman who lived under the thumb of her husband.

Although Rebecca knew they loved her, her parents were unable to provide her with much in life beyond the most basic necessities (this was true of both material and nonmaterial necessities; Rebecca practically parented herself). Nevertheless, Rebecca had used her difficult beginnings to underpin a strong awareness that she wanted to create a better life for herself. She used her firsthand awareness of the pain of poverty as a stimulus to grind hard at school and work till somehow she found herself earning a very nice living on Wall Street.

Rebecca was one of my first clients in private practice, so I was still a little naive regarding exactly how much some Wall Streeters make. I have to say that my jaw dropped a bit when I learned how much she was paid. Let's just say it was *a lot*, especially for someone so young (she bought a large apartment in Columbus Circle during our work together; those apartments are multimillion-dollar gems that are typically out of reach for single young adults without family money). However, as you might guess, hedge funds are usually pretty smart about how they spend money; and they made no mistake investing in Rebecca. Rebecca lived and breathed her hard-won job; she thought constantly and very, very deeply about her work. She even *dreamed* about new ways to analyze the stocks whose performance she was paid to predict.

"I don't stop," Rebecca said with a striking mixture of pride and wistfulness. "Once I set my mind on something, I'm like a dog with a bone." Rebecca's statement, and her ambivalent feelings around it, made complete sense. She was relentless. In her professional life, this was one of her greatest assets—she did *not* let go till she figured out a way to make the proverbial Rubik's Cube of data line up favorably for her portfolio. This same tenacity was also what allowed her to have a damn-near-myopic focus on propelling herself out of squalor and into financial security (or financial luxury, depending on your standards). In relationships, however, her tenacity became a liability.

Remember how I mentioned that Rebecca was "somewhat quirky"? I may have fudged a bit: she was *rather* quirky. One of the ways this quirkiness manifested was in romantic relationships: although she was firm about feeling that, as a woman, she wanted to be pursued by a man, she would compulsively and incessantly *tell her romantic interests how* to pursue her and give them frequent corrective feedback if she felt they weren't doing enough—in other words, she basically ended up pursuing the men herself as she tried to "direct" them to pursue her, and then (here's the kicker!) she would ultimately fault them for making her do all the work. Eventually, the men would retreat from this no-win situation.

Rebecca struggled with profound fears of abandonment. They likely stemmed from the childhood fear that one day her father might leave for one of his other women or allow his gambling to render them completely destitute, or from the way her mother never seemed *fully present* since she seemed to have numbed herself as a coping strategy around her husband's destructive patterns. The retreat of Rebecca's romantic interests would trigger intense feelings of panic and shame from childhood, causing her to engage in what she described as a humiliating pattern of texting and calling men who were clearly rejecting her. She *knew* when she was engaging in a flurry of desperate attempts to reengage them in a pursuit of her, and she *knew* deep down that it wasn't going to give her the result she wanted, but she often felt powerless to stop. A few times, she even pulled out her cell phone during session to compulsively check if a man had responded, and sometimes she couldn't help herself from firing off a quick text right there on my couch.

As self-sabotaging as this pattern was, Rebecca came by it honestly: like many adult daughters of fathers with addictive behaviors or mothers who are a bit "checked out," Rebecca was used to assuming it was *her* job to prod, manage, or entice a man into meeting her needs; and it was very hard for her to step out of this role—particularly with her exceptionally tenacious mind and its uncanny ability to analyze the hell out of almost anything.

Enter: Response Prevention

Rebecca's awareness that she did not *really* want to continue picking up her cell phone to "reach out," "follow up," "close the loop," or any of the other euphemisms she used to rationalize her obsessive behavior during moments of weakness, made her an excellent candidate for Response Prevention. Response Prevention is a popular cognitive behavioral therapy technique that is most often used with clients who are struggling with obsessive-compulsive behaviors. The basic idea is that life presents us with a circumstance that repeatedly leads to an undesirable response, and we can benefit by learning how to *prevent* ourselves from executing that response.

There is often a great deal of therapeutic value in understanding *why* we react in certain undesirable ways, but at a certain point we just want to *stop* reacting in those ways. Rebecca's previous therapist had really helped her to gain insight about why and how she developed a pattern of chasing men, but had done little to help her *change* it. That was why she came to see me. Rebecca and I also spent some time reviewing and understanding the insights she had about herself, but it quickly became clear that she had already analyzed herself to death. At this point, she just needed to learn how to *stop* picking up her phone and texting men compulsively, *especially* men who had clearly rejected her.

Breaking down what felt like an overwhelming, embarrassing, lifelong pattern into a simple, straightforward, predictable interaction of stimulus and response was a helpful framework for Rebecca.

Doing this helped to **externalize something that had previously felt like part of the *fabric of herself* and reslot it as merely a stimulus-response behavior that she wanted to change**. For her, the stimulus was experiencing feelings or events that suggested a man was rejecting her, and her response was to start texting him.

Rebecca wanted her new response to be to *reciprocate* a man's rejection by recognizing him as undesirable. By rejecting her, he clearly *wasn't* pursuing her, which was different than what Rebecca said she wanted. He was also marking himself as unavailable, and she definitely didn't find unavailability to be *desirable*. Rebecca hoped that by recognizing a man as undesirable, it would be easier to quit engaging with him (or even chasing him!) by texting. In a strictly behavioral sense, we couldn't really control whether Rebecca would mentally cease to desire the man, but we could certainly control whether or not she would text him. For Rebecca, who had suffered terrible humiliation after sending hundreds of texts to dozens of men who had rejected her over the years, the idea of at least being able to **stop the texting behavior** was very attractive— and as a psychologist, I agreed it would be in her best interests to do so. Moreover, **when we can change our behavior, our thinking will often follow**—so Rebecca and I decided to focus on how to change her texting behaviors using Response Prevention.

Generally, the best Response Prevention techniques include doing something that makes you literally *unable* to do the undesirable response until the urge passes. The goal is to remove your own willpower from the equation as much as possible: by making your undesirable behavior impossible (at least temporarily), you free yourself from a constant internal "battle of the wills." In milder cases, by simply giving yourself better alternatives, you're able to divert your focus long enough for the urge to pass. Given Rebecca's persistent personality style, we knew we'd have to arm her with some formidable Response Prevention strategies to "save her from herself." The tactics we selected may sound outlandish, but remember that Rebecca's behavior of compulsively texting men who had rejected her was *also* outlandish; and she wanted to ensure it *stopped*. What follows is the protocol we created.

First and foremost, Rebecca locked herself out of her own cell phone account by having a trusted friend reset the account's password without telling Rebecca the new password; and she had the account's email address reset to the friend's email address to make it more difficult for Rebecca to "break into" her account. Rebecca also had her friend call the company to pose as herself and add a verbal passcode on the account to make it more difficult for her to dial the company's customer-service line and get a representative to text her a login, since she wouldn't know the verbal passcode. She knew she could still get into her account eventually if she really needed to (this was Rebecca, after all!), but it would involve faxing in a copy of her driver's license. Taking these steps helped to create more barriers to entry; plus, she felt that if she were to "break into" her account after all this, it would be disrespectful to her friend's willingness to support her.

Next, whenever Rebecca was rejected by a man, she immediately deleted him from her phone so that she couldn't contact him. However, this still left some gray areas: for example, what if a man hadn't actually rejected her, but he at least appeared to be "going quiet" for several days?[1] The following bullet points describe six ideas Rebecca added to her Response Prevention arsenal to consider when she didn't want to delete a man's number altogether for some reason, or when she somehow had the man's number memorized, or when she feared she might be bordering on breaking into her cell phone account to locate old phone numbers of men she'd already deleted. You'll notice that none of these solutions are *permanent* (after all, it's almost impossible to literally, permanently remove an option to communicate), but they did help her to "outsmart" the overactive analyst part of herself that would otherwise go into overdrive modes and come up with ridiculous reasons to rationalize texting unavailable men, only to feel ashamed and angry with herself the following day.

- Leaving her apartment without her cell phone and jumping onto an express subway train or some other place where she would be unable to turn around and run back to her phone on a whim.
- FedExing her phone to herself, just to get it out of her hands for a longer period of time. She happened to live near a FedEx kiosk, so this was actually rather simple.
- Telling a man to ignore any further reach-outs from her, no matter what she might say in the future (this was for a man who had already rejected her several times, whose number she had memorized and was therefore more difficult to block herself from texting, and with whom she knew that any further contact would be unhealthy for her). Telling him this was embarrassing. But she decided it would ultimately be less embarrassing and emotionally draining than continuing in her previous pattern of a mostly one-sided text chain from her which included a combination of booty calls, angry or sad messages about feeling rejected or ignored, and nostalgic messages intended to entice him; with only sporadic responses from him, such as if he was bored or lonely or felt like an ego boost from her attention.
- Powering her phone off or muting notifications from certain contacts while trying to refocus herself on something else so that she could put her full energy into getting into the "something else" rather than constantly checking to see if her latest crush had texted her. This was also helpful since she knew that compulsive checking was often a pre-

cursor to thinking of texts she could send to "nudge" him into asking her for another date.

- Asking a few friends to serve as "lifelines" she could call when she needed support.
- Keeping printouts of some of her most embarrassing text threads in places where she could easily find them to reread. Sometimes this helped her to "snap out of it" when she felt urges to start similar threads with new men.

The last few items on her list are less drastic than the others, but Rebecca found comfort knowing that if these lighter measures weren't enough, she could use some of the stronger options on her menu. Sometimes a drastic measure felt comforting to have in her toolbox, since her urges could feel very powerful. This "stair-stepper" option of escalating levels of Response Prevention also gave her a chance to see how much she could rely on her own willpower before she needed to literally block herself from reaching out.

By practicing the Response Prevention protocol, Rebecca was finally able to experience a different response to the old stimulus of feeling a strong urge to contact a man. When she started to see what it was like to *not* contact a man who had rejected her and discovered how proud she felt the next day when the urge had passed and she had no embarrassing text messages to regret, she finally began to experience a new, positive outcome. She hadn't been able to experience the benefits of holding back on the texts before, since she had always felt so powerless—but experiencing the sense of victory and new identity that emerged with her new behaviors was empowering and helped her to gain momentum. The virtuous circle Rebecca created as she developed a sense of control is a common benefit when we start experiencing success.

By ceasing to send undesirable texts,[2] Rebecca created a new dynamic: instead of constantly feeling like she was digging herself out of a hole, she started to feel like she was in a good place that she wanted to protect and maintain. Plus, she started to notice that by *not* reaching out to men to nudge them to ask her out quickly after a first date, she was sometimes pleasantly surprised that they *would* end up texting her of their own accord, and this dynamic actually pleased her much more than merely having them *respond* to *her* postdate pursuit. I'm not saying Response Prevention made dating completely easy for Rebecca, but a behavioral backstop of Response Prevention definitely helped her to stay on track during challenging moments.

DIY: Put Response Prevention to Work in Your Life

Response Prevention works best on one of life's most frustrating types of behaviors: those that you *know* you're going to do, you know you don't *really* want to do, but you still struggle to stop because at certain (often predictable) vulnerable moments you always feel *so* tempted—and the annoying pattern is so reliable it's almost like clockwork. Whether it's emotional eating, having sex too early in a new relationship, or mindlessly biting your nails while watching TV, Response Prevention can help you interrupt a problematic stimulus-response cycle in your life. Here's what you do:

1. **Define the behavior you'd like to stop.** The behavior must be something you actually *do*, rather than a way you think or a way you feel (check out Thought Replacement, Mental Shortlist, and other techniques in this book if you realize that you can't boil your desired change down to a *specific behavior* that you'd like to stop). Response Prevention works best on behaviors that have obvious starting and stopping points and that are clearly

observable. One simple test to help confirm whether a behavior meets these requirements is if it's something that another person could observe you physically *doing*, even if she was just watching you on a silent TV monitor.

2. **Understand the stimulus that triggers your response.** In Rebecca's case, the stimulus was feeling rejected. In other cases, such as premature sex, the stimulus could be going on a date with a new crush. For emotional eating, the stimulus might be finding yourself presented with a large quantity of comfort food. Response Prevention works best when we have a clearly identifiable trigger for the behavior. The behavior must be observable, but the trigger doesn't have to be observable—it can be a feeling state.

3. **Make a list of all the ways you can deal with the same stimulus without lapsing into your old response.** Aim for at least three ways so that you'll have some flexibility to handle different levels of temptation or circumstances. For example, I've worked with emotional eaters whose Response Prevention arsenal included things like asking the waiter to bring them a half portion or to clear their plate early when they're dining in restaurants, immediately tossing that extra birthday cake or the housewarming gift of delicious banana bread into the garbage after guests leave, and dumping a shaker of salt into the garbage on top of the food if it still seemed to be calling their name (some emotional eaters will eat the food out of the garbage five minutes after dumping it in there if the food seems at all salvageable, depending on their level of emotionality and how delicious that food is likely to taste). These clients would love to be able to

donate their extra food to people in need, but they some-times realize that the food would never actually make it to a donation center because they would consume it before a donation could be coordinated.

I've worked with dating clients who know they have a tendency to rush into sex with an exciting new crush right around the third date, before they really feel as secure in the relationship as they'd like to before having sex; so they'll do things like schedule a check-in call with a friend at 10 P.M. the night of a romantic dinner date as a backstop against extending the date too long after dinner, if that's when the premature sex tends to happen. (Many high functioning clients are very conscientious about other people's time, so having an obligation to a friend *and* a source of social support after the date is often a great way to prevent them from responding to the stim-ulus of an exciting date by staying out late and going too far.) Or they'll give the friend an unflattering photo (of themselves, not of the friend or of anyone else) and ask the friend to post it to Facebook if they don't show up for the 10 P.M. call because they got carried away and didn't want to end their date on the early side as planned (this is just an extra "stair stepper" layer if the client is worried they might be tempted to no-show on their friend due to getting swept away during the date). Or they might preorder a car service for a cer-tain pickup time if they decide to go to their date's apartment "just for one quick nightcap" but are worried it might turn into more. Others might write silly things on their chest and stomach with a water-based marker at home before the date to ruin the potential experience of getting naked. (Yes, this sounds ridiculous and embar-rassing, but for clients who are trying to break a habit of jumping into bed with dates who seem irresistibly special/sexy/sweet before a relationship is ready, this method of Response Prevention seems rather light compared to the heartache they otherwise tend to face.)

Troubleshooting

1. **I can't think of any surefire ways to stop my behavior.**

If you're struggling to think of backstops against certain behaviors, you have a few options:

- **Be patient with yourself.** As you can see from the earlier examples, sometimes it takes a little mental elbow grease to come up with creative ideas like dropping your phone into FedEx or writing something silly on your abdomen as you dress for a date. Sometimes Response Prevention ideas are also a little elaborate, like enlisting a friend to take over your cell phone account. Give yourself at least twenty minutes of really focusing with a pen and paper in hand so you can "whiteboard" ideas before you start to lose patience over drawing a blank.

- **There might be a part of you that doesn't want to stop doing the behavior.** Scratch that—there's *definitely* a part of you that doesn't want to stop doing the behavior, and that part might be secretly blocking you from using your full cognitive capacities to stop said behavior. To solve this, ask yourself what the undesirable behavior is doing for you. Is there a secondary gain you get from the behavior? If yes, see if there are ways you can ensure that part of you will still get its needs met, even if you stop doing the one particular behavior that has previously fulfilled your need. For example, Rebecca realized that sometimes she was just desperate to talk to *someone*, and so she was turning to men habitually as a way to fill that need, even if the behavior ultimately upset the pursuit dynamics she wanted in a romantic relationship. She discovered that sometimes calling a friend or even going into online chat rooms solved her need for connection without involving any regrettable behavior.

- **You might need a friend or therapist to help you brainstorm.** Sometimes we get so stuck in our own patterns, or so down on ourselves about the undesirable behaviors, that it's hard to think creatively about ways to start new patterns. Never underestimate the power of a good talk with a resourceful person who wants to see you meet your goals.

2. I tried some Response Prevention techniques, but they didn't work; I found ways around them.

Let me reframe this as a positive! Okay, maybe not a *total* positive—but on the positive side, it does suggest that you're clever, and at the very least it means that you're engaging with the learning process. What you're doing when you "outsmart" your first effort at Response Prevention is you're gathering information about what works and what doesn't. This empowers you to refine, tweak, or amplify your Response Prevention techniques. This is totally normal and healthy. Don't expect perfection from yourself on the first try; you're wrestling with a stubborn behavior, so give yourself some latitude as you discover the right way to master it.

For example, Rebecca was initially dismayed to learn that merely deleting a man's number wasn't sufficient because she simply dug into her online phone records to locate it. But instead of giving up on herself, she got creative and took the extra step of proactively locking herself out of her cell phone account. Similarly, clients prone to emotional eating, who were extremely humiliated by having dug a box of cupcakes out of the kitchen wastebasket just five minutes after dumping it, have found victory by realizing they just need to dump a shaker of salt onto the cupcakes first, or run the whole box of cupcakes under the kitchen faucet for a moment before dropping it into the trash, or throw the cupcakes down the garbage chute if they live in a high-rise apartment. This extra step refines the "starter idea" of just dumping the sweets into the wastebasket. The point is to not give in to discouragement if you happen to find clever workarounds to your initial ideas. High functioning people often need a couple of go-rounds before finding a "foolproof" Response Prevention method.

3. **Sometimes I don't have a chance to do my Response Prevention technique because I find myself in the middle of actually *doing or having done* my problematic behavior before I was really aware of what I was doing.**

Remember the talk in the Mind Mapping chapter about how the mind deliberately sets up habits to make our neural pathways run quickly and efficiently; and how the unconscious mind sometimes tries to "hide" things from you because it seems easier in the moment than actually dealing with them? That might be part of what's happening here. For example, many nail biters or emotional eaters report sitting down to enjoy a TV show, only to "discover" themselves on the couch forty-five minutes later with their nails nibbled to nubs or an empty plate of food that they barely remember eating. Rebecca sometimes used to find herself engaged in a humiliating text thread with an unavailable man, trying to argue him out of rejecting her, before she had the presence of mind to fully *realize* what she was doing. **The good news is that there are ways you can remedy this problem.** In situations like these, I encourage you to consider the following options:

- **Build your mindfulness skills.** Practice mindfulness skills such as the Three-Part Breath, even when you're not actually battling an urge. Mindfulness skills help *develop* mental muscles that function as an overarching "presence of mind," or metacognition. These mental muscles help you have more perspective and awareness about your thoughts, feelings, and behaviors, even when you're under stress or feeling distracted. Mindfulness is all about *observing* yourself, so the situation of "losing yourself" to the point where you're doing problematic activities *mindlessly* suggests you would benefit from *better self-observation skills.* I realize I can sometimes be almost a militant optimist, but I'd encourage you to think of this as a great opportunity because you now have a strong motivation to learn how to develop mindfulness skills as well as another potential tool to accomplish your goal of Response Prevention. Motivation often increases our energy for learning, and it's great to have a training ground where you can practice your skills—so you may actually be experiencing a moment of great opportunity here.

- **Recognize the patterns.** Start to notice if the "unconscious slips" always seem to happen in certain situations, such as when you've been drinking, sitting in front of the TV, buried in work, or other situations that tend to compromise self-awareness. **If your slips do follow a pattern,** that's *good news* because reliable patterns mean you can start thinking in advance about ways to manage them. Whether it's putting a Post-it Note with the word "THINK!" on top of the TV or on your plate to keep a modicum of self-awareness as you enjoy a TV snack, or setting your cell phone's wallpaper to display a bold new image that grabs your attention and reminds you of whatever you'd like to keep in your awareness during nights on the town, or whatever other ways you can find to introduce a speed bump on the mental fast lane that has been keeping you on a repetitive circuit of certain undesirable habits—please do give yourself the gift of finding ways to stay focused so that you can control (and enjoy!) the ride.

- **Notice H.A.L.T. moments.** The handy habit-breaking acronym "H.A.L.T." can help prevent "surprise attacks." This acronym stands for "hungry, angry, lonely, tired." It is commonly used in addiction therapy because addicts are more likely to relapse when they're experiencing any of these feeling states. These states can be so gripping that they challenge our baseline mindfulness levels. So when you find yourself experiencing any of these four states (hungry, angry, lonely, or tired), give yourself the gift of making an extra effort *not* to make a bad moment worse by lapsing into undesirable problem behaviors. You may even find that successfully staving off an urge during a H.A.L.T. moment can actually brighten that moment because you experience a sense of pride and accomplishment, which can help boost your mood and create positive momentum.

14.

Thought Replacement

You have to work hard to get your thinking clean to make it simple.
But it's worth it in the end because once you get there,
you can move mountains.

—STEVE JOBS

Jack was a sophisticated, handsome advertising executive who came to my office seeking help to manage strong, conflicting feelings around the topic of his wife's repeated infidelity. The couple shared two young daughters, which presented a major point of ambivalence for Jack in trying to decide whether to work on repairing the marriage or simply thank God he had a prenuptial agreement and walk out the door. If not for the kids, he said, he'd leave in a heartbeat—but the fact that they had created a family together gave him pause. He knew that staying in an embittered marriage that modeled habitual disrespect for marital vows wasn't exactly good role modeling for the kids, and he suffered from a sense of disgust every time he thought about his wife's repetitive cheating.

On the other hand, he really did love her and he wanted to believe her when she kept promising it would "never happen again." He felt unsure of what he *wanted* to do, what he felt he *should* do, and whether there was any overlap between those things. He knew that as an advertising executive, he was a *master* at putting a "spin" on things, even to the point of "spinning" his own feelings to himself— so he wanted to be sure he was fully connecting with all the layers of this situation before making any big decisions.

To help Jack strip away the "spin" and unpack his true feelings so he could make whatever decision was ultimately best for him, I asked him to tell me some important context beyond just the pros and cons of divorce. I asked him to tell me about his own childhood, his parents' relationship, and their way of parenting him. I wanted to understand, and I wanted *him* to understand, his foundational beliefs about marriage and parenthood. What I heard was shocking.

Although he presented as an "average" Manhattanite (in New York, this means someone who is educated, at least somewhat gainfully employed, sophisticated, and reasonably fit) to whom success came relatively easily, Jack had actually overcome a set of heartbreaking childhood challenges that would have consigned many to a life of unemployment, brushes with the law, or worse. He was born in rural Appalachia to a mother who was incarcerated for drug smuggling when Jack was a young boy and then succumbed to an overdose shortly after being released on parole. This left Jack in the care of an abusive, narcissistic, often unemployed, severely alcoholic father, who drifted in and out of their squalid apartment, going on binges that grew more frequent as the years went by.

Jack mostly took care of himself, somehow realizing that if he wanted to make a life worth living he'd have to fend for himself. He began working at a local gas station at the age of eleven; earning money helped him build a sense of self-efficacy as well as an ability to treat himself to "new" clothes at the thrift shop on occasion. This was where his skills at "spinning" began, he explained: to be accepted at school, he needed to minimize how bad things were at home. Even for rural Appalachia, where rates of poverty and alcoholism are high, Jack would have been at the bottom of the social ladder unless he learned how to spin things to his classmates, his teachers, and even himself.

As Jack's pride in himself began to blossom through realizing he was capable of earning money and doing well in school, he grew into an increasingly independent young adolescent, and he gradually started to challenge his father by pointing out that none of the other kids at school had to buy all their own groceries or chip in so much for rent, like his dad made him do. Not surprisingly, his father didn't like these reality checks. Push came to shove, literally, when his father began to retaliate physically in order to "show Jack who was boss." For a while, Jack cowered in fear, but eventually he began to fight back—culminating in an all-out fistfight in which Jack was positioned to administer the "knockout punch" but instead just looked at his father with a mix of anger and pity, shook his head, and left for work. He hoped his show of mercy would be a wake-up call to his father, but unfortunately it was not. Jack came home from work that day to find an angry note in a drunken scrawl from his father, telling him that if Jack was such a "big man," then perhaps it was time he lived on his own: his father had abandoned him completely.

Jack never saw his father again, except for a handful of events over the next twenty years when he ran into his father during occasional visits with cousins (his father was still drunk and belligerent then). Instead of trying to chase after his father and make amends with him or wait for him to come banging on the door drunk some late night in the future, Jack left town after getting his father's note of abandonment. He decided his father had actually given him a gift by setting him free of any sense of obligation to him, and he wanted to ensure that his own life was a testament to his vow to be a better man. He was able to obtain a small scholarship for Appalachian youth, as well as take out student loans because of his excellent credit and work history, so he decided to move to New York, go to college, and reinvent himself. That's where his nascent ability to "spin" things bloomed into full-fledged "spin mastery," as he worked to blend in at a private university surrounded by mostly upper-middle-class or higher students. He then worked his way up in the New York advertising world, taking lessons to replace his thick Appalachian accent with a neutral, polished voice. The "spinmaster" was in full swing—no wonder he was so good at his advertising job!

Jack told me this story somewhat calmly, and actually with a fair amount of pride. "I know it sounds crazy, and believe me, I know it's sad," he said. "I wish to God things had been different— but all things considered, I frankly think I made the best choices under the circumstances. So, yeah, that's my story of how I got introduced to the idea of family. Does that help, doc?" he said, cracking a wry joke at the end.

During our treatment, Jack discovered that yet *again* his wife was having an affair. He was brokenhearted and livid, both at the same time. He feared that the environment at home was becoming so toxic that his daughters would *definitely* be better off if he and his wife divorced, so he decided to file. He seemed to be at peace with this decision, until the time came to create a custody agreement. As a loving and engaged father, Jack was adamant that he wanted at least joint custody, which the judge granted. While many fathers would have felt relieved to get joint custody with a fifty-fifty split of parenting time, Jack was horrified. "I cannot abandon my children," he said. For the first time, I saw him cry. He'd told me the story of his childhood in a way that felt emotionally connected, yet without tears. He'd expressed rage and grief over his wife's repeated infidelity, but never cried. The thing that brought him to tears was the idea that he was repeating his father's pattern of abandonment.

I listened supportively and reassured him that he was *not* abandoning his daughters, and he seemed to understand and agree during our therapeutic discussions—but the next week, he'd reappear with the same concern. He knew his daughters would be safe and well cared for during their stays with his soon-to-be ex-wife. (Although her perpetual infidelity was a fatal marital flaw, he said that aside from this she was a responsible and loving mother.) But he would experience constant, intrusive, almost habitual thoughts that he was abandoning his daughters, just like his father had abandoned him.

Enter: Thought Replacement

Once it became clear that insight alone wasn't going to help Jack fix his internal monologue about abandoning his daughters, we decided to introduce Thought Replacement.[1]

The first step was to identify the maladaptive thoughts as maladaptive. In psychology, maladaptive thoughts are those that are inaccurate or counterproductive. Jack's thoughts that centered around self-criticism for abandoning his daughters were both inaccurate *and* counterproductive. Jack was able to see this very easily, but he still struggled to overcome them. What he needed was an adaptive thought with which he could *replace* them. He needed something different from using the Mental Shortlist: the Mental Shortlist technique is great when you just need to quit focusing on a dead-end topic, but Jack's thoughts were too important to just pivot away from—that would have felt (and been) irresponsible. To get real peace and move forward in a healthy way, Jack needed to *correct* his thoughts.

It is imperative that the replacement thoughts be accurate, rather than aspirational, so that clients can fully rely on them during moments of vulnerability. We wanted to avoid over-the-top Thought Replacements like, "I'm a perfect father just the way I am," since of course no father is perfect. The Thought Replacement we created together was, "I'm a good father, I'm a present father, I'm supporting my children, and I'm staying in their lives forever." Naturally, his inner critic tried to poke holes in these statements: How could he say he was a present father when he was gone half the time? Giving the inner critic an appropriate forum in which to challenge the statements is an important step: better to have that conversation with the inner critic while you're in a rational mindset and a supportive environment than in the throes of a moment of vulnerability. Think of it as "due diligence." We wanted to make sure we'd really checked for the inevitable "yeah, buts" that often arise from an active, high functioning mind; so we gave Jack's inner critic ample opportunities to challenge the replacement thoughts before totally committing to them.

Thinking it through in therapy, Jack was able to recognize that, actually, having demanded in court his right to fifty-fifty joint custody and giving his daughters an iPad with a direct FaceTime connection to him to use during stays with their mother if they wanted to reach him *was* being demonstrably present in their lives. Plus, he noted that part of the reason he was in a joint custody situation rather than living with his kids full-time in the first place was at least partially due to concerns about whether he had been *truly* fully present in a marital home where he was so distracted by his wife's infidelity.

Once Jack was able to fully accept his replacement thoughts in therapy, he was able to commit to stick with them in moments of need—he was able to recognize that **although the replacement thoughts might not always feel natural, he could trust that they were accurate, carefully vetted, and accepted as true by his**

most rational self; this was a comfort during moments of self-doubt. Whenever the "old script" would start in his mind, Jack would override it by repeating his replacement thoughts. If he found himself struggling to compete for "airtime" (that is, the old script seemed louder than the Thought Replacements), he would either speak the replacement thoughts aloud (a great way to physically commandeer your brain by bringing your speaking muscles into the picture, as well as your auditory capacity when you literally hear your own *real* voice saying the words on which you want to focus) or write them on paper if he was someplace where speaking aloud to oneself might raise eyebrows (for example, the New York City subway during his daily commute). He would also practice his replacement thoughts when he *wasn't* experiencing intrusions of the old script, just to give his mind a chance to have some focused one-on-one time with the "new normal" that he wanted to create.

While Jack's case may seem "heavy," I want you to know that you can use Thought Replacement for lighter situations, too. For example, I've seen clients use the following Thought Replacements:

- A client with social anxiety replaced maladaptive thoughts such as, "I am so awkward; no one would ever like me," with straightforward Thought Replacements like, "Even if I'm not everyone's cup of tea, I do have at least a few friends that I know like me—so it's likely there are at least a few more in the world if I'm willing to keep trying."

- William, as you know from previous chapters, was a worrywart. He found that every time his heart rate increased during cardiovascular exercise, like running on a treadmill, he'd launch into an internal monologue of hypervigilant thoughts about his elevated heart rate "just in case" it was dangerous. He found himself ruminating about this despite knowing that he was in great health because he'd already talked with his doctor about his concerns and even had an electrocardiogram (commonly known as an EKG) to confirm his cardiovascular health; plus, his doctor had reminded him that elevated heart rates are actually the *point* of cardiovascular exercise. The maladaptive internal monologue would stop him from really enjoying the exercise, much less giving it his full effort. He wasn't panicking; he was just going "WebMD crazy" (he had even actually pulled out his phone to check WebMD right there on the treadmill on more than one occasion). His Thought Replacements in these situations included, "This is safe, this is healthy, this is normal" and, "Elevated heart rates signal cardio workout success!"

- A single client whose people-pleasing tendencies were causing excessive anxiety on dates, keeping her so focused on pleasing her date that she lost touch with whether or not she really liked *him*, used the following Thought Replacement when she found herself stepping onto the mental hamster wheel of quizzing herself on whether her date seemed to like her, how she could make him like her more, and so on. It is important to note that her Thought Replacement is a series of questions, which is totally fine; sometimes directing our minds to ask questions is the healthiest thing we can do: "Is he pleasing me? How do I know? Does he make me feel secure? Does he pursue me the way I like men to do?"

DIY: Put Thought Replacement to Work in Your Life

1. **Identify your "maladaptive thought."** Remember that maladaptive thoughts are just psychology's fancy label for thoughts that are interfering with your ability to cope or adapt well to your situation. Another way to think of this is sometimes: What are your inner critic's go-to statements? *Whatever* annoying script runs through your mind that you know is holding you back could be your maladaptive thought. The only catch is this: if you're thinking of something that you can actually control, then you should *not* necessarily try to replace the thought. For example, if you're thinking, "I'm going to fail my exam" and you haven't studied much, then don't replace that thought—listen to it and go study! It's actually an *adaptive* thought because it's trying to alert you to a real threat, and you have the ability to change the outcome. Maladaptive thoughts are by nature inaccurate, useless, and/or counterproductive.

2. **Write down your maladaptive thought.** Specifically, fold a sheet of paper in half down the center, then write the maladaptive thought on the left side of that sheet. Along with that thought, write any of its "close cousins" (similar or other maladaptive thoughts that you want to replace). Writing the thought down in plain English (or whatever is your preferred language) is important because it forces you to put a fine point on exactly what that thought is so that you can examine it and recognize it clearly when it rears its ugly head.

3. **Write down your replacement thought.** Write your replacement thought on the right-hand side of your paper,

so that you know exactly what to say or think instead whenever the maladaptive thought arises. If you discover that a "yeah, but" response arises from your inner critic (for example, the way Jack's inner critic countered his original Thought Replacement with, "What kind of father is gone half the time?"), write that thought as a new maladaptive thought on the next line of the left-hand side of the paper, then enter your rebuttal to *that* thought on the right-hand side. The idea is that you document every possible maladaptive thought on the left side and accompany it with a logical, accurate counter on the right side.

4. **Practice, practice, practice.** Remember that your maladaptive thoughts may have been with you for a long time. Give yourself ample opportunities to practice your new thoughts, and don't expect your new thoughts to become automatic overnight. Keep your list in your wallet or purse so you can whip it out anytime. I'm a big fan of tangible objects to wrap your mind (and fingers) around, since they can help us to reconnect with the mental state we were in when we chose or created those items. In psychology, we sometimes call these types of things "transitional objects." They're physical objects that help us remember a certain part of ourselves. In psychotherapy literature, they could even be something like a tear-soaked tissue from a meaningful cry over a dead-end relationship during a therapy session; keeping the tissue handy can help one remember that pain and stop pursuing the dead-end relationship. But in this case we're talking about something much more direct: your folded-in-half sheet of Thought Replacements, ideally in your

own actual handwriting rather than just a screen on your phone (although if you're totally into your phone, that's fine, too), will help you to reconnect more easily with your Thought Replacements during an hour of need.

Troubleshooting

1. I've tried affirmations before and they didn't work for me. How is this different?

Good question! As a former yoga teacher and a person who loves self-help, I've spent a lot of time on affirmations, even in my teens and early twenties. When I learned about Thought Replacement in graduate school, I had the same question. Here's where I landed: affirmations are often aspirational and actually *not* representative of a current, accurate belief. For example, a poor person might have an affirmation like, "My bank account is full and I'm living a life of financial abundance," with a belief that by acting "as if" this statement were true, the person would start to attract wealth. Or someone who struggles hard with overeating might say, "My belly is full and satisfied" after eating a moderate meal that actually neither fills nor satisfies his large, half-empty belly. Or a single person with very low self-esteem might repeat the phrase, "I have the love of an amazing partner, and I am unshakable in my sense of self-worth," in the hope of eventually coming to really believe in her self-worth and find an amazing partner. Affirmations have been known to work very well for some people, acting as a "jump start" to help them embody their aspirational selves. However, scientific research has shown that affirmations are often ineffective and can actually make people feel worse when they practice affirmations around topics they feel very insecure about, because deep down, they're aware the statements aren't actually true; and focusing on untruths feels false, escapist, temporary, passive, and disempowering (Wood, Perunovic, and Lee, 2009).

Regardless of whether affirmations work for you, please be assured that **Thought Replacements are *different* from affirmations.** Your Thought Replacements will be carefully crafted to be 100 percent objectively and factually true in your current reality. In fact, part of creating a good Thought Replacement involves inviting your inner critic to "do their worst" at poking holes in your Thought Replacement so that you can keep refining it till you arrive at something that is unassailably true.

2. My Thought Replacements don't feel natural. Intellectually, I know they're accurate, but I'm struggling because they don't *feel* right or normal.

This is actually quite common: if mere insight about the truth were enough to change your patterns, you wouldn't *need* to *practice* Thought Replacement. In fact, if your Thought Replacements feel different or awkward, that actually often means you're doing it right. Just because your Thought Replacement is accurate does *not* mean that your Thought Replacement will always seem *natural* or "feel right" when you say it—but that doesn't mean that it's untrue. Sometimes people have an "aha moment" where, once they arrive at their Thought Replacement, it just feels totally natural, but if that's not the case for you, don't worry—you're normal.

The issue of Thought Replacements not immediately "feeling natural" is similar to the way that a person who has subsisted on junk food for years doesn't initially find healthy meals to be intuitive to prepare or enjoyable to eat; healthy food doesn't feel "natural" to that person at all, at least at first. Their taste buds and body chemistry have acclimated to a certain type of diet; so it takes a little time and concerted effort to create a "new normal." Part of the trick for them is to **learn to reslot moments when they're doing something that feels unnatural as victories rather than as concerns, since those are actually moments when they're very clearly creating *new* and healthy patterns.** So I advise you to keep practicing your Thought Replacement *religiously* for at least ten minutes per day for a good solid month before you start second-guessing yourself by asking if your Thought Replacements should feel more natural. You may not even need that much time, depending on the issue at hand—but if you have a particularly tenacious mind (as many high functioning people do!) then you may need to turn up the volume on your practice sessions. Don't worry, ten minutes per day for a month is a small price to pay for freedom from a thought pattern that's bottlenecking you from a life of emotional well-being, successful goal attainment, or whatever else the Thought Replacement will help you achieve.

15.

Anchoring Statements

Be sure you put your feet in the right place, then stand firm.
—ABRAHAM LINCOLN

Danilo contacted me for sessions via video, since he was far away from my office in New York City—very far; in fact, he was located in the Middle East,[1] running a new location for the well-established family business his uncle had started nearly forty years earlier. Danilo was also far away from his family and friends, who were mostly located in Latin America. Moreover, he was in a city that was experiencing a surge in crime, especially crime targeting wealthy foreigners. He had actually been the victim of an attempted kidnapping somewhat recently. As if all this weren't enough, he was also trying to fulfill his grandfather's wish that he not only spearhead the new location but also gradually assume control of the entire global family business so that his uncle could retire. This was especially challenging because of the company employees' long-time devotion to his uncle and their strong skepticism of Danilo as a young, relatively inexperienced newbie who would likely not be groomed for the role of CEO if not for his family relationship.

Danilo adored and revered his uncle. He wanted nothing more than to allow him the chance to enjoy his golden years without business stress, especially since his grandfather, whom he greatly respected, had explicitly expressed this wish. But Danilo also didn't yet feel capable of leading a global team without frequently reaching out to his uncle. Moreover, his deep respect for his uncle made it difficult to navigate moments when Danilo felt stymied by his uncle's attachment to old ways of doing things. Like many older founders who are ready for the next generation to take the reins, his uncle often vacillated between pressing for Danilo to scale the business with modern technology and insisting that old traditions remain in place. Danilo felt stuck in the middle between wanting to fulfill his uncle's wish that he assume responsibility for the business and simultaneously feeling obligated to accommodate his uncle's resistance to any of the changes that might come with Danilo's individual leadership style.

Danilo's heartfelt wish to free his uncle from the responsibilities of a growing global business as soon as possible was a burden that weighed heavily on him, but he had a hard time acknowledging his struggle, for fear of seeming ungrateful. His uncle had started the business as a poor young man nearly a half century earlier and built it into a global operation. He was a generous man who used his success to help provide Danilo a privileged life,[2] but he always made sure never to do Danilo the disservice of allowing him to become spoiled. He made sure that Danilo was aware and appreciative of his advantages. He sometimes took his efforts to an extreme, telling Danilo that he had "no idea what a bad day was" when comparing Danilo's challenges to the profound poverty he had escaped.

While his uncle's approach was, on balance, much better than allowing Danilo to become an entitled man-child who didn't understand the value of hard work, one drawback was that Danilo grew up reluctant to acknowledge when he was emotionally hurt or struggling. For example, he was quick to question his "right" to feel upset even privately by the way employees devalued him. "I've had so many advantages in life," he would say with a self-conscious shrug, "How could I really be upset about anything? I should just be grateful for all of the opportunities I have." While his attitude was admirable to a certain point, Danilo took it to an extreme that sometimes caused him to push stressors *out of his awareness*, to the point where they would sneak up on him and catch him unawares. For example, he would have trouble sleeping because of nightmares so intense they would cause him to wake in a cold sweat; he'd then try to laugh them off instead of asking if they might signify that something was bothering him. This approach prevented him from giving himself much in the way of self-care or stress management, since he wouldn't give himself permission to even acknowledge stress in the first place.

Finally, as the coup de grâce, Danilo was raised in a very liberal social environment compared to much of the Middle East, and he was used to dating women according to Western norms of respectful dating. He was used to being able to form a close relationship that could include physical closeness and possibly sex. In his new home, however, he found it extremely difficult to date women in a way that felt culturally normal to him; plus he was carrying the legitimate concern that any dating missteps could sabotage his family's effort to establish a successful Middle East arm of the family business. He felt a great deal of pressure at work and did *not* see it as a place to open up about weaknesses. He was in a foreign country (in fact a foreign continent) far away from friends and family, and he had no prospects for dating in what felt like a normal, healthy way, according to his own cultural norms. These circumstances rendered him, in "psychologist speak," a person who was under a great deal of circumstantial stress and who was lacking a social support network.

When a new client calls me, I usually ask the person to explain if any particular recent event prompted them to reach out *now*. As you can see from Danilo's story, there was a long-standing pattern of multiple stressors; but what exactly had made him browse the internet and find me *now*? I asked him. Danilo, who up till then had come across with the smooth swagger of a wealthy CEO globetrotter who was used to enjoying popularity with women, suddenly became diffident as he answered.

He explained that he'd had a recent and terrifying experience during an important business luncheon with several key employees and some potential clients they were hoping to sign. Danilo's main role at the luncheon was to project strength and help build the image of a stable, well-organized family business so that the clients would feel comfortable even as the uncle was phasing out. However, he had completely "choked" when the clients asked him a relatively simple question about the business.

He shook his head with shame and visibly cringed as he recalled how his mind had gone blank, and he'd silently perspired through his shirt while his employees stared at him with a mix of curiosity, concern, and compassion (or schadenfreude, in the case of some employees whom he feared were labeling this incident as proof that he'd never be as good a leader as his uncle, and probably didn't belong in leadership at all). His panic reaction became a vicious circle in which the more alarmed he felt by his momentary lapse, the more alarmed he became *as a response to feeling so alarmed in the first place.* You can imagine how this "panic about panic" can snowball. Perhaps you've even experienced it yourself.

Danilo and I were meeting on video, and I could literally see him blanche as he recounted the story. I sort of already knew what his answer would probably be to the question I was about to ask. But I wanted to confirm, just in case I was wrong—and I wanted him to express it in his own words—so I asked, "What sorts of thoughts were you having during that episode you just described?"

Not surprisingly, he answered, "I wasn't having *any* thoughts! Except maybe that I was about to die. That was the problem! It was like I was in quicksand or had the brain freeze from hell; it was one of the most terrifying moments of my life. And now I'm completely freaked out wondering when an attack like that will strike again. That's why I need your help: this *cannot* happen again. It *cannot*. I've seen my regular medical doctor, and he says there's nothing wrong with my body that could have caused this, and he suggested I try talking to someone, so, please—tell me how to fix this and get rid of my anxiety."

Danilo's pallor began to restore as I explained the good news that, in a weird way, his story made sense to me. He fit a profile: he was a person whose main way of dealing with stress was to discount it and tell himself to "just handle it." I explained that this willingness to "white knuckle" your way through tough times can be really helpful in some situations, but if it becomes a *primary or overused* tool for dealing with stress, then it can lead to a backlog of unaddressed stress that eventually bursts out in an overwhelming "panic mode." I also explained that the goal would not be to "get rid of" his anxiety, but to learn how to *listen* to the anxiety and provide it with support when it was at lower levels so that it wouldn't need to burst out in the form of overwhelming panic in order to get his attention.

"That all sounds nice," he responded, "but I need to know what to do if I get into another one of those situations again in the meantime. You said I need to deal with stress at lower levels—well, this is a big one. I'm walking around totally nervous that this will strike again at any moment. What will I do if it does?"

I assured Danilo that we would be using what I call a "top-down and bottom-up approach," meaning that we would certainly address the question of how to handle an episode of overwhelming panic (that's the "top-down" part, because we're managing the issue from the surface symptoms) as well as understanding how to help him manage stress better so it would be less likely to sneak up on him in the first place (that's the "bottom-up" part, where we dig down into the source). For a case like Danilo's, the bottom-up part includes techniques from this book like mindfulness, the To-Do List with Emotions, Mind Mapping, and other nuanced techniques designed to help people get in touch with their feelings proactively. The top-down approach for dealing with a "fire-alarm situation" centers around simple, direct techniques in this book like deep breathing and Anchoring Statements. You already know at least one deep-breathing technique from the chapter on the Three-Part Breath; now you can also learn about Anchoring Statements.

Enter: Anchoring Statements

When your body and mind seem to be on a "haywire circuit" where you're not even able to track your thoughts because it actually seems like you're not *having* any thoughts other than awareness of how your body is freaking out and your mind is going blank, a helpful remedy may be to restore your mind's ability to think in *language* rather than continuing to experience a visceral awareness of panic that feeds on itself. One way to do this is through an exercise I call Anchoring Statements. (Let me also encourage you to do some deep breathing; getting oxygen almost always helps.) A key feature of a situation in which Anchoring Statements are helpful is that you're drawing a "mind-blank" so profound that you're actually not having any language-based thoughts. It's like you're in a total brain freeze, which is actually alarming in itself for many high functioning people who tend to rely heavily on their thoughts. Anchoring Statements are designed to be short, concrete, *obvious* statements that are relatively easy to use as healthy "anchors" when your mind is experiencing a maelstrom of panic that is wreaking havoc on your ability to think clearly (or at all).

While Anchoring Statements are deliberately plain and straightforward, they are often surprisingly difficult to craft in the midst of a mental maelstrom—so the key is to craft them *in advance* and *practice* them and potentially even carry them in your pocket if needed. This is very similar to the way we deliberately memorize an escape route for fire drills to the point where "our feet know the way," so that if we panic during an actual fire we just have to do the steps we've already drilled into our rote memory. Obviously, each person's ideal Anchoring Statements will be slightly different, but here are some examples in a case like Danilo's:

- "The good news is that my medical doctor has assured me that my body is actually fine. This will pass in about three minutes."
- "My head is above my shoulders. My shoulders are above my stomach. My stomach is above my legs. My legs are above my feet. My head is above my shoulders (repeating the statements). . . ."
- "If this is the worst thing that happens to me, I'm still a lucky man."
- Counting his way through the Three-Part Breath became almost like an anchoring statement for Danilo as well, since he knew this was a rational response that involved simple preset language (labeling each part of the breath as he worked his way through the technique) Counting is a way of reconnecting the mind with language, and doing it with breath often relinks the body and mind in a

way that feels ordered and soothing in moments of panic. In these instances, Danilo would skip the parts of the exercise that involve observing yourself before and after the breath; he would just focus on counting his way through the inhalations and exhalations to restore his faculties of language while simultaneously regaining control of his body.

These Anchoring Statements would *not* likely be helpful in day-to-day life because they would probably bore an intelligent, high functioning person like Danilo to tears if he were operating at his normal level; yet their simplicity is exactly what is needed during a moment of panic. When your mind is short-circuiting, you *need* very simple statements to reactivate the language-based, logical part of your mind. Danilo and I created some of these statements together according to his personal history, but some of them are quite general and could be used by anyone.

Once we had crafted his statements, his next task was to memorize them. We also practiced using them in session by deliberately getting him in touch with the panicky feelings he experienced during the meeting and then having him recall his statements so he could build confidence in his skills to "toggle out of" that state. We'd then have him toggle back into the panicky feelings, and then use his Anchoring Statements to toggle back into his normal state again. In psychology, we call this type of technique "exposure" (because you're deliberately exposing yourself to the fear-inducing situation) and "cognitive rehearsal" (because you're practicing the mental techniques you'd like to be able to execute smoothly when needed).

Not surprisingly, Danilo experienced another episode about a week after we made the statements. He reported with great relief that although the episode was unpleasant, it felt much better knowing that he had anticipated the stressor and provided himself with tools to address it. This prevented the episode from spiraling the way it had the first time, when the panic had built upon itself because he'd felt so unprepared to cope with it. This time, he was able to use his Anchoring Statements at the first whiff of panic and quell it early. In keeping with the fire drill analogy mentioned earlier in this chapter, it is much easier to manage a small fire when you catch it quickly than if you stand there, paralyzed, watching the fire spread before you finally mobilize to address it.

Thanks to the combination of a top-down and bottom-up approach, Danilo never actually experienced another episode like the one that brought him to my office. Like many clients, he found that by learning to detect when he was *starting* to feel stressed out and then dealing with that stress at lower levels, he actually precluded the need for his body to send all-out panic distress signals. Even the act of trying to recall his Anchoring Statements at the first sign of a panicky feeling often presented him with enough of a cognitive challenge that he was able to keep his mind engaged and focused rather than just spiraling down into the nonverbal "fear of fear" state that is central to most panic attacks.

Although Danilo never had another full-on panic attack, he did take comfort in knowing that he *had* his Anchoring Statements ready if ever he needed them. You might say that the act of creating the statements and keeping them ready was *exactly* the sort of thing I was trying to guide him to do when I encouraged him to address anxiety at lower levels. Instead of pushing aside his fear of another jolt of panic and telling himself to "just deal with it," Danilo took the time to give himself tools in case he needed them. Rather than try to stuff away his concern, he dealt with it proactively. This is the sort of self-care that often *prevents* bursts of anxiety in the first place.

DIY: Put Anchoring Statements
to Work in Your Life

Before discussing how to do Anchoring Statements, I want to note that I'll be using the word "panic" to capture the experience of profound physical feelings of fear and the mind-blank that often accompanies such feelings. This is not to suggest that every person who experiences these feelings has the clinical diagnosis of "panic disorder." Many high functioning people have bouts of paniclike feelings in the absence of an actual panic disorder. So please know that when I say "panic" I'm using the term in more of the every-day manner, similar to how people sometimes interchangeably use colloquial phrases like "totally freaking out" or "losing my mind," rather than as a technical clinical term.

The concept of Anchoring Statements can be deceptively simple, so I encourage you to really be patient with yourself if the act of fully preparing your statements happens to challenge you a bit more than you expected ("fully preparing" includes crafting, documenting, and practicing your Anchoring Statements—there's more detail on this in the directions that follow). The good news is that once you have taken the time to craft a good anchoring state-ment and then document it as well as practice it, you may find it to be a surprisingly and wonderfully simple way to ground yourself in the event of a joltlike or "mind-blanking and body freaking" sort of moment.

Remember to check with your medical doctor as well to confirm that your heart and body are in good condition, and that any phys-ical feelings you're attributing to bursts of panic or emotional over-load are not actually signs that you need medical attention. Getting confident about this helps many people move beyond alarm and into a more balanced mental state; and it is certainly important to confirm any questions about your bodily health in order for Anchoring Statements to be appropriate. We wouldn't want you "thinking happy thoughts" or "finally learning to override those panic feelings" if you actually needed to call 911 or see your physician. Don't hesitate to check with your doctor if you are experiencing a racing heart, sweaty palms, dizziness, or other bodily symptoms that are sometimes markers of intense emotion and sometimes markers of a medical issue.

1. **Define your version of "panic."** This might sound surprising, but each person's version of panicky feelings is slightly different. Some people are afraid they're going to be stuck in this moment of "brain/body freeze" forever, while others are afraid they are going to actually drop dead right there on the spot. (I get a fair amount of referrals from emergency rooms dealing with overachievers who thought they were dying but were just having a panic attack.) Others know that the moment will pass and they don't fear that they're *actually* going to die, but they are stuck in a frantic and skittish search for a "light at the end of the tunnel" during their moments of panic. Still others experience total terror that this moment is going to expose them as (gasp) an emotional person to anyone who may witness what's happening. Get clear about what exactly *your* body and mind are imagining during your "panic-button moment."

Putting a very fine point on your visceral sense of panic is key to helping you figure out the best Anchoring Statements to help in an hour of need. Because clients experiencing deep panic often express that part of the problem is that their minds *freeze,* we need to learn how to address their fears using *language*, which is the first and most basic step toward control. Don't worry if your fear seems irrational. In fact, it's almost a given that this fear is irrational: that's part of the way it's able to make itself feel so huge that it creates such an overwhelming feeling of panic.

In situations where your body and mind are reacting in an outsized "the world is ending" manner, things can start to "snowball" such that we start getting alarmed *about* how alarmed we feel—and then we can get stuck in a vicious circle of alarm that we don't really understand (which is partly what's so alarming about it!). So, although it may be unpleasant, please take a moment to get clarity on whatever your personal version of "panic overdrive" is. Having a language-based description will help you understand how to mitigate it.

Here are some stimulators to help you create a detailed definition of what *you* experience during paniclike moments when your "fight, flight, or freeze" system has gone into overdrive:

a. **Body.** What does your body feel like? Do you have a racing heart, sweaty palms, or feel your blood running cold? Do you feel your face getting warm, a sense of dizziness, or a closed-throat feeling? Remember to double-check with your doctor to confirm that these feelings are truly markers of intense emotion rather than a genuine cause for medical alarm. Getting confident about this is essential for step 2 to be successful!

b. **Mind.** What is happening in your mind? Do you feel your mind is blank? Frozen? Are you seeing any visual images? Are you having flashes of fragmented thoughts about how doomsday has arrived? Are you trying to form thoughts but feel unable to complete them? Hint: If you're having full-sentence-based thoughts that are more pesky than doomsday-like, you might want to try Thought Replacement. Anchoring Statements are to rescue you when your most basic faculties of body and mind seem to be escaping you.

c. **Other.** Do you notice any other descriptors or experiences not covered here? Are you experiencing a pulsing feeling that seems to be partly mental and partly physical? Are you feeling like you can't hear very well because you're stuck deep in your head? Are you having a sinking or slowed feeling?

Although it's unpleasant, we want to face the "monster under the bed" and get word-based descriptions of what exactly these "spells" are so that we can wrangle you back into high functioning reality, where you belong!

2. **Craft your Anchoring Statements.** Here's where the rescue begins. Once you nail down an exquisite understanding of your personal experience of panic (challenging, I know!), you are now ready to consider what sorts of statements would be most likely to *soothe* your panic. Common Anchoring Statements are things like the following:

a. "This is certainly uncomfortable, but I will definitely live through it."
b. "I've seen my medical doctor and I'm definitely going to live."
c. "I've experienced this before, and it always passes."

While these statements are common for a reason (they tend to be effective for people who would otherwise go down a mental "rabbit hole" of fear that their burst of panic is more than just a burst of panic),

I encourage you to tailor them to your individual experience of panic. You might also try practicing the S-L-O-W variation of the Three-Part Breath in chapter 6, or any other breathing exercise that helps you reconnect with your body and your sense of logic-based language. A few other examples of stimulators for ideas of possible Anchoring Statements are listed here. The idea is to make sure you choose something that you think will resonate with you in your moment of need based on your knowledge from the "defining" part in step 1.

d. "My number one job right now is to breathe." High functioning people in my office tend to like this one because it gives them a sense of accomplishment and focus at a moment when they're feeling insecure and scattered.

e. "I won't abandon myself. I can count on me." This one is also nice for high functioning people because it activates pride in their sense of personal responsibility and self-efficacy; and it facilitates a sense of control and positive self-regard by simply repeating a statement that they've diligently prepared and rehearsed (see step 3).

f. "I may actually laugh about this later. In fact, I might start right now." Humor is always a nice way to change perspective and restore a sense of control.

g. "Oh, great! It's happening again, just like I predicted. This is my chance to see if introducing language will help anchor me." This type of statement "flips the script" on the panic by having you *welcome it* rather than freak out about it, and reframe it as a predictable training ground where you can experiment with a new skill.

Whatever your Anchoring Statements are, it is *essential* that you write them down. I encourage writing things down frequently throughout this book, but it's specifically important with Anchoring Statements because, by definition, Anchoring Statements are designed to help when your mind is blanking or freezing—so the problem of just relying on your normal memory skills is obvious, right? You can certainly write them down in your phone if that's the only way you'll do this, but I implore you to consider actually writing them down in your own handwriting. Here's why:

As any student of marketing knows, the font in which we read something impacts how we'll "hear" the message—and what could be a stronger way to reconnect with your sense of language than reading your own words *in your own handwriting* that you created deliberately as a gift for yourself in case you ever felt the need to "hear" those words? As a psychologist, I can tell you that memories and feeling states are often triggered by physical things such as locations, objects, or even scents; we call these things "situational cues." So, if you get yourself into a nice, rational, calm state of mind and write down your Anchoring Statements, then having that paper handy during a moment when you're feeling unmoored will help you snap back into the state you were in when you originally wrote the statements. Do yourself a favor and give yourself every possible advantage by writing your statements down on paper if at all feasible!

3. **Rehearse.** Once you have your statements, do your best to commit them to memory. Yes, you'll have them written down, but memorizing them will help you to internalize them; plus it will help if you're in a situation where you don't have access to your written statements. Next, practice toggling into them from an agitated, panicked state

of mind. How to get yourself into such a state? Sit down, close your eyes, and focus on your clearest memories of feeling in whatever panicked state caused you to want to learn Anchoring Statements in the first place. If you start feeling uncomfortable, let me reframe that from a negative to a positive: a sense of discomfort or even full-on panic is exactly what you need to experience so that you can practice toggling from that state into a practice session for your Anchoring Statements. Once you successfully toggle into the statements, toggle back into the panic state. Keep doing this as often as you can; practice helps you to build new neural pathways between these mental states.

If you feel like you "just can't" conjure up a panic feeling no matter how hard you try, consider entering a few practice sessions into your calendar at random times and at least plan to practice your Anchoring Statements "all of a sudden" when those moments pop up. **The idea is to get your brain comfortable pulling up your statements at the drop of a hat.** Think of this the same way you would think of a fire drill: drills happen at random times so we can *practice* the escape route before we're dealing with the confusion and chaos of an actual fire.

4. **Don't forget about the "bottom-up" part.** Consider exercises like Mind Mapping, To-Do List with Emotions, or other tools that help you check in with yourself to see if there's something "in the back of your mind" that needs attention. **Sometimes it's a constellation of small things, sometimes it's one big thing, and sometimes it's just that you've been so busy traveling in a mental or logistical "fast lane" of life that**

your feelings need a way of signaling that it's time to pause and unpack.

Another simple way to guide yourself to be more attuned to your feelings on a day-to-day basis so they don't backlog, is to write a two-sentence journal entry every day, simply listing the high point and the low point of your day. The idea is to make sure you pay attention to your feelings *before* they have to "stomp and shout" to grab your attention. **Of course, some people are totally attuned to themselves yet still experience occasional moments of feeling suddenly overwhelmed with random feelings of panic.** Whether or not your burst of feelings is stemming from a pattern of stuffing away your emotions, it is still an opportunity to try any of the exercises in this chapter to stimulate yourself to cope in a self-aware, proactive manner. Don't hesitate to talk to a therapist if you ever want more help in learning how to explore your feelings in a supportive setting!

Troubleshooting

1. **How are Anchoring Statements different from Thought Replacement? I'm still inserting preset thoughts into my mind, right?**

At first blush, Anchoring Statements have some overlap with Thought Replacement, but there are some important distinctions. Thought Replacements are best for when you have a thought pattern that you previously accepted as rational, but you now recognize as maladaptive and therefore want to revise it. An example is Jack's initial phase of struggling with thoughts that getting shared custody in his divorce was tantamount to his father's abandonment of him, and then learning to replace those thoughts with logical statements affirming that he is a good father who is not abandoning his son. In contrast, Anchoring Statements are for when we are so panicked that we don't even really *have* a clear thought pattern—we're just experiencing a visceral sense of fear. Anchoring Statements tend to be most useful to clients who experience bouts of panic rather than struggling with a fast-talking inner critic or a need to restructure their belief systems around an old, ingrained topic.

2. **Anchoring Statements are great for talking myself down from a flare-up, but is there a way to quit going into semipanic mode in the first place?**

Yes! First of all, I encourage you to see a doctor to confirm if it's possible that these moments actually have nothing to do with psychology. It's possible that you may just have a physiological issue that needs attention (for example, you may have a body issue in which your adrenaline just suddenly spikes for reasons that are actually not driven by anything to do with psychology). On the other hand, if your issue appears to be *psychological*, then I would encourage you to find ways of getting in touch with your stressors in a direct way rather than stuffing them to the back of your mind till they burst out as an overwhelming, amorphous jolt.

How do you "get in touch with your stressors in a direct way"? Good question. As discussed in step 4, things like mindfulness exercises, including but not limited to the Three-Part Breath and others in this book, or the To-Do List with Emotions and Mind Mapping techniques, or even simply writing down the high point and low point of your day on a regular basis. Do these exercises proactively (even spending a total of five minutes on one or some combination of these exercises could make a difference), and certainly do them following any bursts of "random" emotional over-whelming feelings. Please do consider seeing a therapist as well if you want more help.

3. **If I quit having these types of fire alarm reactions to minor issues, will I slowly devolve into a lazy, slovenly loser?**

Ah, I'm so glad you asked! Sometimes, high functioning people purposely become hypersensitive to minor issues so that they'll deliberately "overrespond" to small issues, thereby preventing any small issue from growing into a huge issue. This is similar to the "broken windows" approach in policing, where authorities deliberately pay attention to relatively minor issues like broken windows in a neighborhood because they know that allowing those issues to go unchecked can create a tone of neglect in communities, thereby setting the stage for greater neglect to ensue.

Similarly, high functioning people sometimes pride themselves on having a "panic attack" over relatively minor problems, like arriving a few minutes late to a meeting, because they want to ensure they don't become comfortable with casual drops in their high standards of behavior. This is actually a helpful attitude to a certain degree, but the problem arises when the high functioning person becomes **too good at their own game of creating a sense of alarm over small things,** to the point where they're *actually* panicking over small things. This would be akin to the authorities sending an army of police with guns ablaze to deal with the broken window rather than simply making sure to have an officer visit the home to check on things. While keeping a sharp focus on high standards is important, and your willingness to show concern at the first sign of problems is laudable, there is a tipping point where you start wasting your resources and become *less* productive, reliable, and strong, because you're going berserk over relatively minor problems. So please don't worry that learning to rein in your "fight, flight, or freeze" reactions will make you weak; in fact it will help you to reallocate that panicky energy toward a more productive use!

16.

Moving Forward

Life isn't about finding yourself. Life is about creating yourself.
—GEORGE BERNARD SHAW

Thanks for reading (or at least skimming!) all the way to the end of this book. I hope you've found some practical tips and fresh approaches that will help you achieve your goals while also finding greater connection and fulfillment along the way. Let's conclude with a few key takeaways and reminders for you to keep in your toolbox:

1. **Go easy on yourself.** Rome wasn't built in a day. Please, please, *please* be patient with yourself as you try things on for size. Some techniques might click right away, others might take a little more time to master. You

might need to pick the book up on different days, in different moods, and try the techniques in different situations. Feel free to experiment as you find your stride. On the other hand . . .

2. **You're in charge.** If something feels *wrong* for you, by all means feel free to skip it. Not every technique is a fit for every person. Don't force yourself to do something if the struggle seems more than just a natural process of learning or experiencing something new. New tools often feel awkward at first, but if you're sensing that a tool is really just not a good fit for you, then please do listen to yourself. Take what works from this book and leave the rest!

3. **Stay in touch!** Feel free to keep me posted as you try the techniques! Interact with me on social media![1] (Yes, I know I just used three exclamation points! Now it's even more! I am just really emphatic about this part since the book is ending, and I want you to stay in touch if you liked it!) I love questions and input, and I'm always developing new courses, materials, and workshops around feedback from people like you. Also, if you have questions or ideas on other areas of high functioning life, or further questions about what is addressed in this book, please let me know! I'm open to writing more about how to harness your energy for high functioning parenting, high functioning careers, high functioning relationships, high functioning interior life, and other areas where I think there's a need. I'm also open to writing more about my own journey and how I overcame challenges, to the extent that sharing about these things could be helpful or inspiring to others—so please feel

free to let me know your interests, ideas, or thoughts. I became a psychologist for many reasons, but a big one is that I love connecting with people. . . . So go ahead and connect with me if you want! For a good starting point, visit www.NervousEnergyBook.com to connect more deeply with the material in this book or stay in touch with me if you'd like.

Thanks again for reading, keep in touch, and cheers to you for learning some new skills!

Acknowledgments

Writing this book has been an incredible privilege, and I would like to thank the people who made it possible. Thank you, Jennifer Weis, for taking a chance on me. Thank you, Marc Resnick, for getting my proposal onto Jennifer's desk. Thank you, Serena Jones, for literally pounding the table to help get the meetings I needed. Thank you to my editor Daniela Rapp for your blunt and incisive edits (the best kind!). Thank you, Professor Catherine Monk, for telling a shy undergraduate that you'd mentor her through the process of becoming a clinical psychologist—and then doing it. Thank you to my angelic assistant Donna for taking care of everything else in my life so I had time to focus on this book. Thank you to Amy Summers for telling me I needed to write this book. Thank you to my husband, Jim, and our son, Billy, for making my heart sing every single day. Thank you to the therapists and coaches who have helped me over the years, especially to Ana Tucker. Last but not least, I would like to thank the many clients who teach me invaluable lessons about psychotherapy and coaching during our sessions and workshops; please know that I relish every moment.

Notes

1. INTRODUCTION

1. In this and other vignettes in this book, names and identifying details have been changed to protect the privacy of individuals, and some characters are composites.

2. The term "high functioning" is unpacked more later, but for now just understand that in psychology a "high-functioning person" is someone who goes a step beyond the basics of not frequenting psychiatric emergency rooms; generally not posing any risk of physical harm to self or to others; typically being able to manage their own food, clothing, and shelter; and having at least a few decent relationships with friends or family. In addition to these things, high-functioning people typically demonstrate a few "extra" accomplishments, such as doing really well in school or work (including the work of homemaking, if applicable) or taking especially good care of themselves, their relationships, or their lives in other ways. This describes what many readers may *think* is "just normal adult life." In truth, a person like Amy who meets all these criteria is actually *not* considered average in the world of psychology: someone like her is generally considered "high functioning" in psychology parlance.

3. It was also helpful to have a head start on understanding the specific needs of high-functioning people seeking private sessions: I had fulfilled my postdoctoral licensing hours

at a firm where part of my job was to pair Fortune 500 executives with therapists and coaches. This provided invaluable practical lessons about what many high-functioning people need and want in order to make the investment of time and money in private sessions feel worthwhile, and those lessons informed my approach as well as the techniques in this book!

4. If that's you, please check out my program for therapists in private practice, located at https://www.drchloe.com/for-clinicians/.

5. This is discussed further in the Zone of Control technique in chapter 8.

6. Those of you who are interested in yoga and meditation may be interested to know that the concept of creating a clear blueprint of where you want to be is actually an important part of yogic practices as well. In yoga, when attempting a difficult balancing pose, we use something called a *drishdi*. *Drishdi* is a Sanskrit word meaning "focused gaze." In yoga classes, it refers to a tangible spot where you focus your gaze during balancing poses so that no matter what distractions you experience during that pose, you will be able to center yourself upon a steady point; this helps yogis keep their balance and steady focus. The parallel here strikes me: to keep our balance in a life that can sometimes be hectic or challenging, we benefit from choosing a clear, tangible focal point in order to center our attention and decrease distraction. You will notice that nearly all of the exercises in this book contain directions to write something down; this is because doing so will help you organize yourself and **keep a clear focus on how you want to handle certain situations or feelings.** My yogic and psychological trainings combined with my life experiences have taught me that goals are easier to hit when we have a tangible point of focus—even if that focal point is just a simple piece of paper that contains our plans in cogent, actionable language.

2. WHAT ARE "HIGH FUNCTIONING CLIENTS" AND WHY DOES IT MATTER?

1. Even the concept of "disorder" is fluid and fraught, evidenced by psychologists' ongoing need to revise the *Diagnostic and Statistical Manual of Mental Disorders* (*DSM*). For example, homosexuality was not completely removed from the *DSM* until 1987. I would never rely solely on the *DSM* when considering functioning.

2. If you'd like to learn some techniques to slow yourself down in certain situations, see the S-L-O-W variation of the Three-Part Breath, or Cocoon Breathing, both in chapter 7 of this book.

3. Even if you haven't achieved some of these things but you are working toward realistic plans to do so, or if you've found viable alternatives, you could still be considered high functioning. For example, you may not have a great relationship yet, but you're actively dating in a healthy partner-oriented manner; or you are comfortably single by choice. Or you aren't in great shape yet, but you're on a slow-and-steady pattern of healthy weight loss; or you're still in school but you're attending class regularly and on track for graduation; or you've been able to develop a career without an academic degree. The markers in that list are just examples to help you understand the general idea of a high-functioning person as someone who knows how to create and adhere to multistep, healthy life plans that are a "step beyond" the basics.

4. Exactly how "normal" or unusual is it to be high functioning? Interestingly, data on what proportion of individuals would be considered high functioning are actually rather difficult to obtain, at least in my experience. This is likely because most relevant psychology studies focus on locating and providing support to people in need of help managing symptoms of disorders that are significantly compromising their functioning.

5. If this describes you, please make sure to read this book's sections in chapter 5 on self-discipline and perfectionism!

6. Although there isn't space to unpack these approaches here, please know that supportive therapy, insight-oriented therapy, or motivational interviewing are just a few of the therapeutic approaches that are often helpful in situations like these if you or someone you know needs support. Motivational interviewing and insight-oriented therapy are also helpful in many cases for higher functioning people as well. Also, not all codependent people or addicts are lower functioning (for example, a coffee addict likely poses no harm to others if that's the extent of his addiction; and if you enable your coffee-addict spouse, it's probably fine).

7. Therapy is similar to most service-based fields in that people who have more financial resources often have more freedom when choosing a provider. Generally speaking, most people (including me!) would not *choose* to be treated by a first-year psychology trainee if given a choice; they would prefer to be seen by someone with a greater degree of experience and education. Such therapists typically cost more, especially in a private-practice setting. Higher functioning people often (but not always) have enough financial resources to be more discriminating when choosing a therapist; so most therapists' early training experiences are typically with lower functioning people. This is certainly not to say that every person with financial resources is high functioning (think of Jeffrey Epstein or Bernie Madoff, who were extremely wealthy yet displayed blatant disregard for the welfare of others and for the law, both of which would lower their assessed levels of functioning), nor that people without financial resources aren't high functioning (think of a hardworking single mother who can't afford a pricey private-pay therapist but she makes the most of her sessions with a sharp trainee at a low-fee clinic), nor that all great therapists cost a lot of money, nor that all lower functioning people are without financial resources, nor that all lower functioning people are treated by trainees. But in general, beginning psychology students are not seated in front of ultrahigh functioning CEOs as their first training experiences.

8. Of course, not *all* lower functioning people need weekly visits, but they're more likely to require a higher frequency or intensity of therapeutic services in order to help ensure that their basic needs are met. Sometimes they may even require ongoing inpatient settings, group homes, or what is known as a "continuing outpatient day-treatment program," in which they attend therapeutic programming and activities Monday through Friday, 9 A.M. to 5 P.M., on a long-term basis).

9. For more on this, please see the section "Personal Experience of Seeking Therapy" in chapter 6.

10. Of course, this is not a perfect analogy. As a former yoga teacher, I fully appreciate that a trainer who *specializes* in ultrasafe workouts is often required for someone who has major health challenges. Likewise, many profoundly lower functioning people absolutely require a clinician specializing in their unique challenges—and in my experience, a high functioning person often benefits from an approach that is specifically geared toward his or her level of functioning. The basic idea is just that as our needs and skills become more specialized, it can be harder to find the right fit. I found it harder to find someone who could help me when I was higher functioning than I did when I was lower functioning, and many high functioning clients in my office have expressed relief at finding a therapist who has an appreciation for their unique strengths and vulnerabilities.

4. HOW TO USE THIS BOOK: CHANNEL YOUR NERVOUS ENERGY FOR SUCCESS

1. High functioning people are often interested to learn that psychologists measure various factors of personality, including a factor known as "need for cognition." Need for cognition refers to a person's need for mental activity. Many high functioning people enjoy being mentally active. The trick is to make sure you keep your brain on the right track so that you avoid using that extra mental energy on things that are actually counterproductive (things like excessive worry, self-consciousness, and so on), and instead use that energy for strategic problem-solving, healthy and fulfilling relationships, refreshing stress management, or whatever will really serve your needs best.

2. Even if you didn't have an absent father or you're at a different place in your career than Christina is, you might still identify with Christina's OCD tendencies. For the purposes of this book, the exact reasons *why* Christina developed these tendencies isn't as important as the fact that she *did* develop them and now needs to harness them.

3. Of course, not all children would describe a helicopter parent as a "luxury." But from Christina's childhood standpoint, such parents seemed somewhat enviable.

4. Exactly *how* the Three-Part Breath helps people better recognize, label, and face their interior lives is discussed further in chapter 7 on the Three-Part Breath; but for now let's just say that the University of Massachusetts Memorial Medical Center has an entire program devoted to the benefits of mindfulness meditation, wherein exercises like the Three-Part Breath have been shown to help people increase awareness and control of their thoughts and feelings.

5. ESSENTIALS OF NERVOUS ENERGY: SELF-DISCIPLINE, PERFECTIONISM, AND MINDFULNESS

1. Trait conscientiousness is strongly associated with academic and professional success (Higgins, Peterson, Pihl, and Lee, 2007).

2. Many high functioning people are drawn to perfectionism because being a high achiever has been a ticket to positive attention in their lives. To a certain point, being polished and poised does help you to attract friends, romantic attention, and other positive social responses. However, research has shown that people who are *too* hard on themselves actually tend to experience a decrease in people wanting to be close to them, for an interesting reason: when we can tell that someone is *too* hard on themselves, we tend to worry they'll be "over the top" with us as well. So if you are trying to be "perfect" as a way of people-pleasing, consider that most people are actually more pleased by a person who does well but who is also comfortable with imperfections, including their own.

3. Keep this in mind as you check out Thought Replacement in chapter 14.

4. Mindfulness originated from Buddhism. The sacred parts of Buddhism include the Buddha, the *dharma*, and the *sangha*. These are referred to as the "Three Jewels of Buddhism" in sacred Buddhist texts as well as in modern-day Buddhist teachings. The Buddha is, of course, the actual, original human Buddha; the *dharma* is the teachings of the Buddha (the fact-based material he shared); and the *sangha* is the community (relationship-based). This is partly why a person's true knowledge of mindfulness is hard to grasp without understanding the person's story of contact with it.

5. This means that if you've never had any experience with mindfulness or meditation before, you're actually in a wonderful position as you read this book. Don't let your lack of experience intimidate you as you consider the Three-Part Breath or mindfulness; "beginner's mind" is the specific term for the mindset all yogis and meditators strive to cultivate!

6. If mindfulness seems a little strange and maybe even esoteric to you, please don't feel you need to take my word for it about its benefits: the University of Massachusetts Medical School has an entire center strictly devoted to better understanding exactly why and how mindfulness practices seem to work so darn well for just about every person on the planet. As one of my favorite clinical supervisors who prided herself on a sense of healthy skepticism used to say, "I don't need to 'believe in' mindfulness. It is not a religion. It is a proven science. We don't 'believe in' it, we simply learn it and build skills to use it."

7. "Stat" is short for *statim*, Latin for "instantly." In hospitals, we say we need something "stat" when there is an urgent medical need; the term is usually reserved for life-and-death (or at least extremely time-sensitive) situations.

8. You may notice that these simple examples of mindfulness all reference physical sensations (funny bone, sleeping foot, or paper cut). This is not a coincidence: mindfulness is actually simplest in the context of physical and tangible material situations. In traditional mindfulness training, we begin with practicing nonjudgmental observation of tangible objects (beginning mindfulness students often observe their hands, a raisin, or some other object that is clearly visually defined) and semitangible objects (the breath is considered semitangible), before we graduate to practicing mindfulness with abstract objects like thoughts and emotions. What's really amazing is that this sequence of mindfulness skills (tangible objects, semitangible objects like breath, then abstract thoughts like thoughts and emotions) was part of the ancient Buddhist program of learning; it has now been proven by Western science as an effective way to increase mindfulness skills. This is why we begin with the Three-Part Breath as the first technique, and why all of the example characters earlier in this book used the Three-Part Breath: it is a great foundational technique that can help you understand which tool to reach for in your toolbox.

6. SPECIAL CONSIDERATIONS FOR HIGH FUNCTIONING PEOPLE SEEKING THERAPY

1. The issue of how much agency in "shopping around" is appropriate for people who are incarcerated or involuntarily hospitalized is more complex; but if you're just choosing therapy out of your own desire, then I encourage you to be discriminating (at least a little!).

2. On the other hand, if you've been to half a dozen therapists and didn't feel rapport with any of them, your challenges forming an alliance with your therapist could be what psychologists call "diagnostic," meaning that perhaps you have trouble forming rapport. If you feel this is the case, consider disclosing this at your first session with your next therapist; it may help that person help you. But if you feel that for some reason you just *can't* find a good therapist, consider asking a trusted friend or family member to help you find someone and/or attend a first meeting with you to see if an additional perspective helps. If every therapist you try either refers you out or is someone you dislike, and you don't have any trusted friends or family members but you wish you did, then I would encourage you to explore Dialectical Behavioral Therapy (DBT) or to read a book by its founder, Dr. Marsha Linehan. DBT is great for many people who experience extremely intense emotions in situations, including people who *do* have trusted friends or family members. I am not certified in DBT but I studied it throughout my academic career and I assisted in clinical DBT research at Mount Sinai Hospital during my training. I have seen it work wonders when done by an experienced psychotherapist who is formally credentialed through Linehan's foundation. Of course, if you ever get so lonely or upset by a lack of good therapists or anything else, that you think of hurting yourself, please dial 911 or go to the nearest emergency room!

3. High functioning people tend to have high levels of trait conscientiousness. If your therapist seems "sloppy" to you (e.g., arriving late, seeming to frequently forget material you've shared before, not following up with you on homework, or frequently forgetting to silence a cell phone during sessions), your therapist may be low on conscientiousness or be experiencing life issues that are impacting his or her conscientiousness. You deserve a therapist who will be attentive, organized, and conscientious. So if you have concerns about your therapist, then please feel free to raise your concerns and switch therapists if necessary.

7. THE THREE-PART BREATH

1. As the first technique in this book, the Three-Part Breath *can* actually be used as a starting point for all of the techniques. This chapter is a little longer than the rest, and it doesn't follow the same format as the others do, wherein I start with a clinical story. There's a lot of information here, but I think you'll find it helpful. Always feel free to skip to wherever feels most helpful if another technique is calling your name.

2. If you feel this way, rest assured that this *probably* just means that you're doing the perfect exercise. If you have difficulty filling up your lungs or being able to take a slow breath that contacts all three parts of the Three-Part Breath, it is *likely* that you would either benefit from increasing your lung capacity (lung capacity begins to decrease around age thirty-five, unless you do cardiovascular exercise combined with other remedies, such as breathing exercises) or that you'll benefit from learning to control your breathing pace so you can enjoy slow, deliberate breaths. However, please remember to consult your physician to confirm the specifics of your case if you experience discomfort or dizziness during breathing exercises. Many clients with a self-described "WebMD addiction" will actually benefit more from getting a medical doctor's seal of approval, which they can then even weave into scripted self-talk, like "My doctor says I'm totally fine, I'm just experiencing a healthy growing pain" during this exercise. This helps them learn how to be nonreactive to harmless (and actually helpful) physical challenges. While you are likely to actually benefit from learning to breathe more deeply and more slowly, please check with your medical doctor if there is any concern whatsoever that your case is different.

3. Psychologists are trained to note these reactions partly so that we can try to understand what life must be like for the clients if they typically provoke certain emotions or reactions in people. We do this partly to help ensure that we have the necessary self-awareness to address our own biases if needed, and for many other therapeutic reasons.

4. When you become somewhat practiced at the Three-Part Breath, you'll be able to do it in meetings, on dates, or anytime you need to quickly center yourself in a way that will not be obviously noticeable to others. Much like the way you can "secretly" hold your breath for a few seconds without others immediately noticing, you'll be able to do a few "stealth" Three-Part Breaths without giving it much thought or attracting attention.

8. THE ZONE OF CONTROL

1. I don't mean to imply that other aspects of Sean's makeup, such as issues with self-esteem or a strong desire to prove his capability to his "doubting Thomas" father, were not relevant or important parts of his treatment. The techniques in this book are not a substitute for psychotherapy, and there is no such thing as a "one size fits all" technique. However, I have noticed that certain techniques tend to work reliably enough for a broad population of clients that I felt it would be worthwhile to share these tech-

niques with some general descriptions of the types of people and situations for which these techniques have been helpful. If you feel you need help that is more personalized to your situation and individual history, or if you're unable to apply these techniques to achieve the results you wish, by all means, please seek professional support!

2. If you don't have an assistant but you feel daunted by all of the work that needs to be done, which was my situation when I was first starting my practice on a shoestring budget, just keep putting one foot in front of the other to make progress. Consider asking a friend for help, if appropriate, and perhaps reread the section in this book on self-discipline to find ways you can make the work less stressful—then congratulate yourself on your self-reliance! But also consider getting an assistant. If you think about it, an "executive assistant" is to help *execute*, which is really helpful when you've already done the work of making a super-clear action list. Thanks to the internet, assistants may now be much cheaper than you think. (See my blog at www.USPHJobs.com for more details.)

9. MENTAL SHORTLIST

1. While this item isn't technically one Stephen could "think about" instead of his meeting, playing loud music on his headphones did the trick of forcing his mental monologue off the habitual target of the meeting and onto the lyrics of whatever song he played. Interestingly, an "old school" trick to help severely schizophrenic patients make the voices in their heads stop is to ask them to sing a song. It's almost impossible for the brain to follow two verbal streams at once, so music with catchy lyrics can be a saving grace when we want to change our mental track.

10. TO-DO LIST WITH EMOTICONS

1. Apologies if the strong language offends any of you, dear readers! I wanted to include it to "keep things real" here and convey the intensity of emotion that Sarah discovered was underlying her previous attitude around the housework, which was an attitude marked by such profound detachment that she was struggling to complete the work. When someone who doesn't usually use such strong language starts cursing, it usually demonstrates a powerful, raw feeling; and I wanted to give you the uncensored version here.

11. MIND MAPPING

1. In case you didn't know: "eustress" is the stress we experience from positive life events. Although the event is positive, we can still feel overwhelmed by it: think "tears of joy" at weddings, feelings of pressure to "do great things" after graduation, or feeling a bit listless after accomplishing a big goal.

12. WORRY TIME

1. Due to the fact that I double my private session fee (admittedly already steep) if the client is a therapist seeking individual consultation on building a private practice, I don't usually encounter very many therapists seeking private individual consultations. (After all, I'm selling proprietary business secrets in these situations—and I encourage therapists to use my video programs and monthly group coaching calls rather than having me personally deliver the information to them.)

2. Although therapists don't typically accept gifts of more than a nominal financial value from clients, Kate was not a therapy client—she was a client seeking a business consultation. So, dear reader, in case you're wondering whether there was an ethical conflict

for me because therapists don't generally accept gifts from clients, please rest assured that this was not a therapy relationship. Plus, declining Kate's gift would not only have seemed rude, it might have been culturally insensitive.

3. This is a larger quantity of time than most people choose, but in Kate's case it was appropriate because she was actively building a business and there was actually a fair amount of material for her to consider (and setting aside a very generous amount of time prevented her from worrying that there wouldn't be enough time!).

13. RESPONSE PREVENTION

1. Rebecca knew that her old habit of texting men to nudge them into communicating only served to either push them away or upset the pursuit dynamics that she desired. Moreover, in many situations, these men had been on only one or two dates with her, so texting with multiple messages to "nudge" them often seemed intrusive and left her feeling upset that *they* hadn't pursued *her*. But of course by peppering them with text messages herself, she wasn't giving them a chance to take the lead.

2. It is important to note that the texts were undesirable to her, not undesirable because of anyone else's opinion. In other words, this book is not making a judgment about how much a woman should text or pursue a man; this is just an example of how Rebecca was able to modify a behavior that she herself had labeled as undesirable.

14. THOUGHT REPLACEMENT

1. Please understand that I say "we" rather than "I" in this case because although I introduce the exercise in a psychotherapy session, it is essential that the person *using* the Thought Replacement feels 100 percent on board with the goal of replacing maladaptive thoughts. Client consent is always important in psychotherapy, but I feel it is especially important in techniques like Thought Replacement. It is a very powerful technique.

15. ANCHORING STATEMENTS

1. For any mental health professionals reading this who are curious about licensing issues given that Danilo is overseas: please be assured that if someone is outside of the geographical areas where I'm licensed as a clinical psychologist, I will only offer coaching services rather than psychotherapy to that person; and I will only proceed if the potential client is appropriate for coaching.

2. Danilo's parents did not have the resources that his uncle, whose rise from poverty was quite remarkable, did. Danilo's relationship with his father was somewhat distant: his father was frequently absent on drinking binges that he said were necessary to drown his feelings of inferiority to his successful brother.

16. MOVING FORWARD

1. Twitter and Instagram: @drchloe_; Facebook: @drchloephd; LinkedIn: @chloecarmi chael; blog: www.drchloe.com/blog; newsletter: www.drchloe.com/newsletter YouTube: www.youtube.com/user/drchloecarmichael

Bibliography

Higgins, D. M., J. B. Peterson, R. O. Pihl, and A. G. M. Lee (2007). "Prefrontal Cognitive Ability, Intelligence, Big Five Personality, and the Prediction of Advanced Academic and Workplace Performance." *Journal of Personality and Social Psychology* 93, no. 2: 298–319.

Martin D. J., J. P. Garske, and M. K. Davis (2000). "Relation of the Therapeutic Alliance with Outcome and Other Variables: A Meta-Analytic Review." *Journal of Consulting and Clinical Psychology* 68: 438–50.

Miller, A., A. Isaacs, and E. Haggard (1965). "On the Nature of the Observing Function of the Ego." *British Journal of Medical Psychology* 38, no. 2: 161–69.

Murray, H. A. (1938). *Explorations in Personality.* New York: Oxford University Press, 164.

Wood, J. V., W. Q. Elaine Perunovic, and J. W. Lee (2009). "Positive Self-Statements: Power for Some, Peril for Others." *Psychological Science* 20, no. 7, 860–66.

Zetzel, E. R. (1956). "Current Concepts of Transference." *International Journal of Psychoanalysis* 37: 369–76.

Index